D1232504

The Research and Development Project for the Standardization of Korean Cuisine

The Beauty of Korean Food:

With 100 Best-Loved Recipes

The Research and Development Project for the Standardization of Korean Cuisine

The Beauty of Korean Food:
With 100 Best-Loved Recipes

Text by Institute of Traditional Korean Food

Translated by Kiyung Ham • Richard Harris

Hollym

Elizabeth, NJ·Seoul

The Research and Development Project for the Standardization of Korean Cuisine

The Beauty of Korean Food: With 100 Best-Loved Recipes

First published in 2007
Third printing, 2008
by Hollym International Corp.
18 Donald Place, Elizabeth, New Jersey 07208, U.S.A.
Phone : (908)353-1655 / Fax : (908)353-0255

Published simultaneously in Korea by Hollym Corp., Publishers
13-13 Gwancheol-dong, Jongno-gu, Seoul 110-111, Korea
Phone : (82-2)735-7551~4 / Fax : (82-2)730-8192, 5149

Sponsored by Ministry for Food, Agriculture, Forestry & Fisheries and
Ministry of Culture, Sports & Tourism, Republic of Korea

Photo by Masu Jeong, Gyeongho Baek

ISBN : 978-1-56591-253-3
Library of Conggress Control Number : 2007941002

Printed in Korea

*This book is the results of the "Research and Development Project for Standardization of Korean Cuisine" achieved by Institute of Traditional Korean Food with the supports of Ministry for Food, Agriculture, Forestry & Fisheries and Ministry of Culture, Sports & Tourism, Republic of Korea.

Foreword

Korean food is both a typical slow food and a healthy food, and it is arousing interest in people around the world. As the number of overweight and obese people is increasing worldwide, adult diseases such as diabetes, heart disease, and hypertension are also increasing. The ratio of overweight and obese people in Korea is relatively less than in other countries because Korean food is mainly based on vegetables, and contains suitable carbohydrate, protein, fat, and few calories.

The Good Samaritan hospital in Los Angeles in the U.S.A valuated Korean food as the best food for patients with respect to nutrition, and serves it as meals for patients. The British *Financial Times* newspaper quoted the WHO valuation and stated that Korean food is a model to preserve suitable balanced nutrition. Recently, Health, a U.S.A. health magazine, promoted Korean Kimchi as one of the top 5 worldwide health food.

The native dietary culture of a country provides a typical image of that country and is also a commercial product of high value. Promoting dietary culture overseas increases the export of agricultural products and foodstuffs, sustains the national economy, and improves the country's image. Japan, Italy, Thailand, and other countries have decided to promote their dietary cultures as a national strategy and are endeavoring to put their food on consumers' dining tables around the world.

The Korean government has been making every effort to promote Korean food as a world food. One example of this is a project to standardize the names of Korean food in foreign languages. Based on this goal of globalization of Korean food, the government, academics, and expert researchers have formed a committee and contributed a lot of time and effort to a project called *Research and Development Project for Standardization of Korean Cuisine.*

The result of this project is this book which standardizes recipes so that any foreigner can easily cook Korean food. The book also introduces various stories about Korean food and its ingredients to make people more interested in Korean food. At last, as a result of those efforts, we take great pleasure in publishing this book and distributing it all over the world in local language version. I hope that this book will spread the message about the excellence of Korean food widely, and that it will be a kind of guidebook for the people who want to learn about Korean food. I would like to express my heartful gratitude and recognition to the Head President of the Institute of Traditional Korean Food, Sookja Yoon and all researchers.

Minister for Food, Agriculture, Forestry and Fisheries

Foreword

Food is a culture. As the dining methods and utensils are different in each culture, food is an important factor that represents the cultural background and life style of a country. At present the exchanges between countries are incessant in the global village, and food can play a role to bind the people in different cultures together, and become a representative non-governmental diplomatic measure. Food may also give people who visit foreign countries the opportunity to experience the variety of the heritage and culture of those countries and heighten the joys of the journey.

Recently, food has come to the front as a high value industry worldwide, and a lot of attention is focused on it. In dietary culture, the trend is to change from fast food to slow food, and Korean food is being noticed as a genuine slow food. While the health function of fermented food, including Kimchi, is highlighted, Korean food is becoming the image of healthy food. Korean food decorated with 5 colored garnishes on natural colored foodstuffs is becoming known as a food which charms the eyes and satisfies the taste buds of people around the world.

The purpose of this book, *The Beauty of Korean Food : With 100 Best–Loved Recipes* is to standardize the recipes of the selected typical 100 Korean food and present the pleasure of cooking Korean food easily for everyone.
I believe that this book will be the standard for cooking typical Korean food for both beginners and experts. I also expect that this book, published in Korean, English, Japanese and Chinese versions, will create opportunities to introduce the taste and beauty of Korean food to the world.

Minister of Culture, Sports and Tourism

Preface

The Beauty of Korean Food : With 100 Best-Loved Recipes

Korea has an excellent dietary culture that has developed over several thousands years of history. Cooking methods have evolved with various foodstuffs from plentiful agricultural and marine products produced under the influence of the sea and four seasons. Korean food has been appraised as a scientific food because of the organization with the seasons and regional specialties, harmony of food ingredients and combination of food groups. Fermented food such as fermented sauces, Kimchi and fermented seafoods, which have recently been notified as worldwide health food, and food storage techniques were developed in Korea at an early date.

As Korean culture spreads around Asia through Korean movies and drama, interest in Korean food and culture is growing rapidly. At the Korean food festival in U.N. headquarters and Korean food exhibitions in France, Germany, Japan, China, and the U.S.A., the beauty and excellence of Korean food has won high praise from ambassadors, foreign diplomats, and journalists.

In spite of the high interest in Korean food by foreigners, there have not been any good books introducing Korean food history, ingredients, and table manners so that foreigners or overseas Koreans could learn about traditional Korean food. The existing books about Korean food used ambiguous phrases such as 'about' and 'roughly,' and some may even have incorrect information.

Therefore, the Korean government is driving a project *Research and Development Project for Standardization of Korean Cuisine* to globalize Korean food and to impart precise and accurate information.

This book, published as a part of that project, describes Korean food recipes using international system of units (SI unit) such as grams and centimeters instead of the imprecise terms that were used in the past. Now, Korean food will taste the same no matter where in the world it is cooked, and beginners will be able to easily follow the recipes.

In addition, every effort has been made to present information and stories about the ingredients and food culture for modem people who give priority to health and entertainment. I hope that this book will be an essential guide for foreigners who want to learn about Korean food in depth and for people who has plan to manage Korean food restaurants in foreign countries.

Finally, I would like to express my heartfelt gratitude to all those from the Ministry for Food, Agriculture, Forestry & Fisheries and the Ministry of Culture, Sports & Tourism who provided encouragement, to all members of the Development Committee, and to the consultants who gave advice and heartful devotion.

I would like to thank all participating researchers who, filled with a sense of mission for the globalization of Korean food, have worked with day and night and passed through numerous trials and errors in the process of experimental cooking.

Sookja Yoon

Principal Researcher

Director, Institute of Traditional Korean Food

November 2007

CONTENTS

3. Dessert

於外

CHAPTER I.
AN OVERVIEW OF KOREAN FOOD

1. THE CULTURE OF KOREAN FOOD

With four distinct seasons in the temperate zone, Korea produces a variety of seasonal ingredients such as grains, beans, vegetables and seafood. Main dishes and *banchan* (side dishes) were created with those ingredients as were storable, fermented foods such as fermented sauce, Kimchi (salted fermented vegetables) and salt–fermented seafood. As sharing seasonal food with neighbors was a custom, *sisik* (seasonal food) and *jeolsik* (festival food) thrived, and regional specialties made with local products also developed. In terms of topography, mountains and fields are spread out over the country, and Korea is surrounded by sea on three sides. Therefore, marine products are abundant and Koreans have been farming rice and hunting since early times.

Maekjok who immigrated to Korea from Middle Asia around the time of the Old Stone Age (before 3000 B.C.), was the forefather of Korea. It is believed that the tradition of eating cooked rice as a staple and *banchan* such as Kimchi as a side dish had started from the later part of the Three Kingdoms (*Silla, Baekje, Goguryeo*) era (late 6th – 7th century B.C.) when Korean ancestors lived in a community. In the unified *Silla* era (676 – 935 A.D.), the consumption of meat declined, and dishes with tea and vegetables were preferred due to Buddhism. In the *Goryeo* Dynasty (935 – 1392 A.D.), active trade with northern countries brought salt, black pepper and sugar to *Goryeo*, and famous Korean dishes such as *Goryeo–ssam* (lettuce wraps) and *Goryeo–byeong* (*yakgwa*, a sweet cake) were taken to China.

In the *Joseon* Dynasty (1392 – 1910 A.D.), Confucianism was predominant. Based on the idea of devotion to parents, the culinary tradition of serving ancestors in a patriarchal system was considered to be extremely important. That tradition extends to the Korean way of eating now. The culture of Korean food, harmonized with nature, and social and cultural environments, has developed a cuisine that promotes seasonal and regional characteristics, which are as follows:

A. Main dishes and side dishes have been developed independently.

Main dishes such as *bap* (cooked rice), *juk* (porridge), *tteokguk* (sliced rice pasta soup), *sujebi* and *mandu* (dumplings) are accompanied with side dishes that provide a balanced meal.

B. Various kinds of dishes and recipes

There are various kinds of dishes such as cooked rice, soups, salads, and diverse cooking methods such as grilling, boiling, blanching, steaming, frying and braising.

C. Varieties of taste and appearance

Various seasonings are added during cooking to evoke typical Korean flavors. Nuts, eggs and/or mushrooms are added as garnish to make the food visually appealing.

D. There are two notions about Korean food, which are *eumyangohaeng* (the doctrine of the five natural elements of the positive and negative) and *yaksikdongwon* (food and medicine are of the same origin).

Based on the doctrine of *eumyangohaeng*, ingredients or garnishes in five colors are used in the food, and the concept of *yaksikdongwon* is evident in the recipes.

E. All dishes are served on one table at the same time. All the table settings have been developed based on the table setting for one person.

Prepared dishes are served on one table at the same time. There are 3, 5, 7, 9 and 12–course table settings, but all the table settings are based on the setting for one person.

F. Regional food, seasonal food and storable, fermented food have been developed.

There are various local specialties from every region. Regional food and seasonal food made with those specialties have been enjoyed, and several fermented foods made of seasonal ingredients such as soy sauce, soybean paste, salt–fermented seafood and Kimchi have been developed.

G. The food for initiation ceremonies and table manners has been developed.

Under the influence of Confucianism, food for festivals and rituals such as for the first birthday, marriage, funeral rites and ancestor memorial ceremony, has been developed.

Folding Screen of Feast Celebrating the 60th Wedding Anniversary, Painter–Unidentified, *Joseon*, 18 th Century, (33.5 cm x 45.5 cm) National Museum of Korea

Grains and Beans

2. INGREDIENTS OF KOREAN FOOD

A. Ingredients

1) Grains

Rice is the chief grain in Korea for cooked rice (*bap*), porridges, rice cakes and Korean cookies. Wheat flour is used in making noodles and served at feasts. Barley is used for cooked barley (*boribap*) and various processed foods with wheat. Buckwheat flour is used for noodles, dumplings, jelly and cookies. Foxtail millet, Chinese millet, and African millet are also used in cooking *bap*, porridges, cakes and cookies.

2) Beans

Among beans, soybeans contain more fat and fewer carbohydrates. Red beans, mung beans and peas contain less fat and more carbohydrates. Beans with rice may be cooked for cakes, steamed food or porridges. Beans are used to grow sprouts such as soybean sprouts and mung bean sprouts, and also used as ingredients for fermented foods such as soy sauce and soybean paste.

3) Potatoes

Potatoes and sweet potatoes contain a lot of starch and sugar. They may be substituted for a main course, and used in cakes and fried food. They are also used to produce starch and other processed products.

4) Vegetables

There are various vegetables grown throughout the seasons. They are used as ingredients in soup, Kimchi, salad, *namul* (wild greens) and pickled vegetables, which are an important source of vitamins, minerals and fiber.

5) Mushrooms

Pine mushrooms, brown oak mushrooms, oyster mushrooms, stone mushrooms and snow puff mushrooms are the most edible mushrooms in Korea. Brown oak mushrooms have a good flavor and are often used in braised, steamed, pan–fried and/or stir–fried dishes. Stone mushrooms are often used as garnish.

6) Fish and Clams

Because Korea is surrounded by sea on three sides, various fish and clams are used in cooking. There are white–flesh fish such as sea bream, flatfish, yellow corvina, and red–flesh fish such as mackerel, as well as abalone, mussels, squid, short necked clams, oysters, blue crab among others. They can be braised, simmered in soy sauce, grilled, steamed and cooked in soups.

Fish

Marsh clams

7) Seaweed

Various seaweeds such as laver, brown seaweed, *tot* (brown algae), and sea lettuce are used in soups, fried foods, and salads. Seaweed is a notable health food that is rich in minerals and low in calories.

8) Meat

In Korea, various meat dishes have been developed such as grilled and braised meats as well as dried meat from birds and animals. Beef can have different textures and flavors according to its age, sex, amount of physical exercise, cut, and the level of fermentation. The suitable meat should be selected for a particular recipe. Tenderloin and sirloin are good for grilling and frying. Brisket, shank, gristle, tail and chuck short ribs are the best for soups and braising. Top round, shank and ribs are good for steaming and braising. Top round is the best cut for serving raw, dried or braised in soy sauce. Pork is often used for grilling because pork is more tender than beef, and has different fat distributions according to the cut. Chicken is often used in grilling, frying, steaming and soup because the meat is leaner.

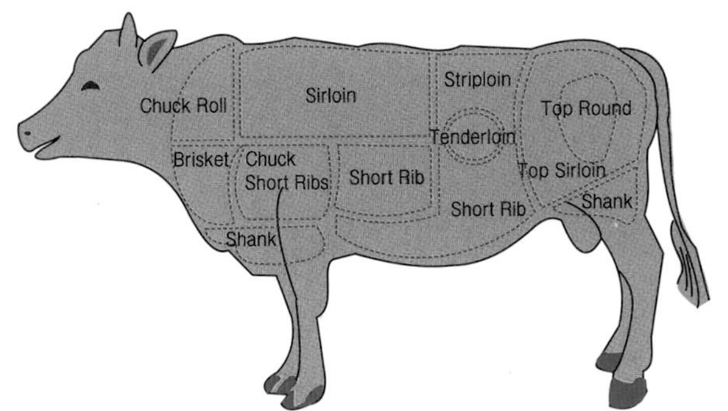

Various beef cuts

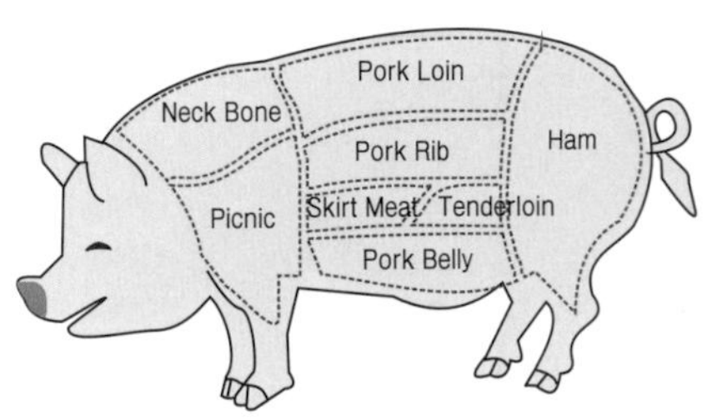

Various pork cuts

9) Eggs

Chicken eggs and quail eggs are often pan-fried or steamed. They are also used for coating fish or vegetables before frying. They may be fried for yellow and white egg garnishes.

10) Fruits

Fresh fruits such as apples, pears, peaches and strawberries may be soaked in wine or vinegar. Persimmons and jujubes may be dried rather than soaked. Hard shell nuts such as chestnuts, walnuts, gingkoes and pine nuts are used as garnish for *gangjeong* cookies, steamed foods, *gujeolpan, sinseollo* and tea.

B. Seasonings

Seasonings enhance taste and flavor, and extend the storage life of foods. *Yangnyeom* (seasoning) is "藥念, *yak-nyeom*" in Chinese. Literally, it means "Keep in mind to be medicine." The flavor of Korean food very much depends upon the selection and quantity of seasonings. There are various seasonings, such as salt, salt-fermented seafood, soy sauce, and soybean paste for saltiness; sugar, glutinous starch syrup and honey for sweetness; vinegar for sourness; ground red pepper, red pepper paste, and black pepper for spiciness; and sesame salt, sesame oil, green onion, ginger, and mustard for additional flavor and color.

1) Salt

Salt is the basic source of salty taste in food. It is classified as *horyeom, jaeyeom,* and table salt according to the size of the crystals. *Horyeom* is coarse bay salt used in making Kimchi, bean sauce or bean paste and marinated fish. *Jaeyeom* is a finer salt called "*kkotsogeum*" (flower salt). It is white and clean, and used as an ordinary salt for seasoning food. Table salt is the finest salt used for seasoning food at the table.

2) Soy sauce

The word for "soy sauce" in Korean means "salty." Soy sauce is made of fermented beans. It is used for seasoning food. It adds saltiness, a savory taste and coloring. Soy sauce is used differently depending on the cooking method. Soup, *jjigae* (stew) and *namul* (wild greens) are seasoned with *gukganjang* (concentrated soy sauce, 24% salinity). *Jinganjang* (less salty soy sauce, 16% salinity) is good for braising, slicing and simmering food and also for meats. Seasoned soy sauce or vinegar soy sauce may accompany fried fish and other fried food.

3) Soybean paste

Doenjang (soybean paste) literally means "thick paste." It is a soybean paste made of the fermented solid ingredients of soy sauce. *Doenjang* is usually used in cooking stews such as *tojangguk* or *doenjangguk.* It is also served as a condiment for *ssam* (lettuce or pumpkin leaves used as wraps), or for *namul* and *jangtteok* (wheat flour pancakes with *doenjang*).

Salt
Coarse salt
Jinganjang
Clear soy sauce
Soybean paste
Red pepper paste
Green onion
Garlic
Ginger
Ground red pepper
Ground black pepper
Ground white pepper
Mustard
Cinnamon
Sesame oil
Wild sesame oil
Soybean oil
Sesame seeds
Sugar
Starch syrup
Honey
Glutinous starch syrup
Vinegar
Ground Chinese pepper

Seasonings

4) Red pepper paste

Red pepper paste is used for stews, soups, fried food, salads, grilled food and *namul*. It is also used in making fried red pepper paste sauce for side dishes, and served with raw fish or mixed noodles.

5) Green onion

Green onions eliminate strong odors from fish and fatty foods. It enhances the taste of food with its unique flavor. They range in size from large to medium to thin. Large green onions are used for seasoning. Finely chopped medium green onions are added to soups such as *seollongtang, gomtang* and *haejangguk*. Thin green onions are added to Kimchi.

6) Garlic

The volatile compound called "allicin" in garlic gives it its spicy taste, and eliminates the strong odors from fat, fish and vegetables. Garlic is also an important seasoning for Kimchi. Minced garlic is used for seasoning. Garlic is usually sliced or shred for flavoring or garnishing, although it may also be added as whole cloves.

7) Ginger

Ginger has a unique flavor and spicy taste which eliminates the strong odors from fish and the fat in pork and chicken, and enhances the taste of food. It is minced, sliced, shred or juiced for seasoning.

8) Ground red pepper

Ground red pepper is made of dried red pepper. It is classified by size as coarse, medium and fine, and classified by spiciness as very spicy, medium and mild. Coarse ground red pepper is used for making Kimchi, the medium size is also used for Kimchi or seasoning, and fine ground red pepper is for red pepper paste or salad.

9) Ground black pepper

Ground black pepper eliminates the strong odors from fat and fish with its pungent taste and flavor, and it stimulates the appetite. The more pungent black pepper is used for meat dishes while the milder white pepper is used for fish. Whole peppercorns are used in making Korean pear pickles, broths and thick soups.

10) Mustard

The mustard seeds in mustard contain the "myrosinase" enzyme. It produces a unique flavor and spicy taste when it is fermented with water at about 40℃. A mustard sauce with salt, sugar and vinegar is used to dress salads such as *gyeojachae* or *naengchae*.

11) Cinnamon

Cinnamon has a unique flavor that enhances the flavor of food. Powdered cinnamon eliminates the strong odors from fatty food. Cinnamon provides a special flavor and color in cinnamon punch, rice cakes and Korean cookies.

12) Edible oil

Varieties of edible oil include sesame oil, perilla (wild sesame) oil and soybean oil. Sesame oil and perilla oil have a unique flavor that stimulates the appetite. They add a nutty aroma to food and prevent moisture evaporation when grilling meat or fish.

13) Sesame salt

Sesame salt is made by washing sesame seeds and stir-frying and grinding them with a small amount of salt while hot. This process produces a sweet taste and flavor. It is used to season *namul* and steamed or braised food.

14) Sugar. Starch syrup. Honey. Glutinous starch syrup

When sugar, starch syrup, honey and glutinous starch syrup are added to the food, they provide sweetness and color to the food. They also make the food soft and glutinous by keeping it moist for a long time. Therefore, they are used for seasoning food, and used in making Korean cookies, such as *gangjeong, junggwa,* and *yumilgwa.*

15) Vinegar

Vinegar is made by fermenting grains or fruit. It adds tartness to food. As a seasoning, vinegar gives a clear and cool taste to the food, stimulates the appetite and helps digestion. It also eliminates the strong odors from fish, makes fish fillets firmer, and acts as an antiseptic.

16) Chinese pepper

Ground Chinese pepper eliminates the strong odors from the fish and fats in fish or meat soups, and it also breaks down the fats.

17) Salt-fermented seafood

Salt-fermented seafood has been marinated with salt and fermented. It is an important side dish since it has a lot of protein. It is harmonized with salty, sweet and savory flavors when making Kimchi or served as a side dish on the dining table.

3. THE KINDS OF KOREAN FOOD

A. Main Dishes

1) *Bap* (Cooked rice)

Bap, a staple of Korean food, is steamed rice. It may also include other grains. There are many kinds of *bap* depending on the ingredients such as *huinbap* (white rice); *japgokbap* (rice with barley, millet, and beans); *byeolmibap* (rice with vegetables, seafood and meat); and *bibimbap* (rice mixed with *namul* and beef).

2) *Juk* (Porridge)

Juk is one of the Korean dishes that was developed in early times. It consists of grains simmered for a long time with 5 to 7 times the volume of water. There are many varieties of *juk* depending on the ingredients. *Juk* is not only served as a main dish but it can also be part of a special meal. It is served to patients and eaten for health.

3) *Guksu* (Noodles)

Korean noodles are made by kneading wheat flour or buckwheat flour and drawing the dough into long coils. Noodles helped develop the use of chopsticks in Korea.

4) *Mandu* and *Tteokguk* (Dumpling and Sliced rice cake pasta soup)

Mandu is a dumpling made of thin wheat flour wrappers stuffed with fillings then steamed, or boiled in *jangguk* (soy sauce soup). It is a specialty of the northern area of Korea. *Tteokguk* consists of diagonally sliced white rice cakes that are simmered in *jangguk.* It is served on the first day of the year without fail.

B. Side Dishes

1) *Guk* (Soup)

Guk is a soup of vegetables, seafood and/or meats boiled in plenty of water. Some varieties are *malgeun-jangguk* (clear soy sauce soup), *tojangguk* (soybean paste soup), *gomguk* (rich beef soup) and *naengguk* (chilled soup). The standard Korean table setting always has *bap* and *guk. Guk* has helped develop the use of spoons in Korea.

2) *Jjigae* (Stew)

Jjigae has less water and more solid ingredients than soup, and it is saltier. Varieties include *malgeun-jjigae* (clear *jjigae*) and *tojang-jjigae* (soybean paste *jjigae*).

3) *Jeongol* (Hot pot)

Jeongol started as a royal court food. It consists of meat, seafood, mushrooms and vegetables simmered in broth at the table just before serving for dinner or as a dish to accompany liquor.

4) *Jjim* (Steamed dish)

Jjim is a dish of main ingredients cooked with seasonings in deep water. It may be boiled with soup just above the solid ingredients, or steamed.

5) *Seon* (Steamed or parboiled stuffed vegetables)

Seon means "good ingredients." It is a dish of vegetables such as pumpkin, cucumber, eggplant and cabbage or tofu stuffed with beef and/or mushrooms that is steamed or parboiled in broth.

6) *Jorim* (Braised dish)

Jorim is a cooking method to braise meat, seafood or vegetables with soy sauce or red pepper paste on low heat. The ingredients are cooked for a long time to allow the flavors to seep in. It may have strong seasonings and can last a long time.

7) *Cho* (*Janggwa*) (Seasoned and braised seafood)

Cho (*janggwa*) is a dish of boiled sea slugs, abalone and mussels with seasoning on low heat. Then starch liquid is added and boiled. The resulting soup is quite thick and glossy.

8) *Bokkeum* (Stir-fried dish)

Bokkeum is a stir-fry of meats, seafood or vegetables. There are two types of *bokkeum* dishes; one is just stir-fried in an oiled frying pan, the other one is stir-fried with soy sauce and sugar.

9) *Gui* (Grilled dish)

Gui is a dish of grilled meats, seafood or vegetables as is, or grilled after seasoning.

10) *Jeon. Jeok* (Pan-fried dish, Brochette)

Jeon is a dish of pan-fried meats, seafood or vegetables after they have been minced or sliced and coated with wheat flour and beaten egg. *Jeok* is a dish of pan-fried ingredients after they have been seasoned and skewered.

11) *Hoe. Pyeonyuk. Jokpyeon* (Raw fish fillets or Raw meat. Pressed meat . Pressed trotters)

Hoe is a dish of raw meat, fish or vegetables seasoned with vinegar soy sauce, vinegar red pepper paste, or mustard. It can also be blanched in boiling water. *Pyeonyuk* is a dish of pressed and sliced beef or pork. *Jokpyeon* is a dish of long-simmered ox-head and ox-feet that is solidified and sliced.

12) *Mareun-chan* (Dry side dish)

Mareun-chan is a dry side dish made of salted and seasoned meat, seafood and/or vegetables that can be stored for a long time. It is enjoyed dried or fried.

13) *Jangajji* (Pickled vegetables)

Jangajji is a side dish of pickled vegetables that include Korean radish, cucumbers, bellflower roots and garlic in soy sauce, soybean paste or red pepper paste. It can be stored for a long time.

14) *Jeotggal* (Salt-fermented seafoods)

Jeotggal is a side dish of marinated shrimp, anchovies or clams with salt that is fermented. It is served as a side dish or used as a seasoning.

15) *Sukchae* (Parboiled vegetables)

Sukchae is a dish of parboiled vegetables. It may be mixed or fried with seasonings. *Sukchae* is a popular basic side dish in Korea.

16) *Saengchae* (Fresh salad)

Saengchae is a seasonal fresh salad dressed with vinegar soy sauce, red pepper paste or mustard. It is sweet and sour. This method of preparation is best for preserving the taste and most of the nutrition in the ingredients.

17) Kimchi (Seasoned and fermented vegetables)

Kimchi is a dish made by marinating Korean cabbage and Korean radish with salt, seasoning it with red pepper, garlic, green onion, ginger and salt-fermented seafood, mixing it thoroughly and letting it ferment. Kimchi is the quintessential side dish in Korea. It is a typical fermented and storable food.

C. Desserts

1) *Tteok* (Rice cake)

Tteok is a dish made by steaming, frying, or boiling rice powder or other grain powder after it has been sprinkled with water. It is served at ceremonies and holidays without fail.

2) *Hangwa* (Korean cookies)

Hangwa are traditional Korean cookies. There are many varieties depending on the ingredients or recipes such as *yumilgwa, gangjeong, sanja, dasik, jeonggwa, suksilgwa , gwapyeon, yeotgangjeong* and *yeot.*

3) *Eumcheong* (Beverages)

Eumcheong are non-alcoholic beverages.

4. TABLE SETTINGS FOR KOREAN FOOD

A. Traditional Table Setting

In the traditional Korean table setting, all dishes are served on one table at the same time as an open space pattern. The basis of the table setting is for one person. Table settings are classified as *bap–sang* (regular dining table) with cooked rice as the main dish, *juk–sang* (porridge table), *myeon–sang* (noodle table), *juan–sang* (liquor table), *dagwa–sang* (refreshment table), and *gyoja–sang* (large dining table).

1) Dining table setting

The ordinary dining table setting features cooked rice as the main dish. *Banchan* (side dishes) are arranged according to the recipes, ingredients, colors and temperature of the food. There are 3, 5, 7, 9, and 12–course table settings according to the number of side dishes.

3–course table setting

5–course table setting

7–course table setting

9–course table setting

2) Porridge table setting

This table setting features porridge as the main dish. Non-salty and mild side dishes such as *nabak-kimchi* (radish water Kimchi), *bugeo-boppuragi* (seasoned dried pollack flakes) and *jeotguk-jjigae* (salt-fermented seafood stew) are good accompaniments to the porridge.

3) Noodle table setting

In the noodle table setting, noodles, *tteokguk*, or dumplings are the main dish. This table setting is good for a lunch or a quick and simple meal.

4) Liquor table setting

The liquor table setting entertains guests with liquor. Some side dishes served with the liquor include dried meat or fish slices, *jeon, pyeonyuk, jjim, jeongol, saengchae*, Kimchi, fruit, rice cakes and/or Korean cookies.

5) Refreshment table setting

The refreshment table setting is for enjoying non-alcoholic beverages. *Gaksaekpyeon, yumilgwa, yugwa, dasik, suksilgwa, saengsilgwa, hwachae* and/or *cha* (tea) may be served.

6) Large dining table setting

This table setting serves food to many people at a large table at the same time on holidays or for ceremonies.

Noodle table setting

Refreshment table setting

B. Table Settings for Foreigners

1) Open Space Pattern Menu

The followings are examples of seasonal Korean dining table settings. All dishes are served on the table at the same time.

Season	Bap(Rice)	Guk(Soup)	Banchan(Side dishes)	Kimchi	Yangnyeomjang (Seasoning sauce)	Husik(Dessert)
Spring	*Bibimbap*	*Naengiguk*	*Saeujeon, Yangpajeon, Deodeok–saengchae, Hobakseon*	*Baekkimchi*	*Cho–ganjang, Yak–gochujang*	*Hobaktteok, Sikhye*
Summer	*Huinbap*	*Samgyetang*	*Gyeojachae, Oigapjanggwa, Gamjajeon, Putgochujeon*	*Kkakdugi*	*Gyeoja–jang, Cho–ganjang, Pa, Sogeum, Huchu*	*Jeungpyeon, Omija–hwachae*
Autumn	*Seomibap*	*Kimchi–jjigae*	*Beoseot–namul, Saengseon–gui, Soe–galbijjim*	*Baechu–kimchi*	*Ganjang*	*Songpyeon, Insamcha*
Winter	*Joraengi–tteokguk*		*Haemul–pajeon, Bugeo–bopuragi, Dotorimuk–muchim*	*Bossam–kimchi, Dongchimi*	*Ganjang, Cho–ganjang*	*Kyeongdan, Sujeonggwa*

Spring table setting

Summer table setting

Autumn table setting

Winter table setting

2) Time Lagging Pattern Menu

Dishes are served one after another along with the side dishes as per the table settings in France, the United States or China.

Course	3 Courses	5 Courses	7 Courses	9 Courses	12 Courses
1	Gyeojachae	Jatjuk	Hobakjuk	Jeonbokjuk	Nokdujuk
2	Mu-malgeunguk, Huinbap	Saengseonjeon	Tangpyeongchae	Oiseon	Eochae
3	Gyeongdan, Sikhye	Bulgogi, Sangchussam	Pyogojeon	Wolgwachae	Gujeolpan
4		Baechusokdaeguk, Wandukongbap	Daehajjim	Bindae-tteok	Juksunchae
5		Dasik, Insamcha	Tteokgalbi	Neobiani	Bugeojeon
6			Dubujeongol, Huinbap	Hwayangjeok	Domijjim
7			Maejakgwa, Sujeonggwa	Dakjjim	Songisanjeok
8				Haemul-jeongol, Kongbap	Jeonbokjjim
9				Hobaktteok, Baesuk	Sinseollo
10					Soe-galbigui
11					Beoseot-jeongol, Huinbap
12					Omija-hwachae, Gangjeong
Basic side dish	Mu-saengchae, Galbijjim Hobakjeon, Nabak-kimchi	Japchae, Sigeumchi-namul Baechu-kimchi	Oi-saengchae, Ojingeo-jeotggal Bossam-kimchi	Deodeok-saengchae, Samhap-janggwa Yeolmu-kimchi	Baechu-kimchi, Jangkimchi Seongyu-kimchi
Seasoning sauce	Choganjang, Gyeojajang	Choganjang, Ssamjang	Choganjang	Choganjang	Choganjang, Gyeojajang

3-course table setting

5-course table setting

7-course table setting

9-course table setting

12-course table setting

5. REGIONAL KOREAN FOOD

Korea is surrounded by sea on three sides, and 70% of the land is mountainous. Therefore, every region is divided by several mountain ranges, and has a different climate and produces various kinds of food. Regional food is characterized by the food that has settled in that area under the influences of the natural, social and cultural environments in that region.

1) Seoul food

Seolleongtang

As Seoul was the capital of *Joseon*, various kinds of foodstuff were centralized in Seoul. Therefore diverse and elegant cuisines were developed there as well as in the cities of *Gaeseong* and *Jeonju*. Seoul cuisine does not feature large portions but it has a lot of variety. It emphasizes small and beautiful presentations which require much time and attention. Meat, fish, vegetables and other ingredients are used equally, and the seasoning is moderate, i.e., not too strong or mild.

Regional food : *Jangguk, Seolleongtang, Gungjung–tteokbokki, Neobiani, Jangkimchi, Yaksik*

2) *Gyeonggi–do* food

Bossam–kimchi

Gyeonggi–do province includes *Gaeseong* which was the capital of the *Goryeo* dynasty. This area faces the mountains and West Sea therefore *Gyeonggi–do* has plenty of seafood, and agricultural products from active dry–field farming and rice farming. The cuisine of *Gaeseong* is known for being luxurious. It requires various ingredients and much time and attention. With the exception of the food in *Gaesong*, *Gyeonggi–do* cuisine is relatively plain in taste, not too strong or mild, but moderate. It may not require much garnish.

Regional food : *Joraengi–tteokguk, Gaeseongmujjim, Honghaesam, Bossam–kimchi*

3) *Gangwon–do* food

Dotorimuk–muchim

Gangwon–do province is mountainous with high mountains and plateaus. Dry–field farming is more prevalent than rice farming. Therefore, plenty of corn, buckwheat and potatoes are produced. Acorns, arrowroot and many wild greens are available from the mountains as well. In the eastern part of *Gangwon–do*, the *Yeongdong* region faces the East Sea. Fresh pollack, squid, brown seaweed, kelp, laver and other marine products are gathered in large numbers. There are various seafood products and salt–fermented foods in this area. *Gangwon–do* cuisine is rather plain, not as luxurious as the food in Seoul, but it is pleasant in taste.

Regional food : *Gamja–bap, Ojingeo–sundae, Dotorimuk–muchim, Chaloksusu–sirutteok, Gamja–tteok*

4) *Chungcheong-do* food

Hobakgoji-jeok

In view of geographical features, agriculture is prevalent in *Chungcheong-do* province and a great deal of wild greens and mushrooms are available in the mountains. *Chungcheong-do* cuisine reflects the heart of the people in that area. The food is served in large quantities, and is mild in taste and unadorned. *Chungcheong-do* cuisine is marked by a small amount of seasonings, and it is light and clean in taste.

Regional food : *Kongnamul-bap, Hobak-beombeok, Hobakjji-jjigae, Hobakgojijeok, Kkotsanbyeong, Gontteok*

5) *Jeolla-do* food

Chueotang

Jeolla-do province faces the sea on the West and South coasts, and has boundless rice fields. Therefore, agricultural and marine products are abundant and the cuisine is luxurious. The climate of this area is warm, and the food is rather salty, spicy and pungent since the food is seasoned with a lot of salt-fermented seafood and seasonings such as ground red pepper.

Regional food : *Jeonju-bibimbap, Chueotang, Nakjihorong, Hongeo-eosiyuk, Godeulbbyaegi-kimchi*

6) *Gyeongsang-do* food

Haemul-pajeon

Because *Gyeongsang-do* province holds good fishing ground on the East and South coasts, it produces much seafood, and also produces plenty of agricultural products from fertile lands along the *Nakdong* river. The food of this region is rather salty, spicy and rustic, but sharp and savory in taste.

Regional food : *Jaecheobguk, Mideodeok, Agujjim, Haemul-pajeon, Andong-sikhye*

7) *Jeju-do* food

Jeonbokjuk

On *Jeju-do* island, lifestyles vary according to the region. In fishing villages, people gathered marine products by fishing or diving. In farming villages, people focused on agriculture in the open field. People who lived in mountains, might have cultivated agricultural products or gathered mushrooms, wild greens or bracken. In *Jeju-do*, rice is scarce, and instead beans, barley, millet, buckwheat, sweet potatoes, sesame, potatoes and mung beans are produced in large quantities. Therefore, the food was developed from these ingredients.

Regional food : *Jeonbokjuk, Jeonbok-kimchi, Gosarijeon, Omegi-tteok*

8) *Hwanghae-do* food

Haengjeok

Hwanghae-do province is a district rich in grains. The rice and grains it produces is high in quality. The flavor of the local pork and chicken is unique since they have been raised on those grains. It is said that the people in this region are good-hearted and life became prosperous because of the abundance of grains. Therefore, the food is large in size and served in large quantities without decoration. The taste is savory, plain and simple.

Regional food : *Kimchi-bap, Haengjeok, Dwaejijok-jorim, Ojaengi-tteok, Yeonan-sikhae*

9) *Pyeongan-do* food

Eobok-jaengban

Even though *Pyeongan-do* province is cold and mountainous, it faces the West coast, and has expanded fields. Therefore, this region has plenty of dry-field products, wild greens and even marine products. It produces more millet than barley since dry-field farming is more prevalent than rice farming. *Pyeongan-do* was a big cultural exchange region between Korea and China from olden days, and the area has been endowed with an enterprising and independent spirit. The food in this region is delicious-looking, large in size and served in large quantities. The taste is less salty, not spicy.

Regional food : *Eobok-jaengban, Nokdu-jijim, Noti*

10) *Hamkyeong-do* food

Bugeo-jeon

Hamkyeong-do is a steep, mountainous province located in the far northern part of Korea. It is the coldest region in Korea, and dry-field farming is more prevalent than rice farming. The food in this region is made large in size without much adornment. Going north, the taste is less salty, light and simple, but red pepper or garlic seasoning may be used more.

Regional food : *Dak-bibimbap, Bugeo-jeon, Gajami-sikhae, Kongnamul-kimchi, Kong-tteok*

6. KOREAN TABLE MANNERS

Dining traditions and utensils may vary from country to country. Accordingly, the table manners will differ for that society and culture.

Korean table manners is as follows:

- When having a meal together with elders, take your seat according to social ranking. After the elders pick up their spoons, others can begin to eat. Try to keep pace with elders while eating. Do not put your spoon and chopsticks on the table earlier than elders at the end of the meal.

- Do not hold the spoon and chopsticks together in one hand. Use the spoon for rice and soup.

- Do not rummage through rice or side dishes with a used spoon. Be hygienic when eating.

- During a meal, do not put bones or scraps on the table. Wrap them in a napkin and dispose of it discreetly.

- Use an individual plate for your own food when platters arrive for the entire table. Be careful not to make noises when eating and drinking. Avoid knocking your spoon, chopsticks or plates around.

- Take food within reach and do not stretch your arms out too far.

- After a meal, return your spoon and chopsticks to the spot where they were placed. Fold the used napkin and put it back on the table.

- When coughing or sneezing during a meal, turn your head to one side and cover your mouth with a hand or handkerchief as to not bother your neighbors.

CHAPTER Ⅱ.
THE BASICS OF COOKING KOREAN FOOD

1. Measuring
2. Adjusting Heat
3. Cutting
4. Preparing Basic Ingredients
5. Cooking Basic Broth
6. Preparing Basic Seasonings
7. Preparing Garnishes

1. MEASURING

A. Measuring Tool

1) Balance

A balance is a weighing instrument that gives the weight of ingredients in grams, kilograms, ounces or pounds. When using a food scale, place it on a flat, horizontal surface and adjust the starting point to zero.

2) Measuring Cup

A measuring cup is a tool for measuring volume. In foreign countries such as the United States, 1 cup equals 240 ml, but in Korea, 1 cup equals 200 ml.

3) Measuring Spoon

A measuring spoon is a tool for measuring small volumes. There are two measuring spoons; "tbsp" stands for tablespoon and "tsp" stands for teaspoon.

4) Thermometer

A thermometer is an instrument for measuring cooking temperature. In general, a kitchen thermometer is a non-contact type infrared thermometer that measures the surface temperature. When measuring the temperature of liquids such as oil or syrup, use a stick liquid thermometer scaled 200–300℃. When measuring the temperature of meat, use a meat thermometer that can measure the interior temperature of the meat with a needle probe sensor.

5) Timer

When measuring cooking time, use a stopwatch or timer.

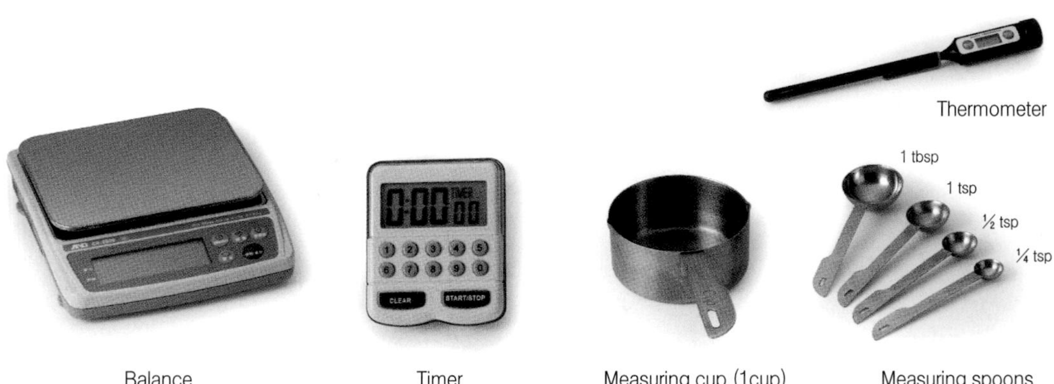

Thermometer

Balance | Timer | Measuring cup (1cup) | Measuring spoons

B. Measuring Method

1) Powder ingredients

To measure powder ingredients such as flour, scoop it out removing lumps, and level the surface without pressing down.

2) Liquid ingredients

To measure liquid ingredients such as oil, soy sauce, water or vinegar, use transparent cups. Because liquids have surface tension, measure them with measuring cups or spoons after filling them up to the edge, or for more accuracy, read the measurement at the bottom line of meniscus of the liquid.

3) Solid ingredients

To measure a solid ingredient such as soybean paste or minced meat, fill a measuring cup or spoon and level the surface.

4) Granular ingredients

To measure granular ingredients such as rice, red beans, black pepper or sesame seeds, fill the measuring cup or spoon and shake it gently to level the surface.

5) Thick ingredients

To measure thick ingredients such as red pepper paste, pack the ingredient into the measuring cup or spoon and level the surface with a straight-edged tool.

C. Measuring unit

1 cup = 1 c = about 13 tbsp +1 tsp = 200 ml water = 200 g water
1 tablespoon = 1 tbsp = 3 tsp = 15 ml water = 15 g water
1 teaspoon = 1 tsp = 5 ml water = 5 g water

2. ADJUSTING HEAT

Even though all the ingredients are prepared well, if the heat adjustments are incorrect, rice may be underdone, fish may burn, beef ribs may be half-done, and you may not get the desired results. The recipes in this book will describe the heat adjustment in detail such as "on medium heat" or "on low heat." These directions are important because they determine the cooking results. Therefore, it is necessary to control the heat as per the recipes in order to obtain the best results.

1) High heat

High heat is a heat level in which the flame touches the entire bottom of the pot on a fully opened gas range. This is the heat level for frying, grilling, steaming or boiling ingredients for the first time, or boiling soup intensely.

2) Medium heat

Medium heat is a heat level in which the flame touches most but not the entire bottom of the pot on a half opened gas range. This is the heat level to continue boiling briskly after high heat.

3) Low heat

Low heat is a heat level in which the flame is very low. Low heat level is less than half of medium heat. This is the heat level for boiling liquids down a long time or simmering soup gently.

Boiling time of water by heat level

Heat source	Water quantity / Heat level	500 g	1 kg	2 kg	Remarks
Gas range	High heat	3 min.	5 min.	9 min.	*Water temperature before boiling 25 ℃ (77 °F) *Based on a 20-cm diameter pot
	Medium heat	6 min.	10 min.	15 min.	
	Low heat	30 min.	45 min.	60 min.	

3. CUTTING

1) *Dunggeul-sseolgi*, Cutting into Rounds

This is a method for cutting cucumbers, carrots, lotus roots, and zucchini into the desired thickness. With this method, it is possible to control the thickness of the ingredients to suit the cooking method. It is generally used when cooking soup, braising or marinating.

2) *Bandal-sseolgi*, Cutting into Half-moon Shapes

This is a method for cutting Korean radishes, potatoes, carrots and zucchini into half-moon shapes after halving the ingredients lengthwise.

3) *Eunhaengip-sseolgi*, Cutting into Gingko Leaf Shapes

This is a method for cutting potatoes, carrots, and Korean radishes into gingko leaf shapes with the desired thickness after cutting the ingredients crisscross lengthwise. This method is generally used when cooking stew or braising.

4) *Yalpak-sseolgi*, Slicing Thinly

This is a method for slicing thinly into the desired thickness after cutting the ingredients into the desired length. This method is generally used for fried food or mixed salads.

5) *Eoseut-sseolgi*, Cutting Diagonally

This is a method for slicing thin and long ingredients such as cucumbers, carrots and green onions diagonally into the desired thickness. This method is generally used for frying or stews.

6) *Golpae-sseolgi*, Cutting into Dominos

This is a method for cutting cylindrical ingredients such as Korean radishes or carrots into domino shapes after cutting them into the desired length then trimming the edges into squares.

7) *Nabak-sseolgi*, Cutting and Slicing into Thin Dominos

This is a method, similar to *golpae-sseolgi*, for cutting cylindrical ingredients such as Korean radishes or carrots into thin domino shapes after cutting them into the desired length then trimming the edges into squares.

8) *Kkakduk-sseolgi*, Cutting into Cubes

This is a method for cutting Korean radishes or potatoes into cubes (about 2 cm per side). This method is generally used to make *kkakduki kimchi*, stews or braised dishes.

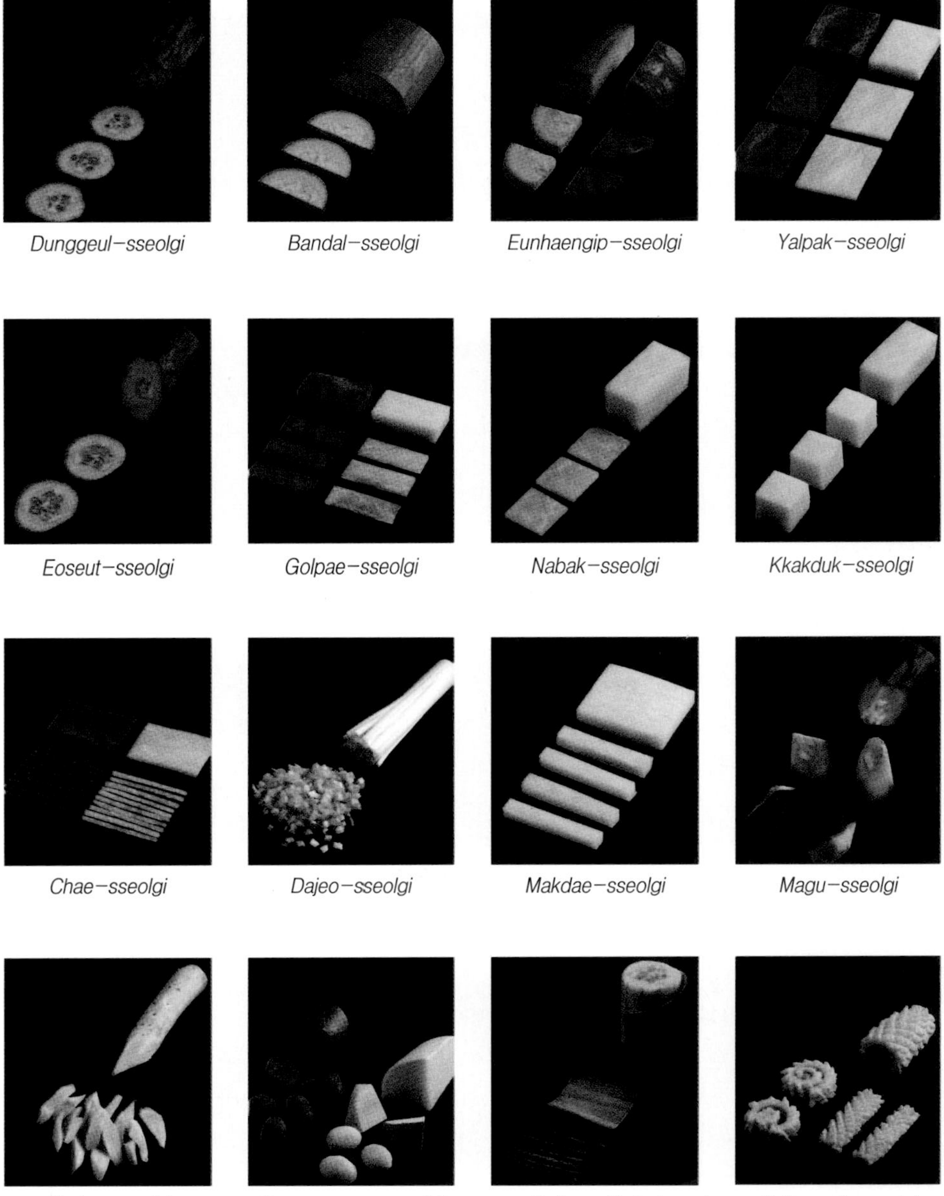

Dunggeul–sseolgi *Bandal–sseolgi* *Eunhaengip–sseolgi* *Yalpak–sseolgi*

Eoseut–sseolgi *Golpae–sseolgi* *Nabak–sseolgi* *Kkakduk–sseolgi*

Chae–sseolgi *Dajeo–sseolgi* *Makdae–sseolgi* *Magu–sseolgi*

Kkaka–sseolgi *Doryeonaeeo–sseolgi* *Dolyeo–kkakgi* *Solbangul–sseolgi*

9) *Chae-sseolgi*, Cutting into Matchsticks

This is a method for cutting Korean radishes, potatoes, cucumbers and zucchini on the diagonal into thin matchsticks. This method is generally used to make *saengchae* (salad), *gujeolpan*, or *mu-chae*.

10) *Dajeo-sseolgi*, Mincing

This is a method for mincing ingredients into small pieces. This method is generally used to make green onion or garlic seasoning sauce. It is best when the ingredients are minced into uniform pieces.

11) *Makdae-sseolgi*, Cutting into Sticks

This is a method for cutting Korean radishes or cucumbers into sticks of the desired length. This method is usually adopted to make *sanjeok* (skewers) or *sukjanggwa* (Korean cookies).

12) *Magu-sseolgi*, Chopping

This is a method for cutting relatively thin and long ingredients such as cucumbers or carrots by turning them to create bite-sized pieces. This method is generally used to make braised vegetables.

13) *Kkaka-sseolgi*, Cutting with Peeling

This is a method for cutting ingredients such as burdock roots by turning them into thin slices. The end part of the knife is used as when trimming a pencil.

14) *Doryeonaeeo-sseolgi*, Cutting and Trimming

This is a method for cutting potatoes or carrots with angles then trimming them to round the edges. This method is generally used for boiling or braising for a long time because the ingredients do not lose their shape.

15) *Dolyeo-kkakgi*, Circular Cutting

This is a method for cutting cucumbers and other ingredients into 5-cm long pieces then peeling the flesh thinly while turning.

16) *Solbangul-sseolgi*, Cutting into Pinecone Shapes

This is a method for cutting squid into big pieces. Use the knife to make diagonal slits on the squid flesh and make cross-hatched slits in the other direction. Blanch the squid in boiling water to create a pinecone shape.

4. PREPARING BASIC INGREDIENTS

A. Grains

1) **Non-glutinous rice:** Wash, remove foreign materials, and soak in water for 30 minutes to 1 hour to make steamed rice. For porridge, soak for 2 hours.

2) **Glutinous rice:** Wash, remove foreign materials, and soak in water for 30 minutes to 1 hour.

3) **Barley:** Wash by rubbing the barley, remove foreign materials, and soak in water for 1 hour.

4) **Glutinous African millet:** Wash by rubbing the millet until the water runs clear, and soak in water for 1 hour.

5) **Glutinous millet:** Wash and remove foreign materials.

B. Beans

1) **Soybeans:** Wash, remove foreign materials, and soak in water for 8 hours.

2) **Red beans:** Wash and remove foreign materials. Add red beans and water to a pot, heat for 2 minutes on high heat. When it boils, discard the boiled water, add additional water, and boil again.

3) **Black beans:** Wash, remove foreign materials, and soak in water for 3 hours.

4) **Mung beans:** Wash, remove foreign materials, and soak in water for 8 hours.

5) **Kidney beans:** Wash, remove foreign materials, and boil in a pot with water.

C. Potatoes

1) **Sweet potato and potato:** Wash, peel and soak in water.

D. Vegetables

1) **Green onion:** Remove root and peel off outer leaves. Use white area for seasonings and green area for broth.

2) **Onion:** Cut off root and stem area, peel and wash. To make onion juice, grate on a grater, wrap with cotton cloths and squeeze the juice out.

3) **Garlic:** Peel and wash. Use the whole clove, or shred or mince for seasonings.

4) **Ginger:** Peel the outer skin and wash. To make ginger juice, grate on a grater, wrap with cotton cloths and squeeze the juice out.

5) **Cucumber:** Rub the skin with salt and wash in water.

6) Burdock and lotus roots: Peel the skin with a special knife or back side of a knife, soak in vinegar water or slightly blanch in vinegar water to prevent discoloration.

7) Spinach: Cut off the roots with knife and remove yellowish leaves. Halve lengthwise if too wide. When blanching, add salt to the boiling water, add spinach root−side down, blanch slightly, and rinse in cold water.

8) Korean cabbage: When trimming tough and heavy cabbage, remove tough outer leaves and cut off the stem end. Use the leaves after removing each one by one. For Kimchi, make a criss−cross with a knife on the stem end of the cabbage, split the cabbage lengthwise and soak in salt water.

9) Korean radish: Cut off leaves and tail; scrub with brush and rinse in water.

10) Red pepper: Wash, remove stem, cut diagonally or halve lengthwise and seed. Cut into thin strips or mince.

11) Zucchini: Wash, halve lengthwise, and cut into half−moon shapes, rounds or matchsticks.

12) Soybean or mung bean sprouts: Remove heads and tails or just tails and wash.

13) Dried vegetables such as bracken: Soak in water for about 8 hours.

E. Fruits

1) Korean pear: Peel and soak in sugar water. Grate on a grater, wrap with cotton cloths and squeeze out juice to make pear juice.

F. Meats

1) Beef: Clean blood off beef, remove tendons, and cut into desired size. Before cooking, pound the beef with a meat tenderizer or the back side of a knife to keep the beef from curling up during cooking, and to make it more tender. When cooking pressed meat, tie it up with kitchen string to make a nice shape, and boil.

2) Pork: Clean blood off pork, pound with a meat tenderizer or the back side of a knife to make the meat tender.

3) Chicken: When cooking whole chicken, trim off the yellow fat, the tail part and wing tips. When cooking chicken pieces, remove the yellow fat.

4) Intestines: Clean by massaging with salt and wheat flour several times; rinse in water.

5) Ox feet. knee bone. Gristle: Soak in water to draw out the blood for about 3 to 4 hours, changing water as needed.

G. Fish and Clams

1) **Sea bream:** Scale from tail to head, remove fins and pleats from inside of the gill with scissors or a knife. Remove internal organs and wash thoroughly.

2) **Yellow corvina:** Scale from tail to head, remove fins and internal organs, and wash thoroughly.

3) **Squid:** Insert hand in between head and legs and remove internal organs, taking care not to tear the body; cut off the internal organs just above eyes. Skin the body and wash thoroughly.

4) **Octopus:** Remove internal organs and eyes, clean by massaging vigorously with salt, rinse in water.

5) **Clam:** Soak in salt water to draw out sediments; rub vigorously with hands under water.

6) **Oyster. Clam meat:** Rinse gently in salt water; drain in a strainer.

7) **Crab:** Scrub the shell with a brush, remove end part of the legs. Separate the top shell from the rest of the body and cook the entire body, or cut into smaller pieces.

8) **Shrimp:** Insert a toothpick or skewer into the back side to remove internal organs. Cook after removing head and shell, or removing just the sharp triangle part above the tail.

H. Seaweed

1) **Kelp:** Wipe with damp cotton cloth, add cold water, boil and drain water.

2) **Brown seaweed:** Soak in water, wash thoroughly and cut into the desired size.

3) **Laver:** Remove foreign elements and toast each sheet on a grill.

I. Others

1) **Black sesame:** Wash thoroughly, remove foreign materials; drain in a strainer and stir-fry on low heat.

2) **Sesame:** Soak in water for about 1 hour, rub with hands; remove foreign materials, drain in a strainer, and stir-fry on medium heat.

3) **Fresh ginseng:** Wash thoroughly and remove the head part.

4) **Cinnamon sticks:** Wash inside and outside and cut into the desired size.

5) ***Omija*:** Wash thoroughly, soak in cold water for about 12 hours, filter through cotton cloths.

6) **Salted yellow corvina:** Slice the flesh. Boil head and bones in water, filter through a strainer and let cool.

7) **Salted shrimp:** Mince the solid ingredients.

5. COOKING BASIC BROTH

1) Cooking Beef Broth

Beef broth goes well with most food. Beef broth is made from simmered brisket and shank. To ensure a tasty broth, select fresh beef. When cooking with more than 300 g of beef, soak the beef in water for 1 hour to draw out the blood. When the beef is less than 300 g, clean off the blood with cotton cloths and boil in water, and skim the foam while boiling. When the beef is well–done, remove it from the pot and strain the broth through cotton cloths. The beef may be served as pressed meat, or shredded into soup.

2) Cooking Chicken Broth

Remove the yellow fat from the chicken, put it in cold water and boil deeply. When the meat is well–done, remove the chicken, strain the broth through cotton cloths. The meat may be shredded and served with seasoning or used for soup.

3) Cooking Anchovy and Kelp Broth

Remove head and internal organs from anchovies and wipe kelp with damp cotton cloths. Heat anchovies and water in a pot. Let it boil and continue to boil on medium heat for 5 to 10 minutes. Add kelp, turn off the heat, and let it sit for 5 minutes. Strain the broth through cotton cloths.

Beef Broth

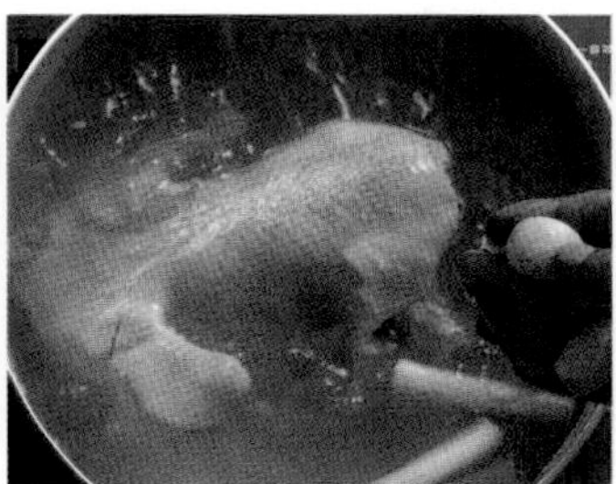

Chicken Broth

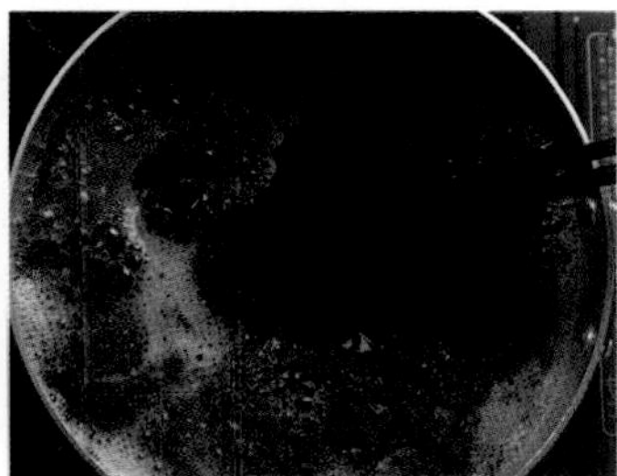

Anchovy and Kelp Broth

6. PREPARING BASIC SEASONINGS

Mustard juice | Soy sauce seasoning | Vinegar soy sauce | Vinegar red pepper paste | *Yaksik* sauce | *Gangjeong* syrup

1) Preparing Mustard Juice

Mustard juice is a seasoning served with vegetables and fermented salads. Mix 1 part mustard powder to 2 parts warm water (about 40℃). Let it ferment for 1 hour at room temperature, or in a warm steaming pot for 10 minutes. Fermented mustard is used for *gujeolpan, gyeojachae,* and other seasonings. Fermented mustard is spicier than raw mustard.

2) Preparing Soy Sauce Seasoning

Soy sauce seasoning is used for beef dishes. For 300 g of beef, mix the following ingredients thoroughly: 36 g (2 tbsp) soy sauce, 12 g (1 tbsp) sugar, 14 g (1 tbsp) minced green onion, 16 g (1 tbsp) minced garlic, 3 g (½ tbsp) sesame seeds, 0.5 g (1/5 tsp) ground black pepper, 13 g (1 tbsp) sesame oil.

Korean pear juice and/or green onion juice may be added (for *bulgogi* seasoning).

3) Preparing Vinegar Soy Sauce

Vinegar soy sauce is a dip for fried dishes. Mix 18 g (1 tbsp) soy sauce, 15 g (1 tbsp) vinegar and 15 g (1 tbsp) water thoroughly.

4) Preparing Vinegar Red Pepper Paste

Vinegar red pepper paste is a seasoning mainly for raw fish. Mix 38 g (2 tbsp) red pepper paste, 15 g (1 tbsp) vinegar and 6 g (½ tsp) of sugar thoroughly.

5) Preparing *Yaksik* Sauce

Heat 24 g (2 tbsp) of sugar in a pot for 3 minutes on medium heat. When the sugar is melted, mix in 4 g (1 tsp) of edible oil. When the liquid turns brown, add a slurry of 2 g (½ tbsp) starch (such as corn starch) and 45 g (3 tbsp) warm water. Boil for about 1 minute while stirring.

6) Preparing *Gangjeong* Syrup

Heat 5 g (1 tsp) water, 12 g (1 tbsp) sugar and 28.5 g (1½ tbsp) glutinous starch syrup in a pot for 1 minute on medium heat.

7. PREPARING GARNISHES

Gomyeong (garnish) is sprinkled or topped on dishes to decorate the food and make it more visually appealing.

1) Preparing Egg Garnish

① Beat egg, separate egg white from yolk and sprinkle each with salt.

② Remove egg cord from the white and stir without letting it foam; strain through a sieve.

③ Preheat a frying pan and oil. Pan-fry white and yolk separately on low heat to the desired thickness.

④ Cut the fried white and yolk into various shapes such as domino or diaper shapes, or thin strips, and garnish.

2) Preparing Watercress Garnish

① Beat egg, season with salt and stir without letting it foam, and strain through a sieve.

② Remove leaves of watercress, cut the stalks into 10-cm lengthwise, and skewer them at both ends.

③ Coat the skewered watercress with wheat flour then the beaten egg. Preheat a frying pan and oil, then pan-fry on low heat.

④ Cut the fried watercress into various shapes such as domino or diaper shapes, and garnish.

3) Preparing Meatballs

① Select lean meat. Clean blood off and mince finely.
② Remove excess water from tofu and mash finely.
③ Add beef to tofu and season with salt, minced green onion, minced garlic, sesame oil, ground black pepper and sesame salt, and mix together thoroughly.
④ Shape the seasoned beef into 1.5-cm diameter meatballs and coat with wheat flour and beaten egg.
⑤ When the frying pan is heated up, oil and pan-fry on low heat while rolling meatballs around so they don' t bum.

4) Preparing Mushroom Garnish

① Soak dried brown oak mushrooms, stone mushrooms and Jew' s ear mushrooms in water for about 1 hour.
② Brown oak mushrooms: Remove the stems, slice and shred into thin strips, and season. Preheat the frying pan with oil, and stir-fry on low heat. It may also be cut into the shape of a gingko leaf, domino or diamond.
③ Stone mushrooms: Wash by rubbing with hands to thoroughly remove moss, remove belly button, roll up, shred into thin strips and season with sesame oil. Preheat the frying pan and oil. Stir-fry on low heat. Or it may be minced finely and mixed with egg white, pan-fried, and cut into domino shapes.
④ Jew' s ear mushrooms: Tear into 3 to 4 pieces, stir-fry after seasoning.

5) Preparing Vegetable Garnish

① Green. Red pepper: Cut diagonally or halve lengthwise, seed, and then cut into thin strips or into domino or diamond shapes, or diagonally.
② Dried red pepper: Seed, cut diagonally or cut into thin strips.
③ Cucumber or zucchini: Wash by rubbing with salt, cut lengthwise, and peel the skin roundly and shred the skin. Marinate with salt and stir-fry. Or cut into domino or diamond shapes.
④ Small green onion: Cut off the roots, remove outer leaves, wash thoroughly, and chop finely or cut lengthwise.

6) Preparing Nut Garnish

① Gingkoes: Preheat a frying pan and oil. Stir–fry, remove skins with dry cotton cloths or paper towels while gingkoes are hot.

② Walnuts: Soak in warm water, peel the inner skin with a stick.

③ Jujubes: Wipe with damp cotton cloths, cut the flesh and flatten with mallet and cut into thin strips. Or create a flower by rolling up the flesh.

④ Pine nuts: Wipe with dry cotton cloths, remove tops, and use as is. Or halve lengthwise like as scale shapes, or grind into powder.

⑤ Chestnuts: Peel off outer shell and inner skin, slice or cut into thin strips.

⑥ Pumpkin seeds: Wipe with damp cotton cloths; use as is, or halve lengthwise.

◆ Notes

Chapter I summarizes the theory of Korean cuisine. The sections on the culture, ingredients, seasonings, types of dishes, regional food, and table manners are brief introductions to Korean food. For a better understanding, more in-depth reading is recommended.

Chapter II describes the necessities for the cooking Korean food. It lists in detail the measuring tools, measuring and cutting methods, and how to prepare basic ingredients, garnishes, broth, and seasonings for standard cooking.

Chapter III arranges standardized recipes for 100 Korean dishes. It includes 22 main dishes, 64 side dishes and 15 desserts. They are suitable for an everyday table setting and table setting for guests.

Please note the following before cooking:

A. This book contains 100 standardized recipes for typical Korean food.
B. The recipes are arranged in order of main dishes, side dishes and desserts.
C. It would be possible to get the same cooking results as in this book when the ingredients are cooked under the presented recipes, which include ingredients, heat sources and cooking tools. Cooking results may vary depending on the ingredients, heat sources and even the season.
D. Weighing ingredients on a scale is the most accurate way to measure ingredients. Results may differ if ingredients are measured by volume such as in tablespoons and teaspoons (which have been provided for reference).
E. The recipes are for four (4) servings except in certain cases.
F. The recipes are based on traditional methods but have been adjusted to modern times.
G. There may be some acceptable allowances in cooking time (heating, boiling, frying, marinating, blanching, fermenting, etc.), and length, weight and volume of the ingredients in this book.

◆ Introduction of Nutrients

1. **Calorie:** Calories represent the total energy created by metabolic action of the nutrients of the food inside the body. 1 g of carbohydrate creates 4 Kcal, 1 g of protein creates 4 Kcal, and 1 g of fat creates 9 Kcal.

2. **Carbohydrate:** Carbohydrates are the most important nutrient to create energy in our body. Carbohydrates can be taken from food made of grains such as cooked rice, cookies, breads, *tteok* and noodles.

3. **Protein:** Protein is the constituent element of our body. Most organs in the human body such as the internal organs, muscles and skin are made of protein. Milk, poultry, fish, eggs and beans contain plenty of protein.

4. **Fat:** Fat is a source of high energy. Fat effectively stores energy for people who require a lot of energy. Fat keeps the body heat and preserves important internal organs by preventing heat emission from the body. Oils such as cooking oil and sesame oil, nuts, and meat contain a lot of fat.

5. **Sodium:** Sodium is an essential mineral for metabolic action in our body. Sodium is the main component of salt. However, consuming large amounts of sodium has been linked to heart disease and other illnesses. Processed foods such as chips, *ramyeon* (instant noodles), and canned food contain high levels of sodium.

*Nutrient analysis has been taken for only edible parts and excludes parts such as skin and bones.

***Cooking terminology**

A. Pre-cleaning meat: Cleaning meat in boiling water shortly.

B. Bring to a boil: A status of boiling over once.

◆ Ingredients Weight Table

Grains

(Unit : g)

Name \ Quantity	1 cup(200 ml)	Name \ Quantity	1 cup(200 ml)
Brown rice	180	Adlay	165
Non-glutinous rice	180	Glutinous millet	170
Non-glutinous rice powder	100	Wheat flour	95
Glutinous rice	180	Soybean	160
Glutinous rice powder	100	Sweet red bean	165
Barley	180	Sesame	120
Glutinous African millet	170	Black sesame	95

Vegetables

(Unit : g)

Name \ Quantity	1 piece(medium size)	Name \ Quantity	1 piece(medium size)
Korean cabbage	2,000	Zucchini	300
Korean radish	1,000	Sguash	1,500
Potato	200	Onion	150
Sweet potato	150	Green pepper	15
Carrot	200	Red pepper	20
Cucumber	200	Dried brown oak mushroom	5

Meats and Seafoods

(Unit : g)

Name \ Quantity	1 (medium size)	Name \ Quantity	1 (medium size)
Chicken	1,200	Dried pollack	70
Egg	55	Octopus	200
Croaker	600	Blue crab	300
Sea-bream	500	Abalone	200

Fruits and Nuts

(Unit : g)

Quantity / Name	1 piece(medium size)	Quantity / Name	1 piece(medium size)
Apple	250	Walnut	5
Korea Pear	500	Jujube	4
Dried persimmons	40	Gingko	2
Chestnut	15	*Omija*	100(1 cup)

Seasonings

(Unit : g)

Quantity / Name	1 tsp(5 ml)	1 tbsp (15 ml)	1 cup (200 ml)	Quantity / Name	1 tsp(5 ml)	1 tbsp (15 ml)	1 cup (200 ml)
Water	5	15	200	Refined rice wine	5	15	200
Coarse salt	4.5	13	160	Coarse red pepper powder	2.2	7	93
Fine salt	4	12		Fine red pepper powder	2.2	7	93
Soy sauce	6	18	240	Black pepper	3	10	
Diluted clear soy sauce	6	18	240	Ground black pepper	2.5	8	
Soybean paste	5	17		Mustard powder	2	6	
Red bean paste	6	19		Pine nuts	3.5	10	120
Sesame oil	4	13		Pine nuts powder	2	6	
Perilla oil	5	15		Starch powder	2.5	8	
Sesame seed	2	7	93	Minced green onion	4.5	14	
Sesame salt	2	6		Minced garlic	5.5	16	
Edible oil	4	13	170	Ginger juice	5.5	16	210
Sugar	4	12	160	Minced ginger	4	12	
Yellow sugar	4	12	150	Onion juice	5	15	200
Honey	6	19	300	Salted shrimps	5	15	200
Starch syrup		19	288	Salted anchovy juice	5	15	200
Vinegar	5	15	200				

◆ Seasonings for Standard Cooking

Seasoning Name	Contents	Seasoning Name	Contents
Gukganjang	Salinity 24%	Honey	Sweetness 76Brix
Jinganjang	Salinity 16%	Glutinous starch syrup	Sweetness 74Brix
Red pepper paste	Salinity 7%, Sweetness 45 Brix	Vinegar	Total acidity 6.0~7.0
Soybean paste	Salinity 11%	Salted anchovy juice	Salinity 22±2%
Ground red pepper	Capsaicin 42.3%	Salted shrimp	Salinity 5.0%
Salt	NaCl over 80%	Salted yellow corvina	Salinity 5.0%

Gukganjang · *Jinganjang* · Red pepper paste · Soybean paste

Ground red pepper · Salt · Honey · Glutinous starch syrup

Vinegar · Salted anchovy juice · Salted shrimp · Salted yellow corvina

◆ Specification of Cooking Utensils

(Unit : cm)

Cooking Utensils	Diameter	Height	Thickness
Single grip pot	16	10	0.2
Double grip pot	18	11	0.2
Double grip pot	20	12	0.2
Double grip pot	24	16	0.2
Double grip pot	28	18	0.2
Double grip pot	32	23	0.5
Simmering pot	28	6	0.2
Steamer	26	16	0.5
Frying pan	30	5.5	0.5
Round pan	28	9	0.5

Single grip pot
Double grip pot(Dia. 20−cm)
Simmering pot
Steamer
Frying pan
Round pan
Stainless steel bowl
Stainless steel rice cake mold
Iron grill
Mallet
Grater
Knife

CHAPTER Ⅲ.
STANDARD RECIPES FOR 100 KOREAN FOOD

1. Main Dishes

2. Side Dishes

3. Dessert

Huinbap 흰밥

Cooked White Rice

Huinbap is cooked only of non-glutinous white rice. Rice was farmed from early times in Korea. Therefore, rice dishes and rice-based foods were developed as well. Rice is the main dish on the table, and the other accompanying dishes are side dishes.

Total weight after cooking	Weight for one serve	Service temperature	Total heating time	Total cooking time	Standard utensil
880 g(4 serves)	220 g	65 ℃	21 min	1 hour	20 cm pot

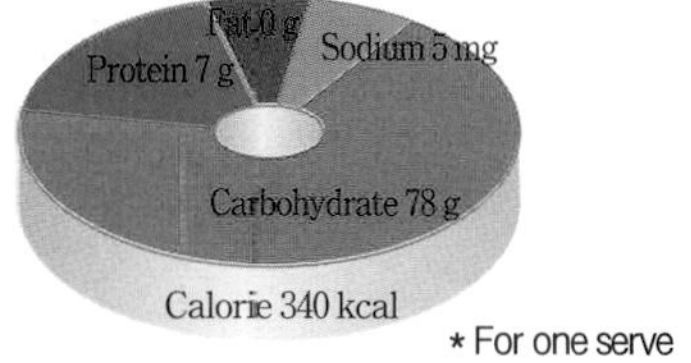

* For one serve

Ingredients & Quantity

450 g (2½ cup) non-glutinous rice
600 g (3 cups) water

Preparation

1. Wash the non-glutinous rice about 3 times and remove foreign elements.
2. Soak the rice in water for 30 min (550 g), drain water on a strainer for 10 min. 【Photo 2】

Recipe

1. Put the rice and water in the pot. 【Photos 3 & 4】
2. Heat it up for 4 min on high heat. When it boils, continue to boil it for another 4 min.
3. Lower the heat to medium, boil for 3 min. When the rice become sodden, lower the heat to low, then steam for 10 min. 【Photo 5】
4. Spread the rice softly with scoop and place in a bowl. 【Photo 6】

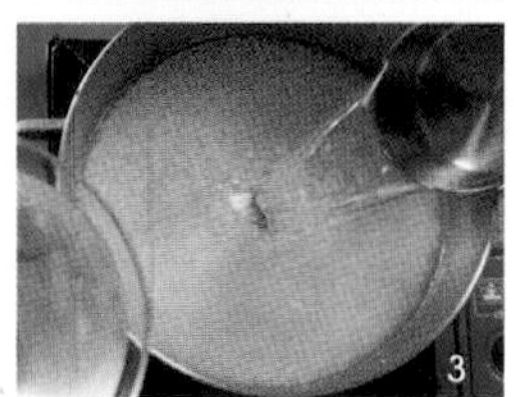

· When rice boiling water overflow during boiling, open the lid shortly and shut down again.
· If rice soaked in water too long, cooked rice may be untasty.

Heating Time	Process	Heat Control
Preparation	Soaking non-glutinous rice	
0 min	Boiling non-glutinous rice with water	H-heat 8 min.
10 min		M-heat 3 min.
20 min	Steaming	L-heat 10 min.

Ogokbap 오곡밥

Five Grain Rice

Ogokbap is cooked of glutinous rice, glutinous African millet, sweet red beans and black beans together. From olden days, Koreans have regarded the first full moon day of the year as an important day. People cooked five-grain rice on that day and shared it with neighbors in hopes of peace and a good harvest.

Total weight after cooking	Weight for one serve	Service temperature	Total heating time	Total cooking time	Standard utensil
1.2 kg(4 serves)	300 g	65 ℃	53 min	4 hours	20 cm pot

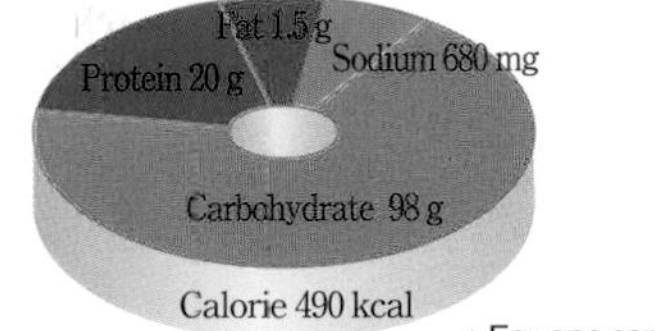

* For one serve

Ingredients & Quantity

360 g (2 cups) glutinous rice
80 g (½ cups) black bean
85 g (½ cups) glutinous African millet
83 g (½ cups) sweet red bean , 300 g (1½ cups) scalding water, 500 g (2½ cups) boiling water
85 g (½ cups) glutinous millet
rice water : 100 g (½ cups) sweet red bean boiled water, 500 g (2½ cups) water, 10.5 g (¾ tbsp) salt

Preparation

1. Wash the glutinous rice, soak in water for 30 min. and drain water on a strainer for 10 min. (440 g).
2. Wash the black bean, soak in water for 3 hours and drain water on a strainer for 10 min. (140 g).
3. Wash the glutinous African millet by rubbing until washing water to be clear, soak in water for 1 hour, and drain water on a strainer for 10 min. (120 g). 【Photo 2】
4. Wash the sweet red bean and remove foreign elements, drain water on a strainer for 10 min.
5. Wash the glutinous millet and drain water on a strainer for 10 min. (114 g).

Recipe

1. Put sweet red bean and scalding water into the pot, heat it up for 2 min. on high heat. When it boils, discard the scalding water. Add fresh water to the sweet red bean, heat it up for 3 min. on high heat. Lower the heat to medium, boil for 20 min. taking care the bean not to be burst, drain through a strainer (131 g). Prepare rice cooking water with sweet red bean boiled water after adding water and salt. 【Photo 3】
2. Put the rice, black bean, glutinous African millet, sweat red bean and rice water into the pot. Heat it up for 2 min. on high heat. When it boils, continue to boil for another 3 min. Lower the heat to medium, add glutinous millet and boil it for 10 min. When the rice become sodden, lower the heat to low, steam for 13 min. Turn the heat off, and let it sit there for 10 min. more to be well-done. 【Photos 4 & 5】
3. Mix them with scoop thoroughly and serve in a bowl. 【Photo 6】

· When cooking five grain rice in a steaming pot or steamer, sprinkle sweet red bean boiled water with salt during steaming.

Heating Time	Process	Heat Control
Preparation	Soaking glutinous rice and black bean. Washing four other grains	
0 min	Boiling sweet red bean	H-heat 5 min. M-heat 20 min.
20 min	Cooking five grain rice	H-heat 2 min. H-heat 3 min.
	Adding glutinous millet	M-heat 10 min.
30 min	Steaming for well-done	L-heat 13 min.
50 min	Steaming for well-done after turning heat off	after heat off 10 min.

Yeongyang-dolsotbap 영양돌솥밥

Norishing Hot Stone Pot

Yeongyang-dolsotbap is a nourishing dish of rice, ginseng, jujubes and chestnuts which are believed to have healing properties. Rice tastes best when cooked in a stone pot because it cooks evenly and stays hot in the pot.

Total weight after cooking	Weight for one serve	Service temperature	Total heating time	Total cooking time	Standard utensil
960 g(4 serves)	240 g	65~80 ℃	23 min	4 hours	15 cm stone pot, 30 cm frying pan

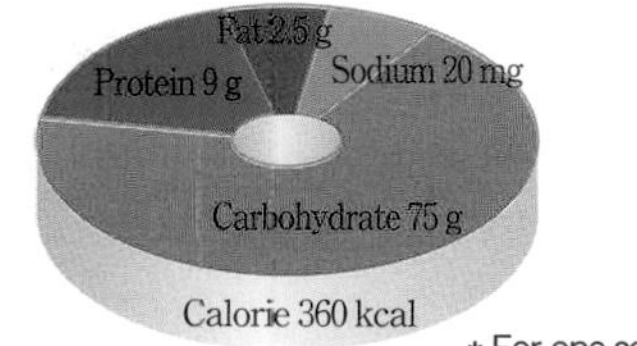

* For one serve

Ingredients & Quantity

360 g (2 cups) non-glutinous rice
90 g (½ cup) glutinous rice
30 g black bean, 60 g (4 ea) chestnut, 32 g (8 ea) jujube, 37 g cultivated pine mushrooms, 24 g (12 ea) gingko
10 g (1 tbsp) pine nuts
25 g ginseng(fresh wet ginseng)
600 g (3 cups) water
seasoning sauce : 54 g (3 tbsp) soy sauce, 14 g (1 tbsp) minced green onion, 5.5 g (1 tsp) minced garlic
1.1 g (½ tsp) ground red pepper, 6 g (1 tbsp) sesame salt
0.3 g (⅛ tsp) ground black pepper, 8 g (2 tsp) sesame oil

1

Preparation

1. Wash the non-glutinous rice and glutinous rice cleanly, soak in water for 30 min., drain water on a strainer for 10 min. (non-glutinous rice 440 g, glutinous rice 110 g).
2. Wash the black bean, soak in water for 3 hours drain water on a strainer for 10 min (63 g).
3. Skin the chestnuts, cut into 2~4 pieces. Wipe the jujube with damp cotton cloths, cut the flesh round, divide into 2~3 pieces.
4. Skin the cultivated pine mushrooms, slice it into 0.7 cm-thick, maintaining the mushroom shape. 【Photo 2】
5. Preheat the frying pan and oil, stir-fry the gingko for 2 min. on medium heat with rolling, skin off. Remove tops of pine nuts, wipe the nuts with dry cotton cloths.
6. Wash the ginseng cleanly, remove the head part, cut into 2 cm-long and 0.7 cm-thick round. 【Photo 3】
7. Blend seasoning sauce. 【Photo 4】

2

3

4

Recipe

1. Put the non-glutinous rice, glutinous rice, black bean, chestnuts, cultivated pine mushrooms, ginseng and water into the stone pot, heat it up for 10min. on high heat. When it boils, continue to boil for another 3 min. 【Photo 5】
2. Lower the heat to low, add the jujube, gingko and pine nuts, boil it for 10 min. Turn off the heat, steam it for 10 min. for well-done. 【Photo 6】
3. When the rice is well-done, mix them thoroughly. Put in a bowl and serve with seasoning sauce.

5

· When the rice boiling water overflow, open the lid shortly and shut down again.
· Cultivated pine mushrooms may be replaced by brown oak mushrooms.
· All the prepared stuffs may be add into the pot from the very beginning.

6

Heating Time	Process	Heat Control
Preparation	Soaking rice in water. Soaking black bean. Preparing vegetables and pine nuts. Stir-frying gingko. Blending seasoning sauce.	
0 min	Boiling after adding stuffs into the stone pot	H-heat 13 min.
10 min	Adding jujube, gingko and pine nuts	L-heat 10 min.
20 min	Steaming for well-done	10 min. after heat off

Bibimbap 비빔밥

Rice Mixed with Vegetables and Beef

Bibimbap is a dish mixed of cooked white rice, vegetables, beef, garnishes and fried red pepper paste. It is said that this dish came from the customs of memorial services and rural villages. This dish is very easy to prepare, just mixing together cooked white rice with various vegetables, *namul* and red pepper paste.

Total weight after cooking	Weight for one serve	Service temperature	Total heating time	Total cooking time	Standard utensil
1.64 kg (4 serves)	410 g	50~65 ℃	43 min	2 hours	24 cm pot, 30 cm frying pan

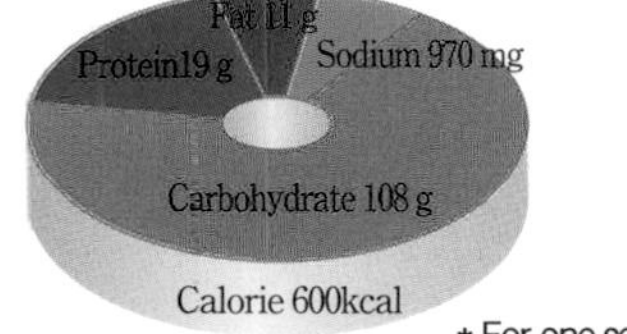

* For one serve

Ingredients & Quantity

450 g (2½ cups) non-glutinous rice, 600 g (3 cups) water
300 g young pumpkin, 2 g (½ tsp) salt
200 g skinned bellflower roots, 4 g (1 tsp) salt
120 g beef (top round), 200 g soaked bracken
seasoning sauce : 18 g (1 tbsp) soy sauce, 6 g (½ tbsp) sugar, 9 g (2 tsp) minced green onion
5.5 g (1 tsp) minced garlic, 2 g (1 tsp) sesame salt, 0.3 g (⅛ tsp) ground black pepper
4 g (1 tsp) sesame oil
2 ea (120 g) egg,
3 g kelps, 26 g (2 tbsp) edible oil
fried red pepper paste : 95 g (5 tbsp) red pepper paste, 20 g minced beef, 9 g (2 tsp) minced green onion
5.5 g (1 tsp) minced garlic, 90 g (6 tbsp) water, 18 g (1½ tbsp) sugar
19 g (1½ tbsp) sesame oil

Preparation

1. Wash the rice, soak in water for 30 min. drain water on a strainer for 10 min. (550 g).
2. Cut the young pumpkin into 5~6 cm-long, then cut them into 0.3 cm-wide/thick round, shred into matchstick, soak with salt for 10 min. wipe water with cotton cloths. Shred bellflower roots into 5~6 cm-long and 0.3 cm-wide/thick, add salt and fumble them with hands, let it sit for 10 min. then rinse and squeeze water out. 【Photo 2】
3. Clean blood of beef with cotton cloths, shred into 6 cm-long and 0.3 cm-wide/thick. Wash the bracken, cut into 5 cm-long. Season beef and bracken with seasoning sauce respectively. 【Photo 3】
4. Panfry egg for yellow/white egg garnish, shred it into 5 cm-long and 0.3 cm-wide/thick.

Recipe

1. Put the rice and water in the pot, heat it up for 4 min. on high heat. When it boils, continue to boil it for another 4 min. then lower the heat to medium, boil it for 3 min. When the rice become sodden, lower the heat to low, steam for 10 min. to be well-done (1.03 kg).
2. Preheat the frying pan and oil, stir-fry pumpkin on high heat for 30 sec. spread out and cool down (80 g).
3. Preheat the frying pan and oil, stir-fry bellflower roots on medium heat for 5 min. (120 g). 【Photo 4】
4. Preheat the frying pan and oil, stir-fry beef and bracken respectively on medium heat for 3 min. (beef 80g, bracken 164g). 【Photo 5】
5. Pour edible oil into the pan, oil fry kelps on medium heat for 10 sec. Crush it into large size.
6. Put the minced beef, green onion, garlic and half of the sesame oil in the pot, stir-fry them on medium heat for 2 min. Add red pepper paste, sugar and sesame oil, stir-fry for 5 min. Add water into it, stir-fry for another 3 min. to make fried red pepper paste (167 g).
7. Serve steamed rice with prepared stuffs and fried red pepper paste on top. 【Photo 6】

· When rice boiling water overflow during boiling, open the lid shortly and shut down again.
· To provide good taste, rice should be cooked properly neither too hard nor too watery.
· When preparing fried red pepper paste with home-made red pepper paste, add sugar a little bit more.
· Fried red pepper paste may be added more, or reduced upon taste.

Heating Time	Process	Heat Control
Preparation	Soaking non-glutinous rice. Preparing beef, vegetables and egg garnish. Cooking steamed rice	
0 min	Stir-frying stuffs	H-heat 8 min. M-heat 3 min. L-heat 10 min.
20 min	Oil frying kelps	H-heat 30 sec. M-heat 11 min.
30 min	Making fried red pepper paste	M-heat 10 sec. M-heat 10 min.

Janggukbap 장국밥

Rice in Beef Soup

Janggukbap is a dish made of cooked white rice in long–simmered beef broth, seasoned with soy sauce. In olden days, when a big event or festival took place in the royal court, *janggukbap* was served to the mobilized soldiers, musicians, dancers and singers because this dish is convenient for serving to the many people.

Total weight after cooking	Weight for one serve	Service temperature	Total heating time	Total cooking time	Standard utensil
2.08 kg(4 serves)	520 g	65~80 ℃	1 hour 57 min	3 hours	20 cm pot, 30 cm frying pan

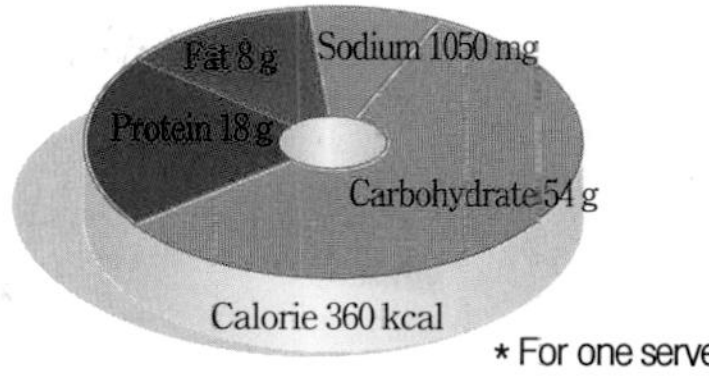

* For one serve

Ingredients & Quantity

300 g (1⅔ cups) non-glutinous rice, 400 g (2 cups) water
broth : 200 g beef (brisket · shank), 200 g (1/5 ea) radish, 2.4 kg (12 cups) water
seasoning sauce① : 6 g (1 tsp) clear soy sauce, 9 g (2 tsp) minced green onion
5.5 g (1 tsp) minced garlic, 0.3 g (⅛ tsp) ground black pepper
80 g soaked bracken
80 g skinned bellflower roots , 4 g (1 tsp) salt
150 g bean sprouts , 100 g (½ cup) water, 1 g (¼ tsp) salt
seasoning sauce② : 9 g (½ tbsp) clear soy sauce, 7 g (½ tbsp) minced green onion
5.5 g (1 tsp) minced garlic, 2 g (1 tsp) sesame salt, 4 g (1 tsp) sesame oil
13 g (1 tbsp) edible oil
6 g (1 tsp) clear soy sauce
6 g (1½ tsp) salt
600 g (4 bowls) warm steamed rice

1

Preparation

1. Wash the non-glutinous rice, soak in water for 30 min. drain water on a strainer for 10 min.
2. Clean blood of beef with cotton cloths, put the beef and radish in the pot. Pour water into the pot and heat it up for 10 min. on high heat. When it boils, lower the heat to medium, boil it for another 20 min. Take the radish out from the pot, and simmer for 40 min. more. Take the beef out and cool the broth down and filter through cotton cloths (1.3 kg).【Photo 2】
3. Cut off durable part of the bracken, wash and cut it into 6 cm-long (75 g).
4. Cut the bellflower roots into 6 cm-long, 0.3 cm wide/thick. Fumble with salt, rinse in water and squeeze the water out (65 g). Remove the heads and tails of bean sprouts, wash them cleanly (140 g).【Photo 3】
5. Blend seasoning sauce ①, ②.

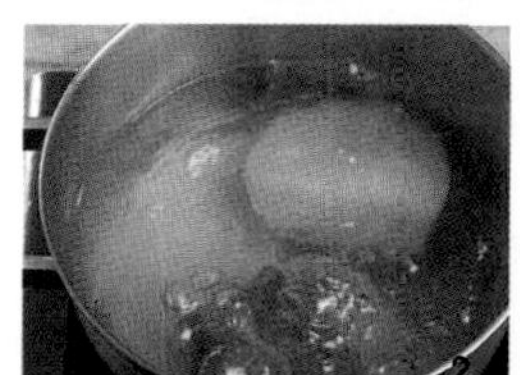
2

3

Recipe

1. Put water and the rice in the pot, heat it up for 3 min. on high heat. When it boils, continue to boil it for another 4 min. lower the heat to medium, boil for 3 min. When the rice become sodden, lower the heat to low, steam it for 10 min.
2. Cut the boiled beef and radish into 2.5 cm-wide, 3 cm-long and 0.5 cm-thick. Season with seasoning sauce①.
3. Season bracken and bellflower with ⅔ of seasoning sauce ②. Preheat the frying pan and oil, stir-fry the bracken and bellflower for 2 min. respectively on medium heat. 【Photo4】
4. Put the bean sprouts, water and salt into the pot, heat it up for 1 min. on high heat. When it boils, lower the heat to medium, boil them for 3 min. and season with remained ⅓ of seasoning sauce ② (110 g).
5. Pour the broth into the pot, heat it up for 5 min. on high heat. When it boils, add the seasoned beef, radish, bracken, bellflower roots and bean sprouts, boil them for 2 min. When it boils again, lower the heat to medium, boil for another 10 min. 【Photo 5】
6. Season with clear soy sauce and salt, bring it to a boil. 【Photo 6】
7. Place warm steamed rice in a bowl and add the beef soup.

4

5

· Do not boil bean sprouts too long, or it may become tough.
· Green onion, salt and/or ground red pepper may be added upon taste.

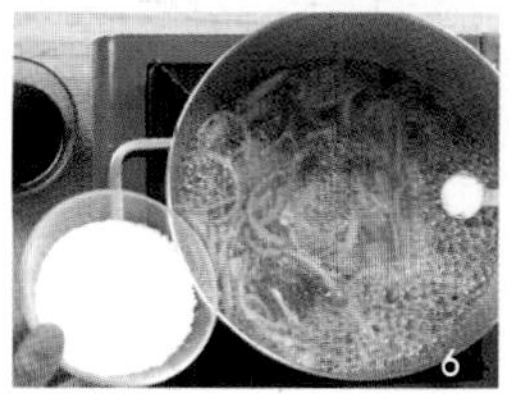
6

Heating Time	Process	Heat Control
Preparation	Soaking non-glutinous rice. Preparing beef and vegetables	
	Blending seasoning sauce	H-heat 7 min. M-heat 3 min. L-heat 10 min.
0 min	Cooking rice	H-heat 10 min. M-heat 60 min.
20 min	Boiling beef and radish	
90 min	Filtering broth. Seasoning beef and radish after cutting	M-heat 4 min.
	Stir-frying bracken and bellflower roots after seasoning	H-heat1 min. M-heat 3 min.
	Boiling bean sprouts and seasoning	H-heat 7 min. M-heat 10 min.
100 min	Boiling broth	M-heat 2 min.
110 min	Seasoning with salt	

Gimbap 김밥

Rice Rolled in Laver

Gimbap is cooked white rice seasoned with sesame oil and salt, then rolled with other ingredients in a sheet of laver. *Gimbap* has been popular since the 1960s. It is good to pack for a picnic as lunch or a snack, because it is convenient to eat and contains many different ingredients and flavors.

Total weight after cooking	Weight for one serve	Service temperature	Total heating time	Total cooking time	Standard utensil
880 kg (4 serves)	22 0g	15~25 ℃	42 min	2 hours	20cm pot, 30 cm frying pan

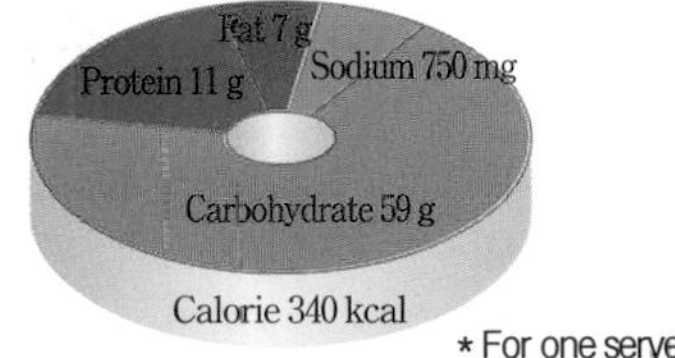

* For one serve

Ingredients & Quantity

360 g (2 cups) non-glutinous rice, 500 g (2½ cups) water
seasoning for rice : 3 g (¾ tsp) salt, 13 g (1 tbsp) sesame oil
50 g (¼ piece) carrot, 1 g (¼ tsp) salt
80 g (½ piece) cucumber, 1 g (¼ tsp) salt
70 g pickled radish
100 g burdock roots, 13 g (1 tbsp) edible oil
diluted vinegar : 17 g (1 tbsp) vinegar ,200 g (1 cup) water
seasoning sauce ① : 27 g (1½ tbsp) soy sauce, 15 g (1 tbsp) water, 6 g (½ tbsp) sugar
5 g (1 tsp) refined rice wine
80 g minced beef
seasoning sauce ② : 12 g (2 tsp) soy sauce, 2 g (½ tsp) sugar, 2.3 g (½ tsp) chopped green onion
1.4 g (¼ tsp) minced garlic, 2 g (1 tsp) sesame salt, 2 g (½ tsp) sesame oil
0.1 g ground black pepper
120 g (2 ea)egg , 1 g (¼ tsp) salt
6 g (4 sheets) dried laver
26 g (2 tbsp) edible oil

Preparation

1. Wash the rice and soak in water for 30 min. drain water on a strainer for 10 min. (440 g).
2. Clean the carrot and skin (40 g). Clean the cucumber by rubbing and cut it into 20 cm–long, 0.7 cm–wide/thick. Take seeds area out (60 g), sprinkle salt and allow it to be marinated for 5 min. wipe excess water with cotton cloths.
3. Slice the pickled radish into 20 cm–long, 0.7 cm–wide and thick.
4. Skin off burdock roots (86 g), cut into 20cm–long, 0.7 cm–wide and thick, and soak in diluted vinegar for 2 min. 【Photo 2】
5. Clean blood of minced beef with cotton cloths and season with seasoning sauce② (70 g).
6. Beat egg and salt.

Recipe

1. Put the rice and water in the pot and boil it on high heat for 4 min. After additional boiling for 4 min. reduce the heat to medium and boil for 3 more min. When the rice become sodden, reduce the heat to low and steam for 10 min. (730 g). Season with salt and sesame oil. 【Photo 3】
2. Preheat the frying pan and oil, stir–fry the carrot and cucumber on high heat for 30 sec. respectively. 【Photo 4】
3. Preheat the frying pan and oil, stir–fry the burdock roots on medium heat for 3 min. add seasoning sauce ①, stir–fry them on low heat for 10 min. 【Photo 5】
4. Preheat the frying pan and oil, stir–fry the beef for 2 min. on medium heat.
5. Preheat the frying pan and oil, fry beaten egg on low heat for 3 min. for front side and 2min. for back side, to be 1cm–thick, cut it into 20 cm–long and 1 cm–wide.
6. Toast the laver on low heat. Upon the laver, layer steamed rice (150 g) evenly and placed the carrot, cucumber, pickled radish, burdock roots, beef and fried egg in the middle. Roll up the laver to create a log with a 3~4 cm diameter. Slice it at intervals of 1.5 cm–wide. 【Photo 6】

· Boiled fish cakes, crab meat, tuna, Kimchi and gourd flesh may be used for filling stuffs.

Heating Time	Process	Heat Control
Preparation 0 min 20 min 40 min	Soaking non–glutinous rice. Preparing ingredients Cooking the rice. Stir–frying carrot and cucumber Stir–frying burdock roots and beef Pan–frying egg for garnish strips Toasting laver Rolling with filling stuffs in laver and slicing	 H–heat 8 min. M–heat 3 min. L–heat 10 min. H–heat 1 min. M–heat 5 min. L–heat 10 min. L–heat 5 min.

Kongjuk 콩죽

Bean and Rice Porridge

Kongjuk is a porridge of ground soybeans and non-glutinous rice. It is sweet, soft and rich in nutrients. Soybeans originated from Manchuria, where *Goguryeo* had been founded. Therefore, Korea developed various dishes using soybeans.

Total weight after cooking	Weight for one serve	Service temperature	Total heating time	Total cooking time	Standard utensil
1.32 kg (4 serves)	330 g	60~65 ℃	1 hour 12 min	over 5 hours	20cm pot

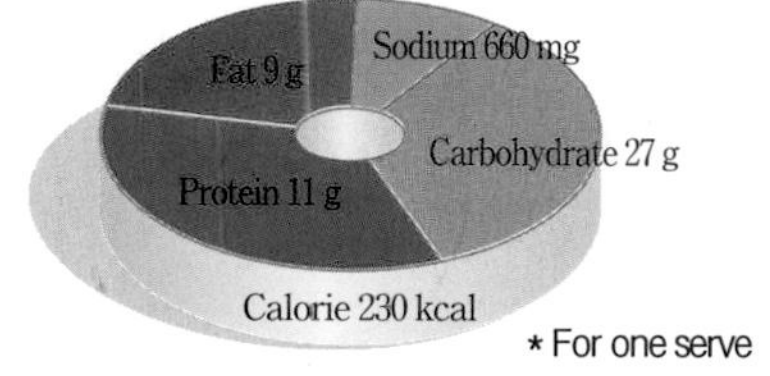

* For one serve

Ingredients & Quantity

160 g (1 cup) white soybean, 1 kg (5 cups) soaking water, 1.6 kg (8 cups) boiling water,
800 g (4 cups) changing water
135 g (¾ cups) non-glutinous rice
1 kg (5 cups) water
8 g (2 tsp) salt

Preparation

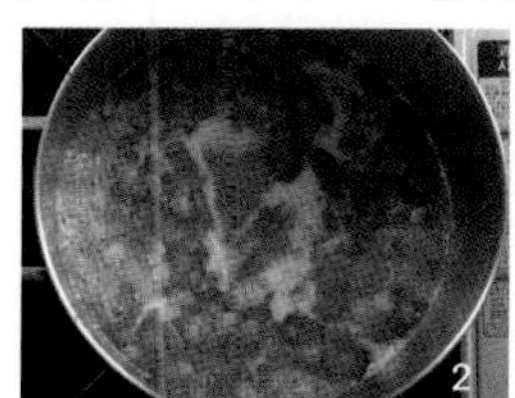

1. Wash the rice and soak in water for 2 hours (220 g). Drain water on a strainer for 10 min.
2. Wash white soybean, soak in water for 8 hours and drain water on a strainer for 10 min. (346 g).

Recipe

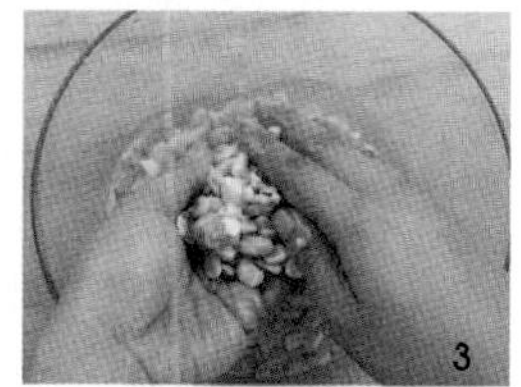

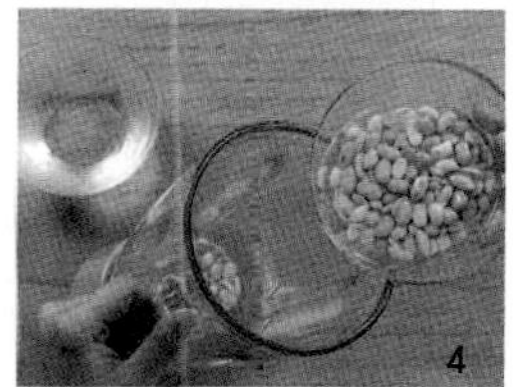

1. Put the soybean and water in the pot, heat it up for 7min. on high heat. When it boils, lower the heat to medium, boil it for 20 min. (369 g). 【Photo 2】
2. Put the soybean on a strainer, skin off by rubbing in water. Put the soybean and water into the mixer, grind it for 2 min. 【Photos 3 & 4】
3. Put the rice and water in the pot, heat it up for 8 min. on high heat. When it boils, lower the heat to medium, boil it for 25 min. with stirring occasionally. When the rice properly sodden, add the ground soybean, boil it for 10 min. Bring it to a boil after season with salt. 【Photos 5 & 6】

· If the soybean has not been sufficiently boiled, it may smell fishy. Take care of boiling time.

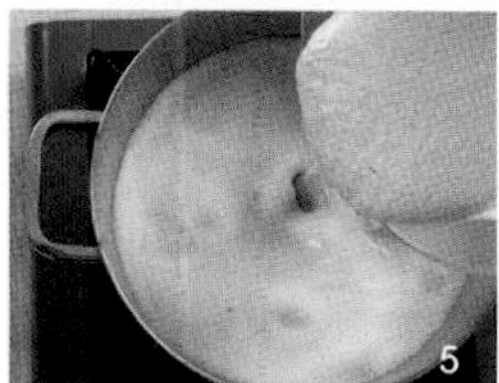

Heating Time	Process	Heat Control
Preparation	Soaking non-glutinous rice. Soaking soybean	
0 min	Boiling soybean. Grinding soybean	H-heat 7 min. M-heat 20 min.
30 min	Boiling porridge	H-heat 8 min. M-heat 25 min.
50 min	Boiling after adding ground soybean	M-heat 12 min.

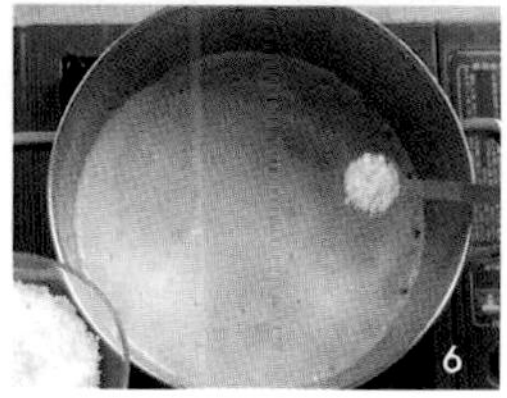

Patjuk 팥죽

Rice and Red Bean Porridge

Patjuk is a porridge of non-glutinous rice and sweet red beans that have been deeply boiled and strained. *Patjuk* is served on the winter solstice (*dongji* day) which has the longest night of the year. It is believed that the red color of the beans can expel devils, and get rid of slight sickness.

Total weight after cooking	Weight for one serve	Service temperature	Total heating time	Total cooking time	Standard utensil
1.24 kg (4 serves)	310 g	60~65 ℃	2 hour 14 min	5 hours	20 cm pot

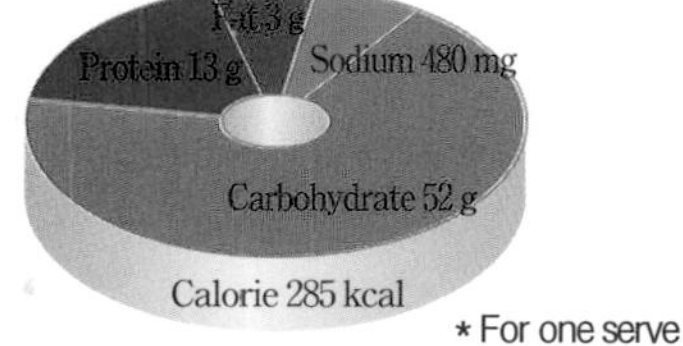

* For one serve

Ingredients & Quantity

90 g (1/2 cups) non-glutinous rice

230 g (1 1/3 cups) sweet red bean, 800 g (4 cups) scalding water, 2.4 kg (12 cups) boiling water

rice ball : 100 g (1 cup) glutinous rice powder, 0.5 g (1/8 tsp) salt, 23 g (1 1/2 tbsp) water

4 g (1 tsp) salt

1

Preparation

1. Wash the rice, soak in water for 2 hours, drain water on a strainer for 10 min. (110 g).
2. Wash the red bean and remove foreign elements if exist. drain water on a strainer for 10 min.

2

Recipe

1. Put red bean and scalding water into the pot, heat it up for 4 min. on high heat. When it boils, continue to boil it for another 3 min. Discard the scalding water, add new boiling water into the pot, heat it up for 10 min. on high heat. Lower the heat to medium, boil it for 1 hour and 20 min. for the red bean to be deeply cooked. 【Photo 2】
2. While the cooked red bean is still hot, put it on a strainer, strain the red bean by mashing with wooden scoop. Make the red bean boiled water is about 1.6 kg (8 cups). Settle down the mashed red bean for 30 min. 【Photo 3】
3. Sprinkle salt on the glutinous rice powder, knead with hot water. Shape rice ball into 1.5 cm−diameter (5 g each, total 25 balls).
4. Put the top red bean water (880 g, 4 cups) and soaked rice into the pot, heat it up for 4 min. on high heat. When it boils, lower the heat to medium, boil for another 20 min. with stirring. 【Photo 4】
5. When the rice is well−sodden, add the red bean sediment. When it boils again, continue to boil for 10 more min. and add rice balls, wait for 1 min. When the rice balls float on, season with salt and bring it to a boil. 【Photos 5 & 6】

3

4

· If the red bean boiled water is not enough, add just water to cook porridge properly.

· The rice ball may be replaced by glutinous rice cake.

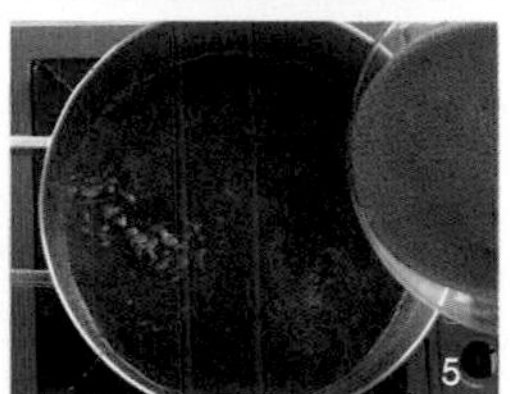
5

Heating Time	Process	Heat Control
Preparation	Soaking non−glutinous rice. Washing red bean	
0 min	Boiling red bean	H−heat 17 min. M−heat 80 min.
90 min	Straining boiled red bean by mashing. Settling down the sediment, Shaping rice balls	
100 min	Cooking red bean porridge	H−heat 4 min. M−heat 30 min.
130 min	Seasoning after adding rice balls	M−heat 3 min.

6

Jatjuk 잣죽

Pine Nut Porridge

Jatjuk is a porridge of skinned and finely ground pine nuts, and non-glutinous rice. *Jatjuk* is sweet and soft. It has been enjoyed by kings in the royal court in olden days, and by men and women of all ages today. Pine nuts have a lot of protein and unsaturated fatty acid. Therefore, it is ranked on top of the whole nuts.

Total weight after cooking	Weight for one serve	Service temperature	Total heating time	Total cooking time	Standard utensil
1.2 kg(4 serves)	300 g	60~65 ℃	27 min	3 hours	20 cm pot

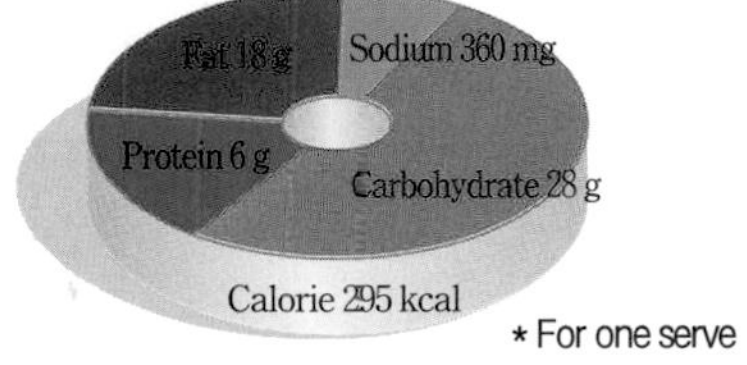

* For one serve

Ingredients & Quantity

180 g (1 cup) non-glutinous rice, 300 g (1½ cups) water
90 g (¾ cups) pine nuts, 100 g (½ cup) water
800 g (4 cups) water, 4 g (1 tsp) salt

Preparation

1. Wash the rice and soak in water for 2 hours, drain water on a strainer for 10 min. (220 g). Grind rice with water in a mixer for 2 min, sieve finely.
2. Remove tops of the pine nuts and wipe the nuts with dry cotton cloth, grind them with water in a mixer and sieve finely. 【Photos 2 & 3】

Recipe

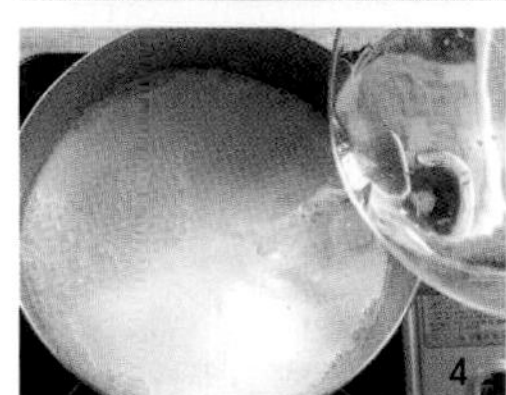

1. Put the ground rice and water in the pot, boil it for 5 min. on high heat with stirring not to be lumped. 【Photo 4】
2. When it boils, reduce the heat to medium, cover the lid on to be steamed, and boil it for 15 min. with stirring occasionally, add ground pine nuts and boil it for 5 min. more. 【Photo 5】
3. When the porridge is well sodden, season with salt, bring it to a boil once more. 【Photo 6】

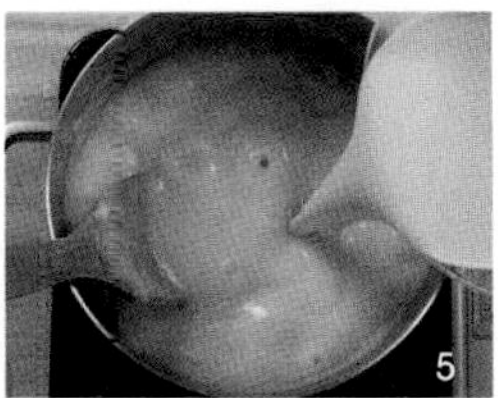

· In the case of grinding rice and pine nuts together, or stirring too strong while porridge is boiling, and/or seasoning at early steps of cooking, the porridge becomes watery and spoils easily.

Heating Time	Process	Heat Control
Preparation	Soaking non-glutinous rice, Grinding the non-glutinous rice and pine nuts	
0 min	Boiling the porridge	H-heat 5 min. M-heat 15 min.
20 min	Boiling after adding pine nuts liquid	M-heat 5 min.
25 min	Seasoning with salt	M-heat 2 min.

Hobakjuk 호박죽

Pumpkin Porridge

Hobakjuk is a porridge of boiled and sieved pumpkin, sweet red beans, soybean and rice cake balls. *Hobakjuk* is a typical Korean porridge; it stimulates the appetite with its sweetness and tender color. *Hobakjuk* is low calories and a good diet food.

Total weight after cooking	Weight for one serve	Service temperature	Total heating time	Total cooking time	Standard utensil
1.4 kg(4 serves)	350 g	60~65 ℃	2 hour 22 min	3 hours	20 ㎝ pot, 26 ㎝ steamer

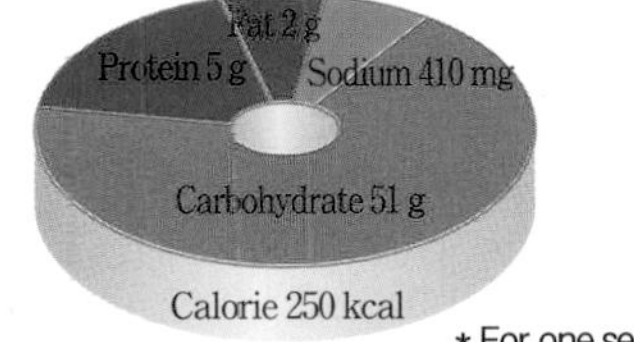

* For one serve

Ingredients & Quantity

700 g (½ ea) **sweet pumpkin**, 1 kg (5 cups) steaming water, 400 g (2 cups) side water
25 g **red bean**, 200 g (1 cup) scalding water, 800 g (4 cups) boiling water
15 g **kidney bean**, 800 g (4 cups) water
100 g (1 cup) glutinous rice powder, 150 g (¾ cups) water
rice cake ball dough : 75 g (¾ cups) glutinous rice powder, 0.5 g (⅛ tsp) salt, 20 g (1⅓ tbsp) water
500 g (2½ cups) water, 36 g (3 tbsp) sugar, 4 g (1 tsp) salt

Preparation

1. Wash and clean the sweet pumpkin, halve the pumpkin, scrape inside stuffs out. (600 g)
2. Mix glutinous rice powder with water uniformly.

Recipe

1. Pour water in the pot and heat it up for 5 min. on high heat. When it boils, put the sweet pumpkin, steam for 15 min. 【Photo 2】
2. Scrape the flesh out (420 g), grind it finely in a mixer with water for 2 min. 【Photo 3】
3. Put the scalding water and red bean in the pot and heat it up for 5 min. on high heat. When it boils, discard the water, add new boiling water. Boil it for 20 min. on medium heat. Reduce the heat to low, boil it for 20 min. more(42 g).
4. Put water and kidney beans in the pot and boil it on high heat for 5 min. Reduce the heat to medium and boil it for 30 min(28 g).
5. Sprinkle salt to the glutinous rice powder and knead with hot water. Shape rice cake ball into 1.5 cm−diameter (around 4~5 g of weight)(20 balls). 【Photo 4】
6. Put the ground sweet pumpkin and water in the pot. Heat it up for 10 min. on high heat. When it boils, reduce the heat to medium, add the mixture of rice powder and water. Boil it for 5 min. with stirring not to be lumped. 【Photo 5】
7. When it boils, reduce the heat to low, cover the lid on to be steamed. Boil it for 20 min. with stirring occasionally. Add the red bean and kidney bean. When it boils, add rice cake balls and boil it for 5 min. on medium heat. 【Photo 6】
8. When the porridge is well−done, season with sugar and salt. Bring it to a boil once more.

· **Mixing ratio of pumpkin and glutinous rice powder may be varied upon taste.**
· **Rice cake balls may be eliminated upon taste.**

Heating Time	Process	Heat Control
Preparation	Trimming sweet pumpkin. Mixing glutinous rice powder with water	
0 min	Grinding sweet pumpkin after steaming	H−heat 20 min.
20 min	Boiling red bean	H−heat 5 min, M−heat 20 min. L−heat 20 min.
60 min	Boiling kidney bean. Shaping rice cake balls	H−heat 5 min. M−heat 30 min.
100 min	Boiling porridge. Steaming for well−done	H−heat 10 min. M−heat 5 min. L−heat 20 min.
130 min	Seasoning after putting red bean, kidney bean and rice cake balls	M−heat 7 min.

1

2

3

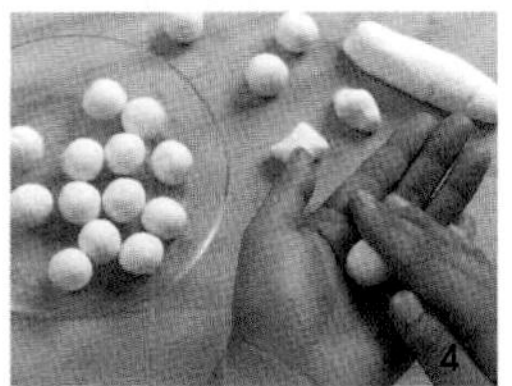
4

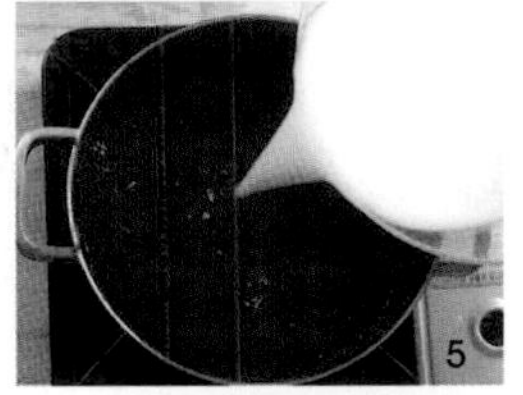
5

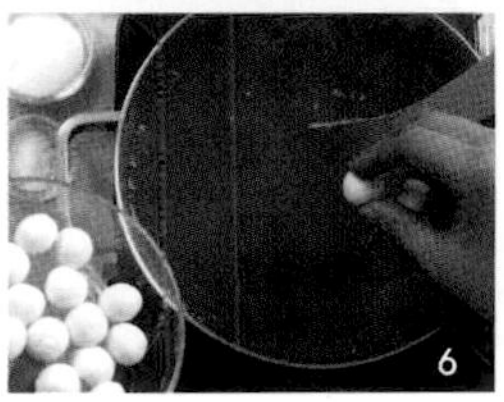
6

Janggukjuk 장국죽

Rice Gruel with Beef Broth

Janggukjuk is a thin rice porridge, made with pounded non–glutinous rice, beef and brown oak mushrooms. *Janggukjuk* is seasoned with soy sauce, and it literally means "soy sauce porridge." It is high in protein and therefore good for recovering patients and the elderly.

Total weight after cooking	Weight for one serve	Service temperature	Total heating time	Total cooking time	Standard utensil
1.36 kg (4 serves)	340 g	60~65 ℃	39 min	3 hours	20 ㎝ pot

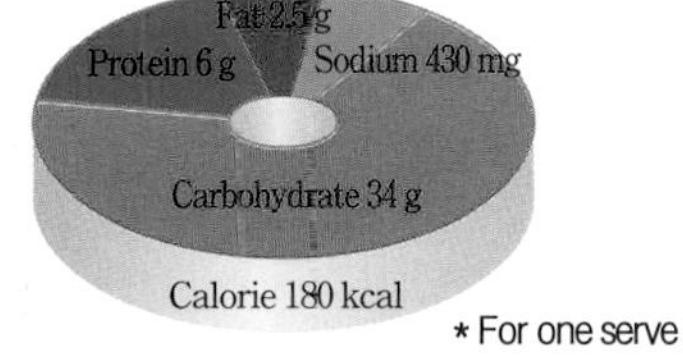

* For one serve

Ingredients & Quantity

180 g (1 cup) non-glutinous rice, 1.4 kg (7 cups) water

50 g beef (eye round), 10 g (2 sheets) brown oak mushrooms

seasoning sauce : 9 g (½ tbsp) soy sauce, 2.3 g (½ tsp) minced green onion, 1.4 g(¼ tsp) minced garlic, 1 g (½ tsp) sesame salt, 0.1 g ground black pepper, 2 g (½ tsp) sesame oil

6.5 g (½ tbsp) sesame oil, 12 g (⅔ tbsp) clear soy sauce, 2 g (½ tsp) salt

1

Preparation

1. Wash the rice and soak in water for 2 hours, drain water on a strainer for 10 min. (220 g).
2. Clean blood of beef and remove tendons. Mince beef (43 g) and season with half of the seasoning sauce.
3. Soak the brown oak mushrooms in water for 1 hour, remove stems, wipe water with cotton cloths, shred into 3 cm–wide/thick (27 g) and season with remained half of the seasoning sauce. 【Photo 2】

2

Recipe

1. Pound the soaked rice with wooden mallet into about half size of rice. 【Photo 3】
2. Heat up the pot and oil with sesame oil. Fry the rice, beef and brown oak mushrooms on medium heat for 2 min. 【Photo 4】
3. Add water, boil for 5 min. on high heat. Reduce the heat to medium, cover the lid on to be steamed, boil for 10 more min. with stirring occasionally. 【Photo 5】
4. When the porridge become sodden, reduce the heat to low and boil it slowly for 20 min. with stirring occasionally. Season with clear soy sauce and salt. Bring it to a boil. 【Photo 6】

3

4

· To prevent the porridge spoiled easily, seasoning should be done at the last step and bring it to a boil once more.

5

Heating Time	Process	Heat Control
Preparation	Soaking non–glutinous rice.	
	Trimming beef and brown oak mushrooms	
0 min	Pounding the non–glutinous rice	
	Pan–frying the rice, beef and brown oak mushrooms	M–heat 2 min.
	Boiling after adding water	H–heat 5 min. M–heat 10 min.
20 min	Boiling porridge. Seasoning with salt	L–heat 22 min.

6

Jeonbokjuk 전복죽

Rice Porridge with Abalone

Jeonbokjuk is a delicacy made of sliced abalone and non-glutinous rice. It has a sweet taste, nice aroma and is rich in nutrients. It has been served as a noble dish in the royal courts since early days. Blue *jeonbokjuk* is a special delicacy cooked with abalone entrails. It is blue in color and has a bitter taste.

Total weight after cooking	Weight for one serve	Service temperature	Total heating time	Total cooking time	Standard utensil
1.4 kg(4 serves)	350 g	60~65 ℃	41 min	3 hours	20 cm pot

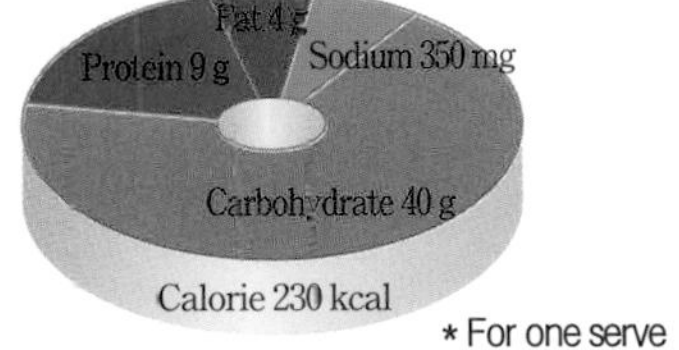

* For one serve

Ingredients & Quantity

225 g (1¼ cups) non-glutinous rice
400 g (2 ea) abalone
13 g (1 tbsp) sesame oil
1.6 kg (8 cups) water
6 g (1 tsp) clear soy sauce
2 g (½ tsp) salt

Preparation

1. Wash the rice, soak in water for 2 hours, drain water on a strainer for 10 min. (275 g).
2. Wash and clean the abalones with brush, take out the flesh by spoon, remove the entrails and slice into 0.3 cm-thick (150 g). 【Photo 2】

Recipe

1. 1. Preheat the pot and oil with sesame oil, stir-fry rice for 1 min. on medium heat, add abalones, stir-fry together for 2 min. 【Photos 3 & 4】
2. Add water, boil it for 6 min. on high heat. When it boils, lower the heat to medium, cover the lid, and boil for another 30 min. with stirring occasionally. 【Photo 5】
3. When the porridge is well-done, season with clear soy sauce and salt, bring it to a boil. 【Photo 6】

· Cooking abalone porridge with abalones entrails, in blue color, may be an another choice.
· Sliced abalones may be replaced by minced abalones.

Heating Time	Process	Heat Control
Preparation	Soaking non-glutinous rice. Preparing abalones	
0 min	Stir-frying non-glutinous rice with abalones	M-heat 3 min.
	Boiling after adding water	H-heat 6 min. M-heat 30 min.
40 min	Seasoning	M-heat 2 min.

1

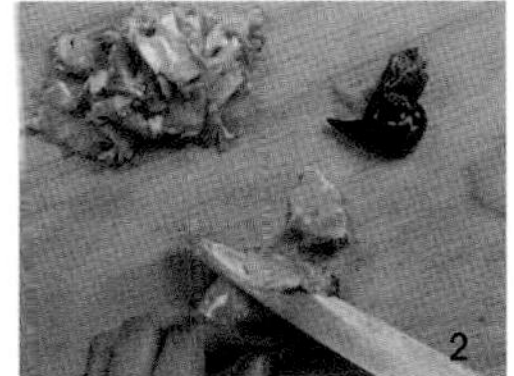
2

3

4

5

6

Heugimjajuk 흑임자죽

Black Sesame and Rice Porridge

Heugimjajuk is a porridge of finely ground black sesame and non-glutinous rice. It is sweet in taste and easily digested, so it is a good nourishing meal. According to Oriental medicine, *heugimja* (black sesame) promotes health, makes hair healthy, and keeps weight off.

Total weight after cooking	Weight for one serve	Service temperature	Total heating time	Total cooking time	Standard utensil
2.2 kg (4 serves)	550 g	65~70 ℃	38 min	1 hour	20 cm pot

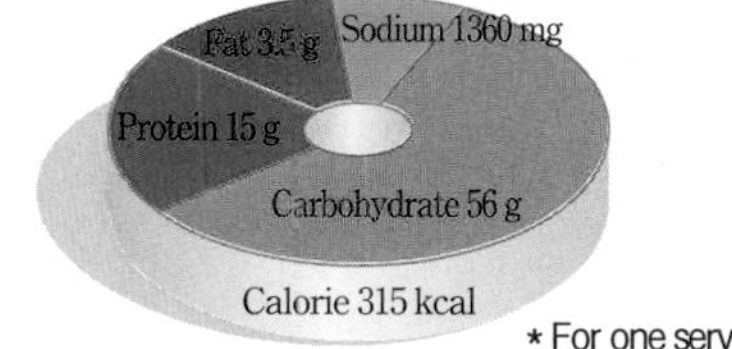

* For one serve

Ingredients & Quantity

190 g (2 cups) wheat flour, 4 g (1 tsp) salt, 60 g (1 ea) egg, 50 g (¼ cups) water
14 g (2 tbsp) wheat flour (additional flour)
hand rolled noodles soup : 2.2 kg (11 cups) water, 50 g radish, 30 g anchovies, 10 g dried shrimp, 20 g kelps, 3 g (½ tsp) clear soy sauce, 4 g (1 tsp) salt
50 g (¼ ea) potato, 50 g pumpkin, 20 g green onion, 5.5 g (1 tsp) minced garlic
50 g shrimp, 200 g (1 cup) water, 1 g (¼ tsp) salt
30 g oyster, 200 g (1 cup) water, 4 g (1 tsp) salt
200 g thin shelled surf clam, 400 g (2 cups) water, 6 g (½ tbsp) salt

1

Preparation

1. Add salt, beaten egg and water into the wheat flour and knead. Wrap it with cotton cloths and let it sit for 30 min. (350 g). Press and roll it with wooden roller to be 0.2 cm of thick. Sprinkle additional flour all over the top surface. Roll the sheet again and cut it into 0.2 cm of width. 【Photo 2】
2. Wash the radish for the soup cleanly and skin (45 g).
3. Remove the head and internal organs of the anchovies (26 g). Wipe the kelps with damp cotton cloths.
4. Wash the potato, skin and cut it into 0.5 cm–thick as half moon shape (45 g). Clean the pumpkin, peel the skin off into flat strips, shred into 0.3 cm–wide (30 g). Clean the green onion and cut them diagonally (17 g). 【Photo 3】
5. Wash the shrimps and oysters by soft swinging in the salt water. Put salt and water to the thin shelled surf clams and let it sit for 30 min. for the clams to spit out the watery sediment. 【Photo 4】

2

3

Recipe

1. Preheat the frying pan and stir–fry anchovies and dried shrimps on medium heat for 2 min.
2. Put the radish, anchovies and dried shrimps in the soup water, boil it on high heat for 10 min. When it boils, add the kelps, reduce the heat to medium, boil it for 10 min. more. Strain the soup, and blend noodles soup with salt and clear soy sauce (1.8 kg). 【Photo 5】
3. Pour the blended soup in the pot and heat it up on high heat for 9 min. When it boils, add the noodles, potato, pumpkin and seafoods, boil it for another 5 min. Season with minced garlic and green onion, bring it to a boil. 【Photo 6】

4

- Some raw bean powder may be added to the noodle dough.
- Hand rolled noodles may be available in the market.

5

Heating Time	Process	Heat Control
Preparation	Kneading noodles dough	
	Preparing soup stuffs. vegetables and seafoods	
0 min	Stir–frying anchovies and shrimps	M–heat 2 min.
	Boiling soup. Seasoning	H–heat 10 min. M–heat 10 min.
20 min	Boiling the noodle soup	H–heat 16 min.

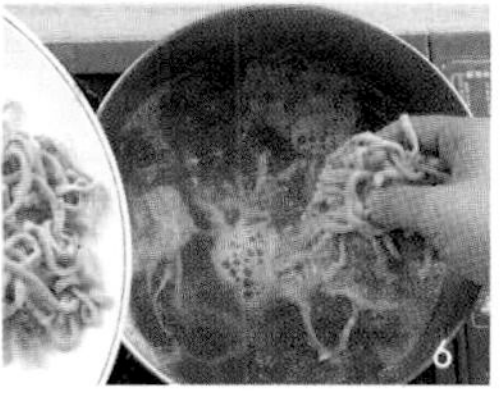
6

Kong-guksu 콩국수

Noodles in Chilled White Bean Soup

Kong-guksu is a dish of cold noodles in a chilled soybean puree which is made of ground white soybeans after soaked, boiled and skinned. *Kong-guksu* is sweet and rich in nutrition. It is a summer specialty for people who are easily exhausted from the hot weather.

Total weight after cooking	Weight for one serve	Service temperature	Total heating time	Total cooking time	Standard utensil
2.16 kg (4 serves)	540 g	4~8 ℃	22 min	over 5 hours	24 cm pot

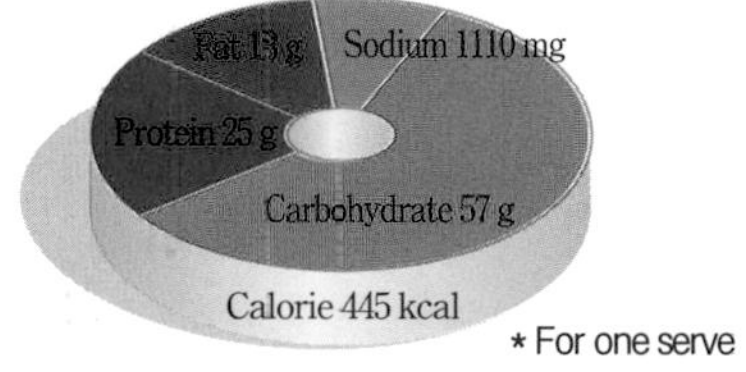

* For one serve

Ingredients & Quantity

200 g (¼ cup) white bean, 1 kg (5 cups) soaking water, 800 g (4 cups) boiling water,
900 g (4½ cup) grinding water
12 g (1 tbsp) salt
350 g noodles (thin noodles), 2 kg (10 cups) boiling water, 200 g (1 cups) additional boiling water
70 g (½ ea) cucumber, 100 g (½ ea) tomato

1

Preparation

1. Wash the bean cleanly and remove useless elements. Soak in water for 8 hours (420 g).
2. Clean cucumber by rubbing with salt, cut into 5 cm-long and 0.3 cm-wide diagonally. Shred them at intervals of 0.3 cm-thick, dip in cold water.
3. Halve tomato lengthwise, cut into 2 cm-thick. 【Photo 2】

2

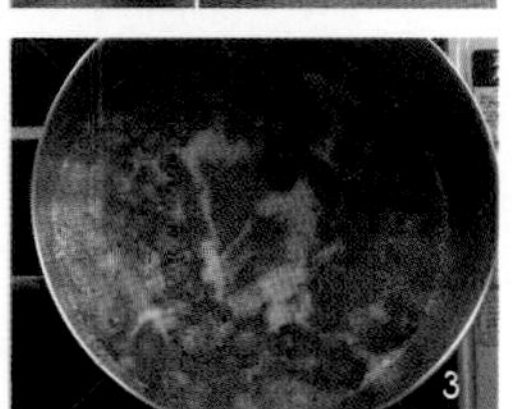
3

Recipe

1. Put the soaked bean and water in the pot, heat it up for 5 min. on high heat. When it boils, continue to boil it for another 5 min. (440 g). 【Photo 3】
2. Put the boiled bean on a tray in water and peel the skin by rubbing with hands (410 g). 【Photo 4】
3. Put the bean and grinding water in a mixer, grind finely (1.27 kg), filter through a strainer and season with salt. 【Photo 5】
4. Pour water in the pot and heat it up for 9 min. on high heat. When it boils, put noodles and boil for 1 min. When it boils over, add 100 g of water, let it sit for 1 min. Repeat adding 100 g of water and boil it for 30 sec. more.
5. Take out the noodles from the pot, rinse in cold water, make coils with noodles, drain water through a strainer (954 g).
6. Place the noodles in a bowl, garnish with cucumber and tomatoes, finally pour the bean soup. 【Photo 6】

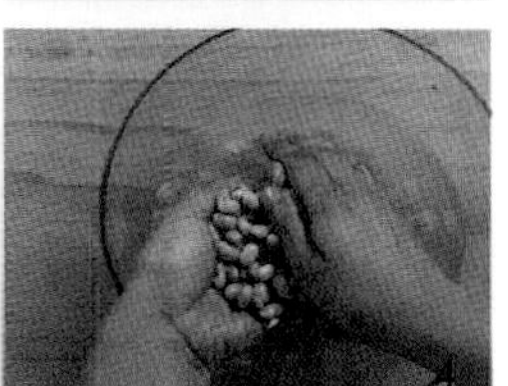

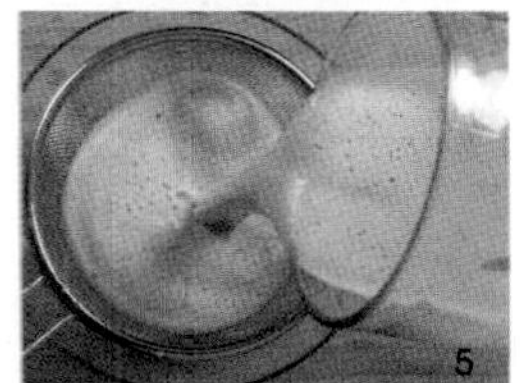
5

· Soak the bean in water for 5 hours in summer, 8 hours in winter.
· If the bean boiled rarely, it may smell fishy. If boiled too long, it may not be tasty. Take care of boiling time.
· Serve cold cucumber after dipping in cold water.

Heating Time	Process	Heat Control
Preparation	Soaking bean in water. Preparing vegetables	
0 min	Boiling white bean. Grinding white bean	H-heat 10 min.
10 min	Boiling noodles	H-heat 11 min. 30 sec.
20 min	Placing in a bowl and garnishing	

6

Mul-naengmyeon 물냉면

Buckwheat Noodles in Chilled Broth

Mul-naengmyeon is a dish of buckwheat noodles in chilled broth that is garnished with radish Kimchi, pickled cucumber, Korean pear and slices of pressed beef. Originally it was had thin ice over it and was served in the winter, but nowadays people enjoy this dish all year round.

Total weight after cooking	Weight for one serve	Service temperature	Total heating time	Total cooking time	Standard utensil
2 kg(4serves)	500 g	4~8 ℃	2 hours 11 min	3 hours	24 cm pot

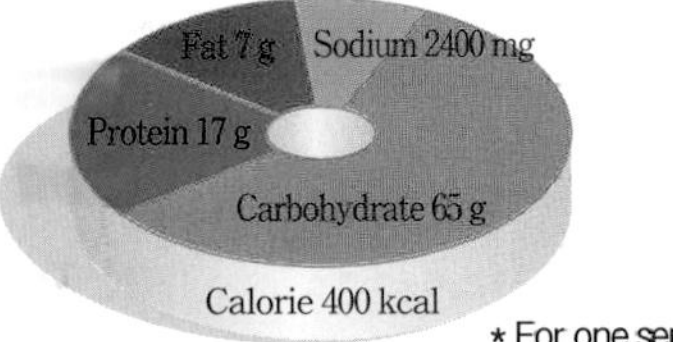

* For one serve

Ingredients & Quantity

400 g buckwheat noodles (dried), 3 kg (15 cups) water
300 g beef (brisket · shank), 1.6 kg (8 cups) water,
fragrant seasoning : 20 g green onion, 20 g garlic
seasoning sauce : 9 g (½ tbsp) clear soy sauce, 24 g (2 tbsp) sugar, 45 g (3 tbsp) vinegar
24 g (2 tbsp) salt, 5.4 g (½ tbsp) fermented mustard
50 g cucumber, 2 g (½ tsp) salt, 15 g (1 tbsp) water
170 g radish, 4 g (1 tsp) salt, 12 g (1 tbsp) sugar, 15 g (1 tbsp) vinegar
2.2 g (1 tsp) fine ground red pepper
100 g (1/5 ea) pear, 100 g (½ cup) water, 4 g (1 tsp) sugar,
120 g (2 ea) egg, 1 kg water, 4 g (1 tsp) salt
10 g (1 tbsp) pine nuts, 0.5 g shred red pepper

1

Preparation

1. Clean blood of beef with cotton cloths. Wash the fragrant seasoning cleanly.
2. Put the beef and water in the pot, heat it up for 10 min. on high heat. When it boils, lower the heat to medium, simmer for 1 hour, add green onion and garlic, simmer for another 30 min. (1 kg). 【Photo 2】
3. Take the beef (300 g) out from the broth, slice it into 4 cm−wide, 2 cm−long and 0.2 cm−thick. After the broth cooled down, skim fats, season with seasoning sauce. 【Photo3】
4. Wash the cucumber and halve lengthwise, slice at intervals of 0.2 cm−thick diagonally, soak it in salt water for 20 min, then wipe water with cotton cloths (43 g).
5. Shred the radish into 5 cm−long, 2 cm−wide and 0.2 cm−thick, marinate with salt, sugar, vinegar and fine ground red pepper for 20 min. (100 g). Peel the pear, cut it into half−moon shape, dip in sugar water (70 g). 【Photo4】
6. Remove tops of the pine nuts, wipe the nuts with dry cotton cloths. Cut the shred red pepper into 2~3 cm of length.

2

3

Recipe

1. Put the eggs, water and salt in the pot, heat it up for 5 min. on high heat. When it boils, lower the heat to medium, boil for another12min. Take out the eggs, put in cold water, then peel eggshell, cut them into two pieces.
2. Pour water in the pot, heat it up for 12 min. on high heat. When it boils, add noodles, boil for 2 min. Take the noodles out from the pot, wash in cold water by rubbing, make coils with noodles and drain water on a strainer (830 g). 【Photo5】
3. Place the noodles in a bowl, garnish with beef, cucumber, radish, egg, pear, pine nuts and shred red pepper, then pour the cold broth. 【Photo6】

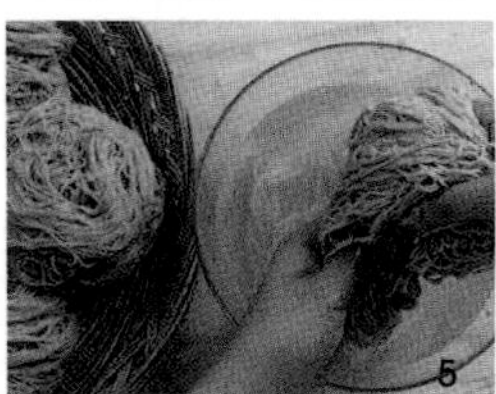
5

- Cold radish pickled Kimchi juice in the beef broth, or only Kimchi juice may be another choice for the broth.
- In summer season, young summer radish Kimchi may be a tasteful broth.
- More fermented mustard and/or more vinegar in the dish is an option.

6

Heating Time	Process	Heat Control
Preparation	Preparing beef. Trimming vegetables	
0 min	Simmering broth	H−heat 10 min. M−heat 60 min. M−heat 30 min.
100 min	Boiling eggs	H−heat 5 min. M−heat 12 min.
120 min	Boiling noodles	H−heat 14 min

Bibim-naengmyeon 비빔냉면

Mixed Cold Buckwheat Noodles

Bibim-naengmyeon is a dish of cold buckwheat noodles mixed with a spicy and thick red pepper sauce. It may be garnished with raw fish. It is also called '*Hamheung-naengmyeon*' because it was a regional food of the *Hamheung* district in *Hamkyeong-do* province.

Total weight after cooking	Weight for one serve	Service temperature	Total heating time	Total cooking time	Standard utensil
1.64 kg(4 serves)	410 g	4~8 ℃	33 min	1 hour	24 cm pot, 30 cm frying pan

Fat 6 g
Sodium 1230 mg
Protein 15 g
Carbohydrate 73 g
Calorie 410 kcal
* For one serve

Ingredients & Quantity

600 g buckwheat noodles (dried), 3 kg (15 cups) water
100 g minced beef
seasoning sauce① : 9 g (½ tbsp) soy sauce, 2 g (½ tsp) sugar, 2.8 g (½ tsp) minced green onion
1.3 g (¼ tsp) minced garlic, 0.3 g (⅛ tsp) ground black pepper
1 g (½ tsp) sesame salt, 2 g (½ tsp) sesame oil
50 g (1 ea) cucumber, 15 g (1 tbsp) water, 2 g (½ tsp) salt
100 g radish, 2 g (½ tsp) salt, 6 g (½ tbsp) sugar, 7.5 g (½ tbsp) vinegar,
100 g (1/5 ea) pear, 100 g (½ cup) pear dipping water, 4 g (1 tsp) sugar
120 g (2 ea) egg, 1 kg (5 cups) water, 4 g (1 tsp) salt
seasoning sauce② : 250 g (½ ea) pear, 30 g (¼ ea) onion, 18 g (1½ tbsp) salt
16 g (1 tbsp) minced garlic, 36 g (3 tbsp) sugar, 90 g (6 tbsp) vinegar
10 g (4 ea) dried red pepper, 28 g (4 tbsp) coarse red pepper powder

Preparation

1. Clean blood of beef with cotton cloths, season with seasoning sauce ① (85 g).
2. Wash cucumber cleanly, cut into two pieces lengthwise, shred into 4 cm-long and 0.2 cm-thick diagonally. Marinate them with salt water for 20 min. wipe water with cotton cloths (47 g). 【Photo 2】
3. Wash radish, shred into 6 cm-long,1.5 cm-wide and 0.2 cm-thick, then marinate with salt, sugar and vinegar for 20 min (85 g). 【Photo 3】
4. Peel the pear and cut into half moon shape. Dip it in sugar water for 5 min (70 g).
5. Peel and shred the pear and onion for seasoning sauce ②.
6. Wipe dried red pepper with damp cotton cloths, cut them diagonally and take seed.
7. Grind seasoning sauce② without red pepper powder in the mixer first, then add coarse red pepper powder and mix together. 【Photo 4】

Recipe

1. Preheat the frying pan, stir-fry beef for 2 min. on medium heat (66 g).
2. Put water, salt and eggs in the pot, heat it up for 5 min. on high heat. When it boils, lower the heat to medium, boil it for 12 min. take them into cold water. Peel off eggshell, halve them.
3. Pour water in the pot, heat it up for 12 min. on high heat. When it boils, boil noodles for 2 min, Rinse in cold water by rubbing with hand, make coils with noodles and drain water on a tray. 【Photo 5】
4. Place the noodles in the bowl, top with prepared beef, cucumber, radish, pear, egg and seasoning sauce ② tastefully. 【Photo 6】

· Fresh wet noodles may be used.
· Pre-mixed noodles with seasoning sauce may be served.

Heating Time	Process	Heat Control
Preparation	Preparing beef and vegetables. Preparing mixing seasonings	
0 min	Pan-frying beef	M-heat 2 min.
	Boiling eggs	H-heat 5 min. M-heat 12 min.
20 min	Boiling cold noodles	H-heat 14 min.
30 min	Placing in a bowl	

Mandutguk 만둣국

Dumpling Soup

Mandutguk is a soup made of dumplings simmered in beef broth, often served in the winter. The dumplings have wheat flour wrappers stuffed with fillings such as meat, tofu, Kimchi and other vegetables. People enjoy *mandutguk* on lunar new year's day because it represents fortunes wrapped in the dumplings.

Total weight after cooking	Weight for one serve	Service temperature	Total heating time	Total cooking time	Standard utensil
2.04 kg(4 serves)	510 g	65~80 ℃	1 hour 21 min	2 hours	20 cm pot, 30 cm frying pan

Fat 19 g
Sodium 1390 mg
Carbohydrate 26 g
Protein 19 g
Calorie 355 kcal
* For one serve

Ingredients & Quantity

broth : 300 g beef (brisket · shank), 2.2 kg (11 cups) water
fragrant seasoning : 50 g green onion, 20 g (4 cloves) garlic
dough for dumpling skin : 143 g (1½ cups) wheat flour, 2 g (½ tsp) salt, 75 g (5 tbsp) water
160 g minced beef(top round)
160 g cabbage kimchi
160 g (⅓ cake) tofu
200 g mung bean sprouts, 1 kg (5 cups) water, 4 g (1 tsp) salt
10 g watercress, 7 g (1 tbsp) wheat flour, 13 g (1 tbsp) edible oil
seasoning : 4 g (1 tsp) salt, 9 g (2 tsp) minced green onion, 5.5 g (1 tsp) minced garlic, 6 g (1 tbsp) sesame salt, 0.3 g (⅛ tsp) ground black pepper, 13 g (1 tbsp) sesame oil
9 g (½ tbsp) clear soy sauce, 4 g (1 tsp) salt
vinegar soy sauce : 18 g (1 tbsp) soy sauce, 15 g (1 tbsp) vinegar, 15 g (1 tbsp) water

1

Preparation

1. Clean blood of beef with cotton cloths. Wash and clean fragrant seasoning. Put the beef and water into the pot, heat it up for 10 min. on high heat. When it boils, lower the heat to medium, continue to simmer it for 30 min. Add fragrant seasoning, simmer for another 20 min. Take out the beef from the broth, cool the broths down and filter through cotton cloths (1.6 kg). 【Photo 2】
2. Sprinkle salt on the wheat flour and knead with water. Wrap it with damp cotton cloths and let it sit for 30 min. (220g).
3. Remove the inside stuffs from cabbage Kimchi,, chop the Kimchi finely, squeeze the Kimchi juice out (85 g). Wrap the tofu with cotton cloths, mash by squeezing (100 g). Wash the mung bean sprouts. 【Photo 3】
4. Panfry the watercress after coating with wheat flour and beaten egg. Panfry egg for garnish, cut them into 2 cm diaper shape.
5. Blend vinegar soy sauce.

2

3

Recipe

1. Pour water into the pot, heat it up for 5 min. on high heat. When it boils, scald mung bean sprouts with salt for 2 min. chop it into 0.5 cm-long, and squeeze water out (100 g).
2. Mix minced beef, Kimchi, tofu, and mung bean sprouts all together, and season with seasoning (460 g). 【Photo 4】
3. Roll and press dumpling dough into 0.2 cm-thick and 7~8 cm diameter round disk.
4. Put the filling stuffs (23 g) onto the dumpling skin, fold it into half. Pinch the both edges together roundly. (20 ea) 【Photo 5】
5. Pour the broth into the pot, heat it up for 6 min. on high heat. When it boils, season with clear soy sauce and salt to make dumpling soup. When it boils again, add dumplings, boil it for 4 min. When the dumplings float on the surface of the broth, lower the heat to medium, continue to boil it for another 4 min. Fill the dumpling soup in a bowl, garnish with watercress and egg strips. Serve with vinegar soy sauce. 【Photo 6】

4

· Pork may be an another good meat for dumpling filling stuffs.
· Squeeze the dumpling filling stuffs slightly, or it may become too hard.

5

Heating Time	Process	Heat Control
Preparation	Preparing beef. Kneading wheat flour dough.	
	Preparing vegetables. Blending vinegar soy sauce	
	Simmering broth	
0 min	Adding fragrant seasoning. Filtering broth	H-heat 10 min. M-heat 30 min.
40 min	Scalding mung bean sprouts	M-heat 20 min.
60 min	Preparing filling stuffs and dumpling skin. Shaping dumplings	H-heat 7 min.
	Boiling dumpling soup	
70 min	Garnishing	H-heat 10 min. M-heat 4 min.

6

Pyeonsu 편수

Square Dumpling

Pyeonsu is a steamed square dumpling stuffed with vegetables and beef. *Pyeonsu* is served chilled or floating in a cool soy sauce soup. It is a summer delicacy. The dish gets its name from the Chinese characters for the word, '*pyeonsu*' which means 'a small fragment on the water.'

Total weight after cooking	Weight for one serve	Service temperature	Total heating time	Total cooking time	Standard utensil
2kg(4 serves)	500 g	4~10 ℃	1 hour 27 min	3 hours	20 ㎝ pot, 26 ㎝ steamer, 30 ㎝ frying pan

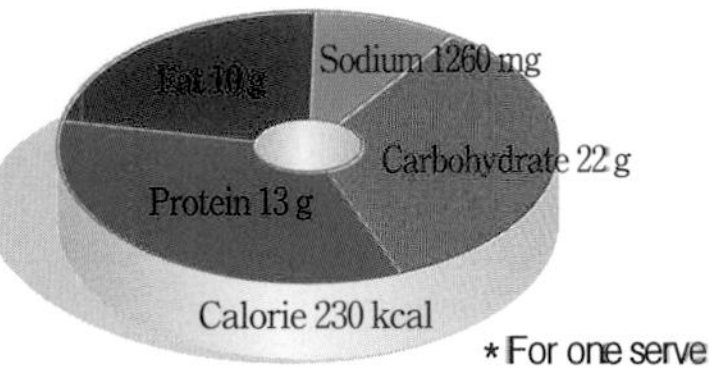

* For one serve

Ingredients & Quantity

broth : 200 g beef(brisket, shank), 2 kg (10 cups) water, 9 g (½ tbsp) clear soy sauce, 8 g (2 tsp) salt
fragrant seasoning : 20 g green onion, 20 g (4 cloves) garlic
dumpling skin : 190 g (2 cups) wheat flour, 2 g (½ tsp) salt, 90 g (6 tbsp) water
150 g minced beef (top round), 15 g (3 stems) brown oak mushrooms
seasoning sauce : 18 g (1 tbsp) soy sauce, 4 g (1 tsp) sugar, 4.5 g (1 tsp) minced green onion
2.8 g (½ tsp) minced garlic, 0.3 g (⅛ tsp) ground black pepper, 2 g (1 tsp) sesame salt
4 g (1 tsp) sesame oil
150 g (½ ea) pumpkin, 1 g (¼ tsp) salt
250 g mung bean sprouts, 1 kg (5 cups) water, 2 g (½ tsp) salt
10 g (1 tbsp) pine nuts
2 kg (10 cups) steaming water
60 g (1 ea) egg, 15 g (3 stalks) watercress, 3.5 g (½ tbsp) wheat flour, 13 g (1 tbsp) edible oil
vinegar soy sauce : 18 g (1 tbsp) soy sauce, 15 g (1 tbsp) vinegar, 15 g (1 tbsp) water
3 g (½ tbsp) pine nuts powder

Preparation

1. Clean blood of beef for broth with cotton cloths (190 g). Trim and wash the fragrant seasoning. Put the beef and water in the pot and boil it on high heat for 9 min. Reduce the heat to medium and simmer it for 30 min. Add the fragrant seasoning and simmer it for 20 min. more. Strain it through cotton cloths, season with salt and cool it down (1.4 kg).
2. Add salt and water to the wheat flour and knead (280 g). Wrap it with cotton cloths and let it sit for 30 min. 【Photo 2】
3. Clean blood of minced beef with cotton cloths (140 g). Soak the brown oak mushrooms in water for 1 hour, remove the stems. Wipe excess water with cotton cloths and shred it into 0.2 cm−thick and wide, season them respectively (40 g).
4. Clean the pumpkin and cut it into 4 cm−long. Peel the skin off into 0.2 cm−thick round and shred it into 0.2cm−wide. Marinate with salt for 10 min, wipe water with cotton cloths (82 g). Remove the tails of mung bean sprouts and wash (230 g). Remove tops of the pine nuts and wipe the nuts with dry cotton cloths. 【Photo 3】
5. Panfry the egg for yellow/white garnish (thin sheet and then cut it into strips). Panfry the watercress after thick coating with wheat flour liquid and beaten egg. Cut them into 2 cm of diaper pattern.
6. Blend vinegar soy sauce.

1

2

Recipe

1. Preheat the frying pan and oil. Stir−fry the beef and mushrooms for 3 min. respectively on medium heat. 【Photo 4】
2. Pour water in the pot and boil it on high heat for 5 min. When it boils, add the mung bean sprouts and salt, scald it for about 2 min. Drain water. Chop them into 0.5 cm−long (140 g). Preheat the frying pan and oil, stir−fry pumpkin for 10 sec. on high heat, maintaining green color, cool it down.
3. Provide filling stuffs with the mixture of beef, mushrooms, mung bean sprouts and pumpkin. Press and roll the kneaded dough with wooden roller to be 0.2 cm thickness, cut it into 7 cm square for dumpling skin. Stuff the dumpling skin with 13~15 g of fillings in the middle, put two pine nuts on it. Pinch four corners together to form square shape. 【Photo 5】
4. Pour water in the steaming pot, heat it up for 9 min. on high heat. When it gives off steam, layer damp cotton cloths on the bottom of the pot, place the square dumplings on the damp cloths and steam it for 5 min. on high heat. 【Photo6】
5. Place the square dumplings on a dish and pour the broth, top with fried egg strips and watercress. Serve it with vinegar soy sauce.

4

· When seasoning the broth with soy sauce and salt, it may be better taste and better color.
· Steamed square dumplings may be served with vinegar soy sauce without broth.

Heating Time	Process	Heat Control
Preparation	Soaking brown oak mushrooms. Kneading dumpling skin dough Preparing sub stuffs	
0 min	Simmering broth	H−heat 9 min. M−heat 30 min.
40 min	Adding fragrant seasoning Stir−frying beef and brown oak mushrooms	M−heat 20 min.
60 min	Scalding mung bean sprouts. Stir−frying pumpkin	M−heat 6 min. H−heat 7 min. H−heat 10 sec.
70 min	Shaping square dumplings and steaming	H−heat 14 min.

6

Eomandu 어만두

Fish Fillet Dumpling

Eomandu is thinly sliced white fish fillet (croaker, sea bream, flatfish or gray mullet) that is stuffed with beef and vegetables, coated with starch, then steamed. The white fish fillet as dumpling skin is unique, light and sweet in taste. It was originally a summer dish but now people enjoy it on special occasions all year round.

Total weight after cooking	Weight for one serve	Service temperature	Total heating time	Total cooking time	Standard utensil
720 g(4 serves)	180 g(5 ea)	55~65 ℃	1 hour 27 min	2 hours	18 cm pot, 26 cm steamer, 30 cm frying pan

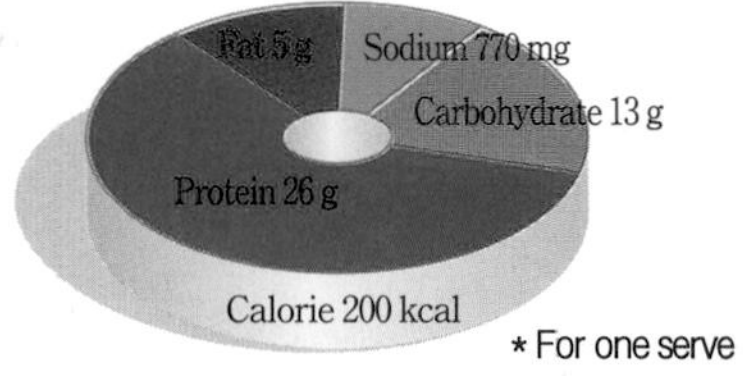

* For one serve

Ingredients & Quantity

700 g (3 sheets) white fillet fish (croaker, codfish, frozen pollack) slices, 2 g (½ tsp) salt,
0.5 g (¼ tsp) ground white pepper
70 g minced beef (top round), 15 g (3 sheets) brown oak mushrooms, 4 g Jew's ear mushrooms
seasoning sauce : 9 g (½ tbsp) soy sauce, 2 g (½ tsp) sugar, 2.3 g (½ tsp) minced green onion
1.4 g (¼ tsp) minced garlic, 1 g (½ tsp) sesame salt, 0.3 g (⅛ tsp) ground black pepper
2 g (½ tsp) sesame oil
100 g (½ ea) cucumber, 1 g (¼ tsp) salt
100 g mung bean sprouts, 1 kg (5 cups) water, 2 g (½ tsp) salt
60 g (1 cup) starch, 7 g (2 tsp) pine nuts
2 kg (10 cups) steaming water, 13 g (1 tbsp) edible oil
vinegar soy sauce : 18 g (1 tbsp) soy sauce, 15 g (1 tbsp) vinegar, 15 g (1 tbsp) water
3 g (½ tbsp)pine nuts powder
mustard juice : 6 g (½ tbsp) fermented mustard, 15 g (1 tbsp) vinegar, 4 g (1 tsp) sugar, 2 g (½ tsp) salt
9.5 g (½ tbsp) honey, 15 g broth (or 1 tbsp water)

1

Preparation

1. Cut and slice the fish fillet into 7 cm-square and 0.3 cm-thick (540 g), sprinkle salt and ground white pepper on it, and let it sit for 10 min. pad dry with cotton cloths. 【Photo 2】
2. Clean blood of minced beef with cotton cloths (67 g), season with half of the seasoning sauce.
3. Soak the mushrooms in water for 1 hour, remove stems of the brown oak mushrooms and shred it into 2 cm-long, and 0.2 cm-wide (43 g). Rip up the Jew's ear mushrooms into small size (32 g), season with remained half of the seasoning sauce respectively.
4. Wash and clean cucumber by rubbing with salt, cut them into 2 cm-long, and peel the skin with 0.2 cm-thick, shred the skin into 0.2 cm-wide. Marinate them with salt for 10 min. wipe water with cotton cloths (50 g). Remove tails of mung bean sprouts and wash (90 g). 【Photo 3】
5. Blend vinegar soy sauce and mustard juice.

2

3

Recipe

1. Preheat the frying pan and oil. Stir-fry the beef, brown oak mushrooms, and Jew's ear mushrooms for 2 min. respectively on medium heat.
2. Preheat the frying pan and oil. Stir-fry the cucumber on high heat for 10 sec. maintaining green color, and cool it down. 【Photo 4】
3. Pour water in the pot and heat it up for 5 min. on high heat. When it boils, put salt and mung bean sprouts, scald for 2 min. Drain water and chop them into 0.5 cm-long finely.
4. Prepare filling stuffs with the mixture of beef, mushrooms, cucumber and mung bean sprouts.
5. Pot dry the sliced fish fillet and coat inside with starch. Put 10 g of filling stuffs on the sliced fillet, add two pine nuts. Roll it round and coat with starch all over the surface. 【Photo 5】
6. Pour water in the steaming pot and heat it up for 9 min. on high heat. When it boils, place the fish dumplings on the damp cotton cloths and steam it for 5 min. Serve it with vinegar soy sauce and mustard juice. 【Photo 6】

4

5

· The thinner slices of fillet may make the job easier and better shape.
· Two frozen pollack (4 kg) may be enough for 4 serves.

Heating Time	Process	Heat Control
Preparation	Preparing white fillet fish. Soaking mushrooms Preparing beef and vegetables	
0 min	Stir-frying beef and mushrooms. Stir-frying cucumber	M-heat 6 min. H-heat 10 sec.
10 min	Scalding mung bean sprouts Preparing filling stuffs for dumplings. Shaping dumplings	H-heat 7 min.
20 min	steaming dumplings	H-heat 14 min.

6

Tteokguk 떡국

Sliced Rice Cake Pasta Soup

Tteokguk is a soup made of diagonally sliced rice cakes simmered in beef broth, garnished with pressed meat, and fried egg white and yolk strips. People enjoy *tteokguk* made with sliced *garaetteok* on the first day of the year. *Garaetteok* is a rice cake rod that pulled it into a long rod. It is eaten in hopes of expanding one's property like the rice cake rod.

Total weight after cooking	Weight for one serve	Service temperature	Total heating time	Total cooking time	Standard utensil
2 kg(4 serves)	500 g	65~80 ℃	1 hour 17 min	2 hours	24 cm pot, 30 cm frying pan

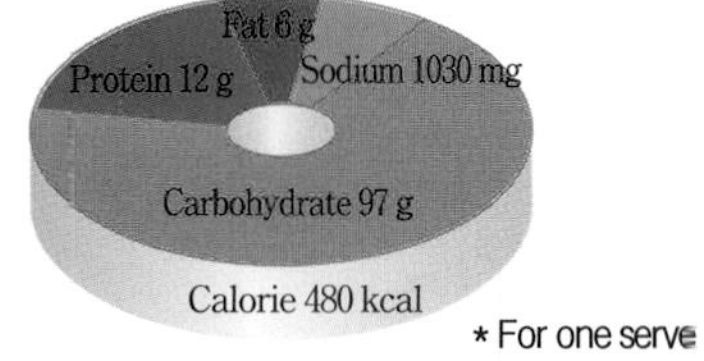

* For one serve

Ingredients & Quantity

600 g white rice cake
300 g beef (brisket · shank), 1.6 kg (8 cups) water
fragrant seasoning : 20 g green onion, 10 g garlic
seasoning sauce : 3 g clear soy sauce, 1.1 g (¼ tsp) minced green onion, 1.4 g (¼ tsp) minced garlic
0.1 g black pepper
6 g (1 tsp) clear soy sauce, 6 g (1½ tsp) salt
20 g green onion, 60 g (1 ea) egg, 1 g shred red pepper

Preparation

1. Clean blood of beef with cotton cloths. Wash the fragrant seasoning cleanly.
2. Put the beef and water in the pot, heat it up for 7 min. on high heat. When it boils, lower the heat to medium, simmer it for 30 min. Add the fragrant seasoning, simmer it for another 30 min. 【Photo 2】
3. Shred the white rice cake 4 cm-long, 0.2 cm-thick diagonally. 【Photo 3】
4. Wash the green onion and cut it into 2 cm-long lengthwise diagonally.
5. Pan-fry eggs for yellow/white garnish and cut into 2 cm of diaper shape.
6. Cut the shred red pepper into 2 cm-long.

Recipe

1. Filter the simmered broth (1.4 kg) through cotton cloths, rip up the beef along with the texture (160 g). 【Photo 4】
2. Pour the broth in the pot, heat it up for 5 min. on high heat. When it boils, add the sliced rice cake, boil for 3 min. When the rice cake float on the surface, season with clear soy sauce and salt, add green onion, bring it to a boil once more. 【Photo 5】
3. Dip up the soup in a bowl, garnish with beef (80 g), egg and shred red pepper. 【Photo 6】

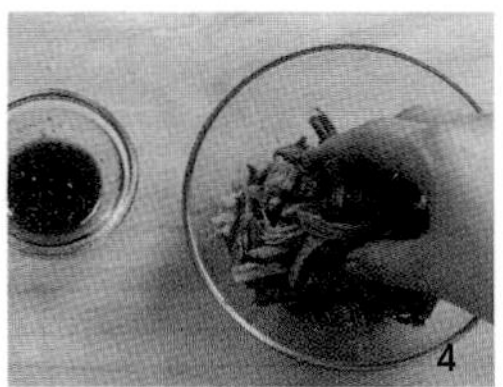

· Simmered ox knee bone broth, or brisket and shank may be an another choice for the broth.
· Pan-fried skewered beef garnish may be an option.

Heating Time	Process	Heat Control
Preparation	Preparing beef. rice cake and green onion. Pan-frying egg for garnish	
0 min	Boiling broth	H-heat 7 min. M-heat 60 min.
70 min	Boiling rice pasta soup	H-heat 10 min.
80 min	Placing in a bowl. Garnishing	

Bugeotguk 북엇국

Dried Pollack Soup

Bugeotguk is a soup made by boiling seasoned *bugeo* (dried pollack) after it has been soaked and ripped. *Bugeo* is available year-round at a low price in Korea, therefore, *bugeotguk* is an everyday soup for Koreans. It is believed that *bugeo* protects the liver and many people have *bugeotguk* after drinking alcohol.

Total weight after cooking	Weight for one serve	Service temperature	Total heating time	Total cooking time	Standard utensil
1.36 kg(4 serves)	340 g	65~80 ℃	30 min.	1 hour	20 cm pot

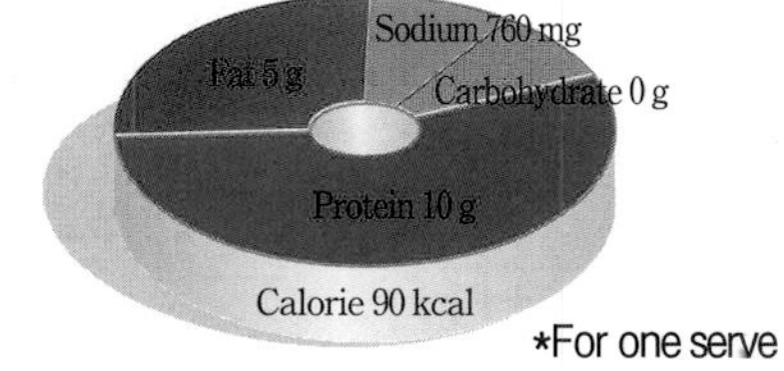

*For one serve

Ingredients & Quantity

70 g (1 body) dried pollack (skinned yellowish dried pollack)
seasoning : 7 g (½ tbsp) minced green onion, 5.5 g (1 tsp) minced garlic
0.3 g (⅛ tsp) ground white pepper, 6.5 g (½ tbsp) sesame oil
100 g radish, 20 g small green onion, 5 g (¼ ea) red pepper
4 g (1 tsp) sesame oil
1.4 kg (7 cups) water, 6 g (1 tsp) clear soy sauce, 6 g (½ tbsp) salt
60 g (1 ea) egg

Preparation

1. Remove the head, tail and fins of the dried pollack (55 g) and soak in water for 10 sec. wrap it with damp cotton cloths and let it sit for 30 min.
2. When the dried pollack is soften, take out bone and spines from the pollack. rip it up into about 5 cm− long and season it (120 g). 【Photos 2 & 3】
3. Trim and clean the radish, shred it into 3 cm−square and 0.3 cm−thick (90 g).
4. Trim and clean the small green onion, cut it into 3~4 cm−long (15 g). Halve the red pepper and seed, then cut it into 3 cm−long and 0.3 cm−wide (4 g). 【Photo 4】
5. Beat egg.

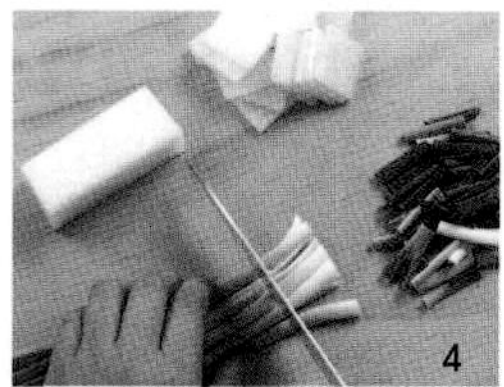

Recipe

1. When the pot preheated, oil and stir−fry the dried pollack and radish together for 1 min. on medium heat. Add water and boil it on high heat for 7 min. 【Photo 5】
2. Reduce the heat to medium and boil it for 20 min. more. Season with diluted soy sauce and salt. Put small green onion and red pepper, draw lines with beaten egg on top and bring it to a boil. 【Photo 6】

· Shred dried pollack may be used for dried pollack soup.
· Bean sprouts may make the soup cool in taste.

Heating Time	Process	Heat Control
Preparation	Preparing dried pollack and vegetables, Beating egg	
0 min	Stir−frying dried pollack and radish	M−heat 1 min. H−heat 7 min.
10 min	Boiling dried pollack soup	M−heat 20 min.
30 min	Seasoning with salt,Boiling after adding small green onion red pepper and egg	M−heat 2 min.

Jogaetang 조개탕

Clam Soup

Jogaetang is a soup made by boiling whole clams after they have been soaked to expel sediment. *Jogaetang* has a light, refreshing taste. It is enjoyed after drinking alcohol because clams are high in taurine which is believed to protect the liver.

Total weight after cooking	Weight for one serve	Service temperature	Total heating time	Total cooking time	Standard utensil
1.4 kg(4 serves)	350 g	65~80 ℃	14 min.	4 hours	20 cm pot

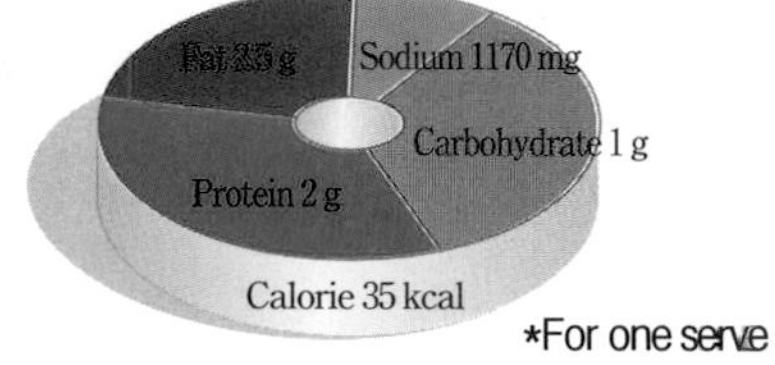

*For one serve

Ingredients & Quantity

300 g short necked clam, 600 g (3 cups) water, 8 g (2 tsp) salt
20 g small green onion
10 g (½ ea) red pepper
1.2 kg (6 cups) water
5 g (1 clove) garlic
8 g (2 tsp) salt

Preparation

1. Wash and clean the clam's shell, put in the salt water for 3 hours for the clams spit out watery sediment. 【Photo 2】
2. Trim and wash the garlic, mince finely. 【Photo 3】
3. Cut the small green onion into 3cm-long.
4. Shred the red pepper into 3cm-long and 0.3 cm-wide/thick. 【Photo 4】

Recipe

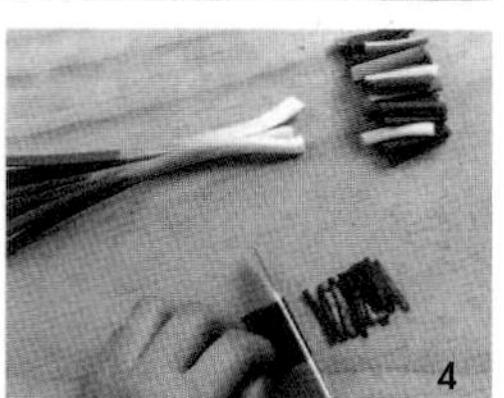

1. Put the short necked clams and water into the pot, heat it up for 7 min. on high heat. When it boils, lower the heat to medium, boil it for another 5 min. 【Photo 5】
2. When the clams open the shell, add small green onion, red pepper and minced garlic, season with salt, bring it to a boil. 【Photo 6】

· Clams must be alive, then it will give good taste without fishy smell.
· Do not boil clams too long, or clam flesh may be tough and untasty.

Heating Time	Process	Heat Control
Preparation	Clams spitting watery sediments. Preparing vegetables	
0 min	Boiling after adding clam and water	H-heat 7 min. M-heat 5 min.
10 min	Seasoning with salt after adding small green onion red pepper and minced garlic.	M-heat 2 min.

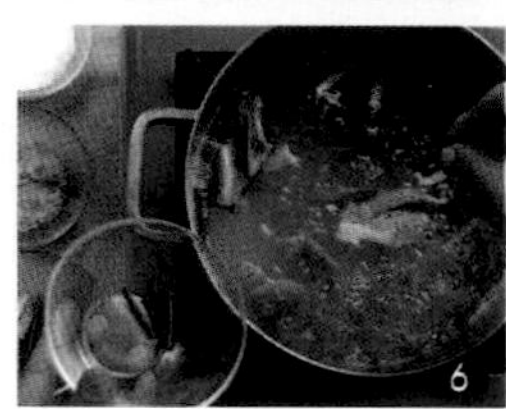

Miyeokguk 미역국

Seaweed Soup

Miyeokguk is a soup boiled with soaked brown seaweed, shredded beef and soy sauce seasoning. From olden days, *miyeokguk* was served without fail to women after childbirth, or for birthdays because *miyeok* (brown seaweed) is believed to ease swelling by eliminating waste and salt from the body.

Total weight after cooking	Weight for one serve	Service temperature	Total heating time	Total cooking time	Standard utensil
1.32 kg(4 serves)	330 g	65~80 ℃	32 min.	1 hour	20 cm pot

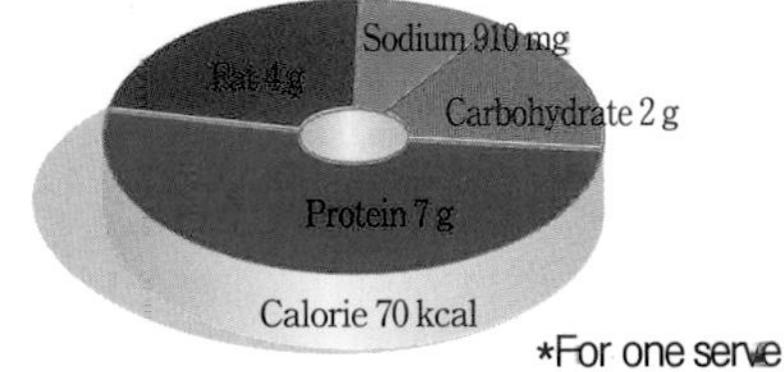

*For one serve

Ingredients & Quantity

20 g dried brown seaweed
100 g beef (shank)
seasoning sauce : 3 g (½ tsp) clear soy sauce, 2.8 g (½ tsp) minced garlic, 0.1 g ground black pepper
13 g (1 tbsp) sesame oil
1.6 kg (8 cups) water
6 g (1 tsp) clear soy sauce
8 g (2 tsp) salt

1

Preparation

1. Soak dried brown seaweed in water for 30 min. remove foreign elements such as sands if exist. Squeeze the water out and cut it into 4 cm-long (260 g). 【Photo 2】
2. Clean blood of beef with cotton cloths, cut it into 2.5 cm-square and 0.2 cm-thick, season with seasoning sauce. 【Photo 3】

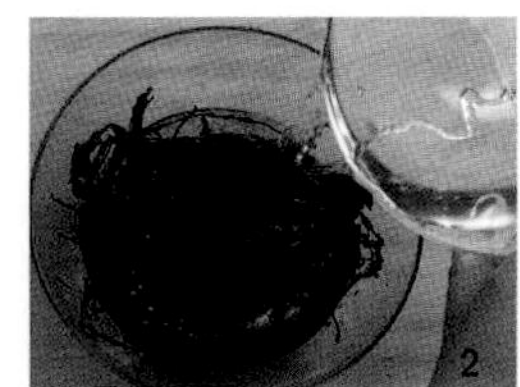
2

3

Recipe

1. Preheat the pot and oil with sesame oil, stir-fry the beef for 2 min. on medium heat. Add soaked brown seaweed, fry them for another 3 min. 【Photos 4 & 5】
2. Add water into the pot, boil it for 5 min. on high heat. When it boils, lower the heat to medium, continue to boil for 20 min. When the soup soaked tastefully, season with clear soy sauce and salt, bring it to a boil. 【Photo 6】

4

- When the dried brown seaweed is soaked in water for 30 min. it grows 15 times in volume.
- Frying seaweed with only sesame oil, without beef, may be an another choice.

5

Heating Time	Process	Heat Control
Preparation	Soaking dried brown seaweed. Preparing beef	
0 min	Stir-frying beef	M-heat 2 min.
	Stir-frying brown seaweed	M-heat 3 min.
	Boiling after adding water	H-heat 5 min. M-heat 20 min.
30 min	Seasoning	M-heat 2 min.

6

Mu-malgeunjangguk 무맑은장국

Clear White Radish Soup

Mu-malgeunjangguk is a soup made with sliced squares of Korean radish boiled in water. It is seasoned with soy sauce and salt. *Mu-malgeunjangguk* is a basic everyday soup that is easily digested and thus good for children and the elderly. According to Oriental medicine, Korean radish quenches thirst, stops coughing and helps digestion.

Total weight after cooking	Weight for one serve	Service temperature	Total heating time	Total cooking time	Standard utensil
1.12 kg (4 serves)	280 g	65~80 ℃	1 hour 16 min.	2 hours	20 cm pot

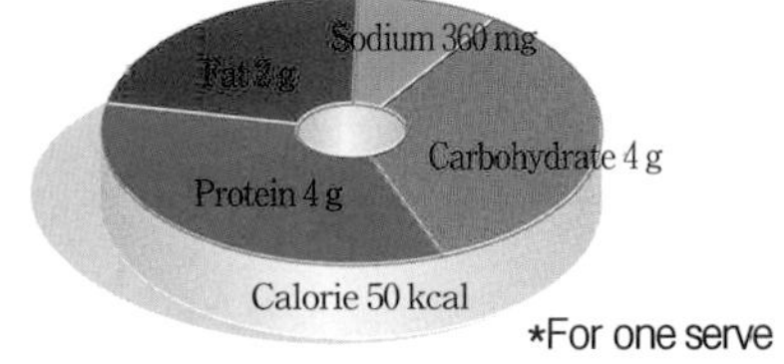

*For one serve

Ingredients & Quantity

300 g beef (brisket, shank), 1.6 kg (8 cups) water
fragrant seasoning : 20 g green onion, 10 g garlic
seasoning sauce : 3 g (½ tsp) clear soy sauce, 1.1 g (¼ tsp) minced green onion
1.4 g (¼ tsp) mince onion, 0.1 g ground black pepper
300 g radish, 5 g kelps
3 g (½ tsp) clear soy sauce, 6 g (1½ tsp) salt
20 g green onion

Preparation

1. Clean blood of beef with cotton cloths, and wash fragrant seasoning.
2. Put the beef and water in the pot, boil it on high heat for 7 min. When it boils, lower the heat to medium, simmer for 30 min. Add fragrant seasoning, simmer it for another 30 min. 【Photo 2】
3. Cut the radish into 2.5 cm-square and 0.5 cm-thick (260 g).
4. Wipe the kelps with damp cotton cloths, cut it into 2.5 cm-square. Cut the green onion into 2 cm-long diagonally. 【Photo 3】

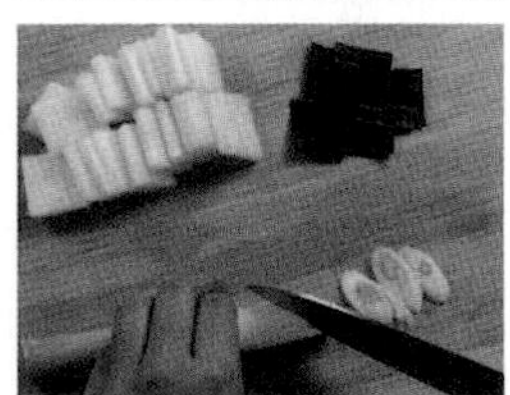

Recipe

1. Take the beef out from the broth, cut it into 2.5 cm-square and season. Filter the soup through strainer. 【Photo 4】
2. Add radish and kelps in the pot, boil for 7 min. Season with clear soy sauce and salt. 【Photo 5】
3. Add green onion and bring it to a boil. 【Photo 6】

· Autumn radish is more sweet and tasteful.

Heating Time	Process	Heat Control
Preparation	Preparing beef and radish	
0 min	Simmering beef	H-heat 7 min. M-heat 60 min.
70 min	Boiling after adding radish and kelps. Seasoning	M-heat 7 min.
80 min	Bringing to a boil after adding green onion	M-heat 2 min.

Galbitang 갈비탕

Beef Rib Soup

Galbitang is a soup made by slowly simmering beef ribs. It is gamished and served with steamed rice at the table. Beef ribs are a tasty cut that is well-marbled with fat. Therefore, beef ribs are also grilled and steamed.

Total weight after cooking	Weight for one serve	Service temperature	Total heating time	Total cooking time	Standard utensil
2.1 kg (4 serves)	525 g	65~80 ℃	3 hours 32 min.	over 5 hours	24 cm pot, 30 cm frying pan

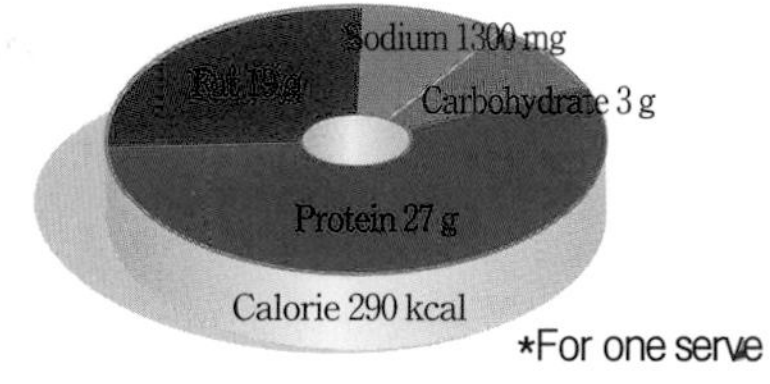

*For one serve

Ingredients & Quantity

600 g beef ribs, 1 kg (5 cups) precleaning water
5 kg (25 cups) boiling water
200 g radish
fragrant seasoning : 40 g (1 root) green onion, 42 g (6 cloves) garlic, 130 g (½ head) onion
36 g (2 tbsp) clear soy sauce, 8 g (2 tsp) salt
60 g (1 ea) egg
seasoning : 28 g (2 tbsp) minced green onion, 16 g (1 tbsp) minced garlic, 0.3 g (⅛ tsp) ground black pepper

1

Preparation

1. Cut the beef ribs into 5 cm–long, soak in cold water for 3 hours to draw out the blood, changing the soaking water every 1 hour. 【Photo 2】
2. Remove fats and tendons from the beef ribs. 【Photo 3】
3. Trim and wash the radish, peel skin (180 g), cut into 6 cm–long.
4. Panfry egg for yellow/white egg garnish, and cut into 2 cm–long of diaper shape.
5. Blend seasoning.

2

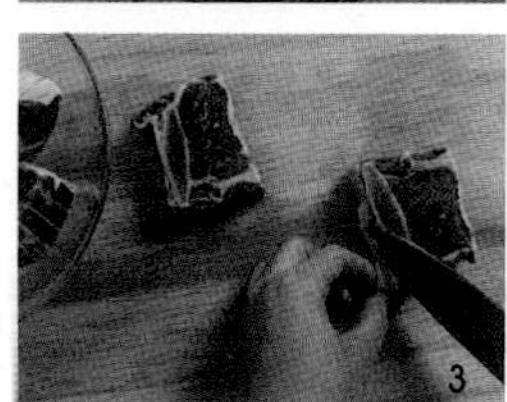

3

Recipe

1. Pour water in the pot and heat it for 5 min. on high heat. When it boils, add the beef ribs, and boil it another 2 min. Discard boiling water. 【Photo 4】
2. Pour cold water and beef ribs in the pot, boil it for 20 min. on high heat, then lower the heat to medium, simmer it for 2 hours Add radish and fragrant seasoning together, boil for 1 hour, while skim the fats. 【Photo 5】
3. When radish is well–done, take out the radish, cut into 3 cm–wide, 4 cm–long and 0.5 cm–thick. Remove out the fragrant seasoning from the pot.
4. Cool down the broth, filter through cotton cloths, skim fats off. Season with clear soy sauce and salt. Put beef ribs (420 g) and radish into the broth, boil it for 5 min. on medium heat. 【Photo 6】
5. Place the beef rib soup in a bowl, top with egg garnish, then serve with seasoning sauce.

4

- Beef rib soup may be boiled with seasonings from the beginning.
- Boiled potato starch noodles may be added upon taste.
- Chopped green onion and red pepper powder may be added upon taste.
- Summer radish may have strong smell. Scald summer radish in water before adding into the broth.

5

Heating Time	Process	Heat Control
Preparation	Preparing beef ribs and radish. Blending seasoning Pan–frying egg for garnish	
0 min	Precleaning beef ribs by boiling shortly	H–heat 7 min.
10 min	Boiling beef ribs. Adding radish and fragrant seasoning	H–heat 20 min. M–heat 120 min.
150 min		M–heat 60 min.
210 min	Boiling beef ribs in broth	M–heat 5 min.

6

Seolleongtang 설렁탕

Ox-Bone Soup

Seolleongtang is a soup made by simmering ox bones, intestines and shank for a long time. The name of the soup comes from a story in which the king held a memorial service at the *seonnongdan* (an altar) with his officers, and offered an ox as a sacrifice and shared ox bone soup afterwards with the attendants.

Total weight after cooking	Weight for one serve	Service temperature	Total heating time	Total cooking time	Standard utensil
2.6 kg(4 serves)	650 g	65~80 ℃	8 hours 55 min.	over 5 hours	32 cm pot

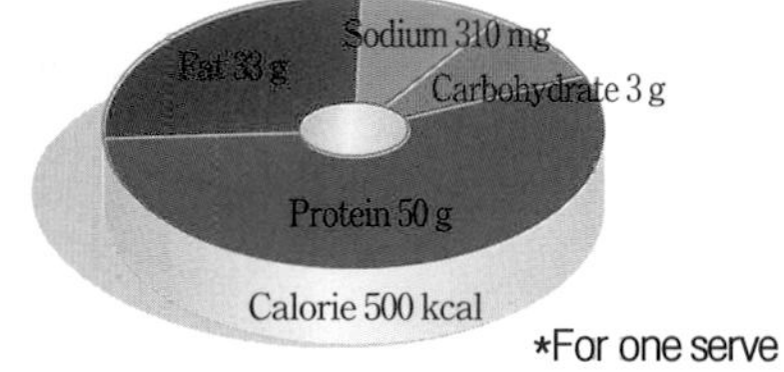

*For one serve

Ingredients & Quantity

1 kg ox-knee bone, 600 g gristle, 700 g ox-tongue, 5 kg (25 cups) precleaning water
200 g beef (brisket), 200 g beef (shank)
7 kg (35 cups) boiling water
fragrant seasoning : 30 g green onion, 65 g garlic, 20 g ginger, 50 g onion
seasonings : 40 g green onion, 8 g (⅔ tbsp) salt, 0.3 g (⅛ tsp) ground black pepper

1

Preparation

1. Wash and clean ox-knee bone, gristle and ox-tongue, soak in water for 5~6 hours to draw out the blood.
2. Wipe blood of brisket and shank with cotton cloths. Wash fragrant seasoning cleanly.
3. Trim and wash vegetables for fragrant seasoning and green onion cleanly. Chop green onion finely.

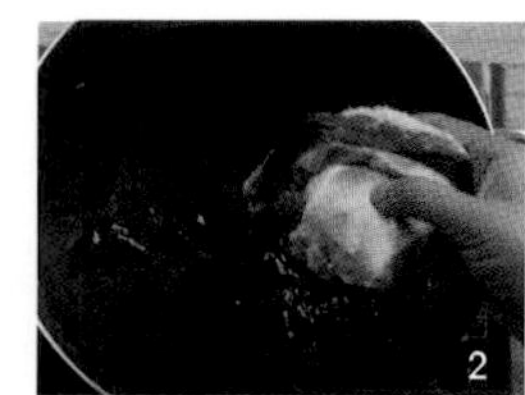
2

Recipe

1. Pour water in the pot and heat it up for 10 min. on high heat. When it boils, add ox-knee bone, gristle and ox-tongue, and boil it for 5 min. for precleaning, then discard boiling water. 【Photo 2 · 3】
2. Put water, ox-knee bone and gristle in the pot, boil it for 1 hour on high heat. Then lower the heat to medium, simmer it for 5 hours while skim the foam and fats. Add ox-tongue, brisket and shank in the pot, boil for 1 hour. Add the fragrant seasoning, boil for 1 hour, then boil it for another 30 min. after reduce the heat to low. 【Photo 4】
3. When ox-tongue and beef are well-done, take them out from the broth, cut into 3 cm-wide, 4 cm-long and 0.2 cm-thick. Cool down the broth, skim fats, and boil for 10 min. on high heat. 【Photo 5】
4. Place the cut beef in a bowl, pour broth and serve with seasonings. 【Photo 6】

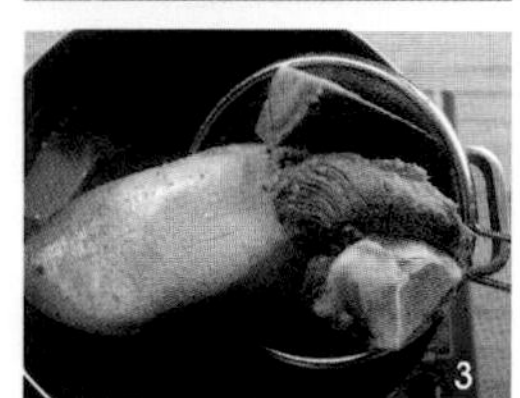
3

4

· Ox-head meat, ox-hooves and/or breast meat may be added.
· Large size onion and radish in the soup may be more tasteful.
· Ground red pepper may be added upon taste.

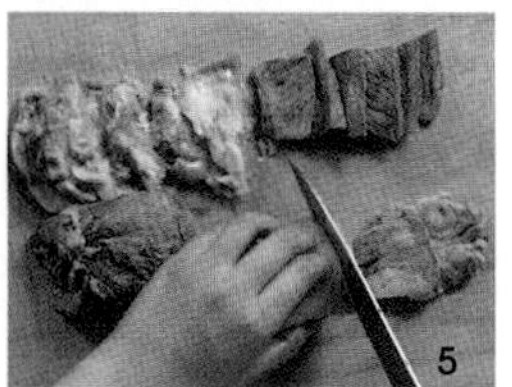
5

Heating Time	Process	Heat Control
Preparation	Drawing out blood from ox-knee bone, gristle and ox-tongue	
0 min	Precleaning meat by boiling shortly	H-heat 15 min.
10 min	Simmering after adding ox-knee bone and gristle	H-heat 60 min. M-heat 300 min.
370 min	Simmering broth after adding ox-tongue, brisket and shank	M-heat 60 min.
430 min	Boiling broth after adding fragrant seasoning	M-heat 60 min. L-heat 30 min.
500 min	Cooling broth, skimming fats, seasoning and boiling again	H-heat 10 min.

6

Samgyetang 삼계탕

Ginseng Chicken Soup

Samgyetang is a chicken soup made by stuffing a young chicken cavity with glutinous rice, ginseng, jujubes and garlic, then simmering it for a long time. In Korea, there are three traditional hottest days (*sambok*) in the summer. People have *samgyetang* on those hottest days to overcome the hot weather.

Total weight after cooking	Weight for one serve	Service temperature	Total heating time	Total cooking time	Standard utensil
3.6 kg(4 serves)	900 g	65~80 ℃	2 hours 10 min.	4 hours	32 cm pot

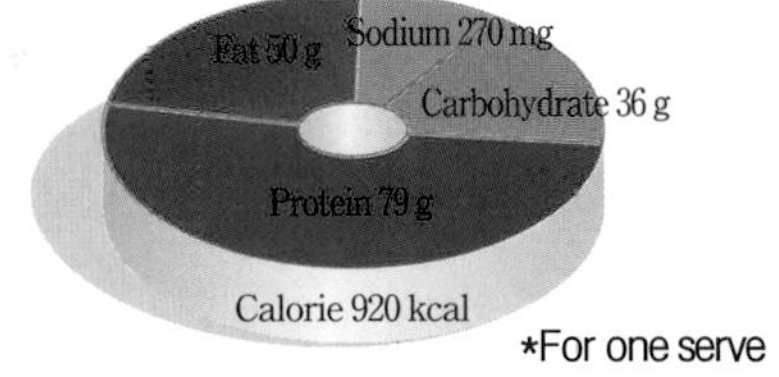

*For one serve

Ingredients & Quantity

4 heads (2.2 kg) young chicken
180 g (1 cup) glutinous rice
milk vetch water : 20g (4 roots) milk vetch roots, 3 kg (15 cups) water
40 g (4 roots) fresh wet ginseng, 20 g (4 heads) garlic, 16g (4 ea) jujube
2.6 kg (13 cups) water
20 g green onion, 12 g (1 tbsp) salt, 0.3 g (⅛ tsp) ground black pepper

1

Preparation

1. Remove internal organs and excess fat from the chicken through under the stomach, and wash it cleanly (500 g).
2. Wash the glutinous rice and soak in water for 2 hours, drain water on a strainer for 10min. (220 g).
3. Wash the milk vetch roots and soak in water for 2 hours.
4. Wash and clean the fresh wet ginseng and cut the head part (35 g). Wash and clean garlic and jujube. 【Photo 2】
5. Wash green onion and chop them finely (16 g).

2

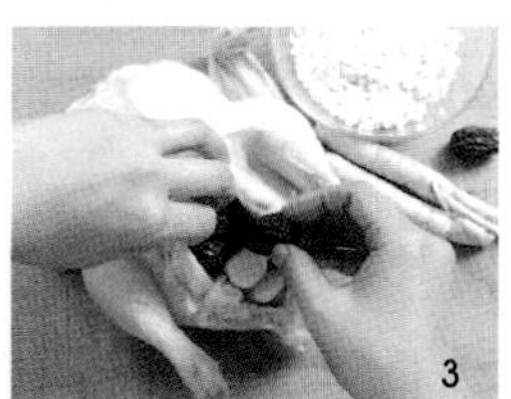

3

Recipe

1. Put the milk vetch roots and water in the pot, heat it up for 20 min. on high heat. When it boils, lower the heat to medium, simmer it for 40 min, filter it through a strainer to make milk vetch water (2.6 kg).
2. Stuff each chicken cavity with the rice, ginseng, garlic and jujube. Criss-cross the legs of each chicken to keep the stuffs inside. 【Photos 3 & 4】
3. Put the chicken and milk vetch water in the pot, boil it for 20 min. on high heat. Reduce the heat down to medium and simmer it for 50 min. until the soup turns milky white. 【Photos 5 & 6】
4. Serve it with green onion, salt and ground black pepper.

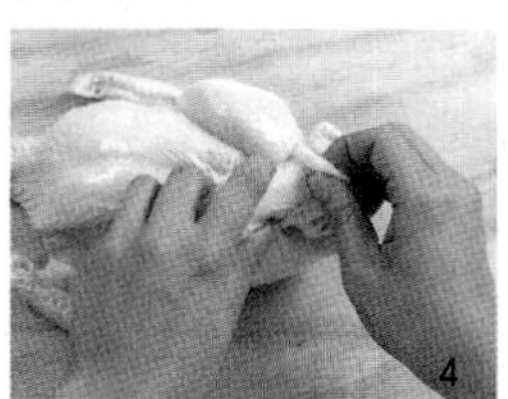

4

· Do not boil the chicken soup too long, or it may be untasty because of crushed meat.

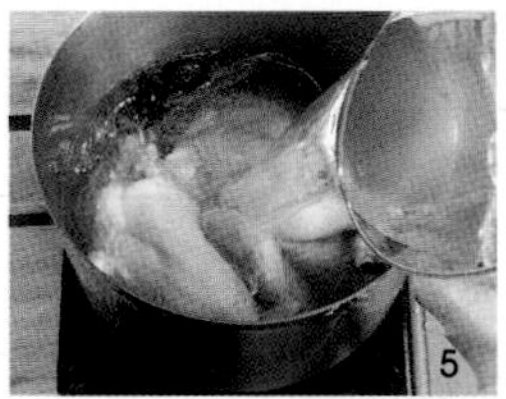

5

Heating Time	Process	Heat Control
Preparation	Preparing young chicken. Preparing glutinous rice Soaking milk vetch roots Trimming and cleaning fresh ginseng, garlic, jujube and green onion.	
0 min	Boiling milk vetch water	H-heat 20 min. M-heat 40 min.
60 min	Stuffing chicken cavity	
	Simmering ginseng chicken soup	H-heat 20 min. M-heat 50 min.

6

Yukgaejang 육개장

Spicy Beef and Leek Soup

Yukgaejang is a spicy soup made by boiling beef with various vegetables, such as green onion, bracken, mung bean sprouts and taro stalks. It is a good soup for the summer to stimulate appetite and recoup physical strength with its high protein content.

Total weight after cooking	Weight for one serve	Service temperature	Total heating time	Total cooking time	Standard utensil
2.44 kg(4 serves)	610 g	65~80 ℃	2 hours 45 min.	4 hours	20 cm pot, 32 cm pot

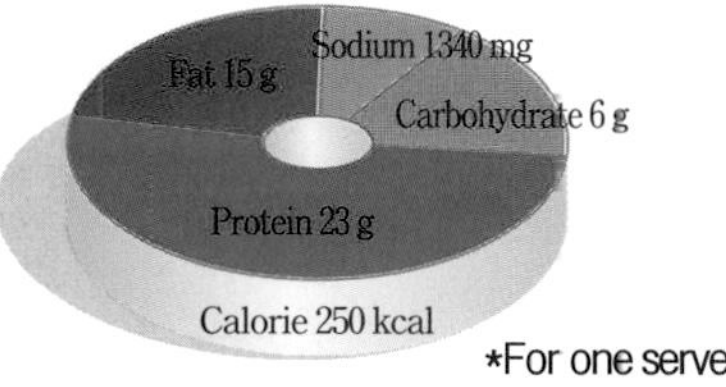

*For one serve

Ingredients & Quantity

broth : 400 g beef (brisket), 4 kg (20 cups) water fragrant seasoning : 100 g green onion , 42 g (6 cloves) garlic
seasoning sauce ① : 18 g (1 tbsp) clear soy sauce, 28 g (2 tbsp) minced green onion
16 g (1 tbsp) minced garlic, 26 g (2 tbsp) red pepper oil, 6.5 g (½ tbsp) sesame oil
100 g soaked bracken, 100 g soaked taro stalks
200 g mung bean sprouts, 100 g green onion, 600 g (3 cups) water, 2 g (½ tsp) salt
seasoning sauce ② : 18 g (1 tbsp) clear soy sauce, 14 g (2 tbsp) ground red pepper
28 g (2 tbsp) minced green onion, 16 g (1 tbsp) minced garlic , 6.5 g (½ tbsp) sesame oil
8 g (2 tsp) salt

Preparation

1. Soak the beef in water for 1 hour to draw out the blood. Trim and wash fragrant seasoning. Put the beef and water into the pot, heat it up for 17 min. on high heat. When it boils, lower the heat to medium, simmer it for 1 hour. Add fragrant seasoning and continue to simmer for another 30 min. 【Photo 2】
2. When the beef is well-done, take the beef out and filter the broth through cotton cloths (2.6 kg). 【Photo 3】
3. Wash soaked bracken and taro stalks, cut them into 7 cm-long. Rip up taro stalks into 0.5 cm-wide (90 g).
4. Remove the tails of mung been sprouts and wash.
5. Cut the green onion into half of the length, then shred into 7 cm-long. 【Photo 4】
6. Blend seasoning sauce ①, ②.

1

2

Recipe

1. Rip up the beef into 6 cm-long and 0.5 cm-wide/thick along with the texture, mix seasoning sauce ① together.
2. Pour water into the pot, heat it up for 3 min. on high heat. When it boils, scald the mung bean sprouts with salt for 2 min. (158 g). Scald the green onion for 1min. (115 g).
3. Mix the soaked bracken, soaked taro stalks, mung bean sprouts and green onion with seasoning sauce ② together. 【Photo 5】
4. Pour the broth into the pot, heat it up for 10 min. on high heat. When it boils, add the seasoned stuffs, lower the heat to medium, boil for another 40 min. When the broth cooked tastefully, season with salt, bring it to a boil. 【Photo 6】

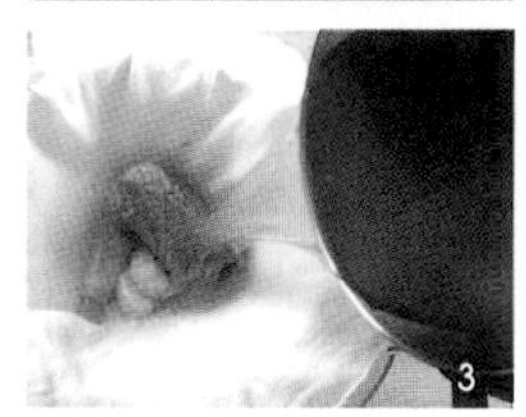
3

4

· Because raw taro stalk is acrid, it should be boiled and soaked in water sufficiently before cooking.
· Putting more ground red pepper in the soup is an option.
· When green onion added later, it may show better color.
· To blend red pepper oil, heat up 39 g (3 tbsp) of edible oil in a pot, add 7 g (1 tbsp) of ground red pepper and 2.8 g (½ tsp) of minced garlic into the oil. Then turn off the heat, wait for 2 min. with stirring. Filter it through fine sieve.

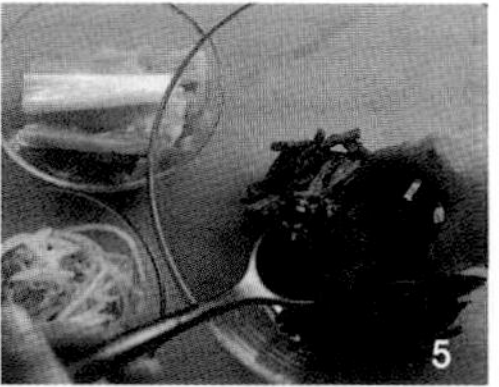
5

Heating Time	Process	Heat Control
Preparation	Preparing beef and vegetables. Blend seasoning sauce	
0 min	Simmering broth	H-heat 17 min. M-heat 60 min.
70 min	Adding fragrant seasoning	M-heat 30 min.
100 min	Filtering broth	
	Seasoning boiled beef	H-heat 6 min.
110 min	Scalding mung bean and green onion. Seasoning bracken, taro stalks. mung bean and green onion,	H-heat 10 min. M-heat 40 min.
160 min	Seasoning with salt	M-heat 2 min.

6

Imjasutang 임자수탕

Chilled Chicken Soup

Imjasutang is a cold soup with chicken meat in a chilled broth that is a mixture of ground roasted sesame seeds and chicken stock. "*Imja*" refers to white sesame. *Imjasutang* may also be called '*kkaekkuktang*.' It is believed to maintain health in the summer. This soup was enjoyed by royalty and noble families in olden days.

Total weight after cooking	Weight for one serve	Service temperature	Total heating time	Total cooking time	Standard utensil
2 kg(4 serves)	500 g	4~10 ℃	60 min.	2 hours	24 cm pot, 30 cm frying pan

Fat 20 g, Sodium 760 mg, Carbohydrate 8 g, Protein 31 g, Calorie 340 kcal

*For one serve

Ingredients & Quantity

1.2 kg (1 head) chicken : 2 kg (10 cups) water, 1 g (¼ tsp) salt
fragrant seasoning : 20 g green onion, 15 g (3 cloves) garlic, 5 g ginger
sesame broth : 1.4 kg (7 cups) broth, 100 g sesame seeds, 6 g(½ tbsp) salt
dumpling : 80 g minced beef(top round), 20 g tofu, 60 g (1 ea) egg, 14 g (2 tbsp) wheat flour
seasoning sauce : 2 g (⅓ tsp) clear soy sauce, 0.5 g (⅛ tsp) salt, 4.5 g (1 tsp) minced green onion 2.8 g (½ tsp) minced garlic, 0.1 g ground black pepper, 2 g (½ tsp) sesame oil
100 g (½ ea) cucumber, 2 g (½ tsp) salt
15 g (3 stems) brown oak mushrooms
20 g (1 ea) red pepper, 3.5 g (1 tsp) pine nuts
60 g (1 ea) egg , 24 g (3 tbsp) starch powder

Preparation

1. Remove internal organs and fats from the chicken and wash cleanly (1.1 kg).
2. Soak the sesame in water for 1 hour, wash it by rubbing and drain water on a strainer for 15 min (160 g).
3. Clean blood of the minced beef with cotton cloths (75 g). Mash the tofu (15 g) and season with seasoning sauce. Shape dumplings with 2.5 g of the stuff into 1.5 cm diameter (dumplings 32 ea).
4. Wash and clean the cucumber by rubbing with salt, cut it into 1.5 cm–wide, 3 cm–long and 0.3 cm–thick (40 g), marinate it with salt for 5 min. wipe water with cotton cloths. Soak brown oak mushrooms in water for 1 hour and cut it into same size of the cucumber (30 g). Halve the red pepper, seed and cut into same size of the cucumber (6 g).
5. Remove tops of the pine nuts and wipe the nuts with dry cotton cloths.
6. Panfry the egg for yellow/white egg garnish and cut it into 1.5 cm–wide and 3 cm–long.

Recipe

1. Put the chicken in the pot and add water, boil it for 10 min. on high heat. Reduce the heat to medium, boil it for 10 min. Boil it for another 20 min. after adding fragrant seasoning. 【Photo 2】
2. Take out the chicken from the pot, separate the meat from bone, rip up the meat into 0.5 cm–thick (430 g) and season with salt. Cool down the soup and strain through cotton cloths to provide broth (1.4 kg). 【Photo 3】
3. Stir–fry the sesame seeds for about 10~15 min. on medium heat (90 g). Grind it with 400 g of chicken broth finely in the mixer, then strain it. To blend sesame liquid, add remained broth (1 kg) and season with salt (1.4 kg). 【Photo 4】
4. Coat the dumplings with wheat flour and beaten egg. Preheat the frying pan and oil, panfry dumplings with rolling for 5 min. on medium heat.
5. Coat the cucumber, mushrooms and red pepper with starch powder, scald it in water for about 20~30 sec. and rinse in cold water. 【Photo 5】
6. Place the chicken meat on a dish, lay out the provided several vegetables around the dish, pour the sesame broth, and then top the pine nuts on it.【Photo 6】

· In summer, ice cubes may be served in the soup.

Heating Time	Process	Heat Control
Preparation	Trimming and cleaning chicken. Soaking brown oak mushrooms Preparing sesame seeds, beef and vegetables	
0 min	Simmering broth	H–heat 10 min. M–heat 30 min.
40 min	Stir–frying sesame seeds and grinding. Pan–frying dumplings	M–heat 15 min. M–heat 5 min.
60 min	Scalding vegetables. Placing in the dish and pouring the sesame broth	H–heat 20~30 sec.

1

2

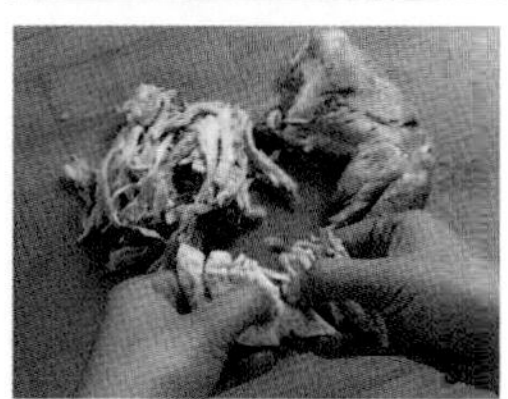

4

5

6

Doenjang-jjigae 된장찌개

Soybean Paste Stew

Doenjang-jjigae is a stew made of tofu, zucchini, and other ingredients seasoned with soybean paste. *Doenjang-jjigae* is an everyday Korean stew. It tastes best when boiled in unglazed pottery. Certain studies have shown that the lecithin in soybean paste may prevent arteriosclerosis and other diseases.

Total weight after cooking	Weight for one serve	Service temperature	Total heating time	Total cooking time	Standard utensil
960 g(4 serves)	240 g	65~80 ℃	19 min.	2 hours	20 cm pot

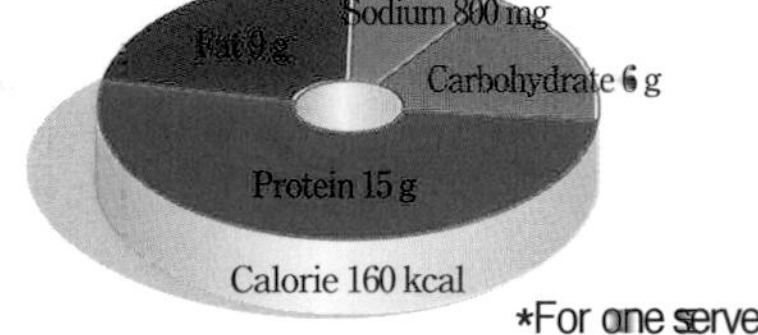

*For one serve

Ingredients & Quantity

90 g beef (top round · sirloin)
15 g (3 sheets) brown oak mushrooms
seasoning sauce : 9 g (½ tbsp) clear soy sauce, 4.5 g (1 tsp) minced green onion
2.8 g (½ tsp) minced garlic, 0.5 g (⅓ tsp) sesame salt
0.3 g (⅛ tsp) ground black pepper, 4 g (1 tsp) sesame oil
700 g (3½ cup) rice washed water, 75 g (5 tbsp) soybean paste, 250 g (½ cake) tofu
2.2 g (1 tsp) coarse red pepper powder
20 g (½ roots) green onion, 15 g (1 ea) green pepper, 20 g (1 ea) red pepper

Preparation

1. Clean blood of beef with cotton cloths, cut into 2.5 cm–square and 0.5 cm–thick.
2. Soak brown oak mushrooms in water for 1 hour (50 g), remove stems, wipe water and shred into 4 cm–long and 0.5 cm–wide.
3. Cut the tofu into 2 cm–wide, 3 cm–long and 1 cm–thick. 【Photo 2】
4. Mix beef and mushrooms with seasoning sauce respectively. 【Photo 3】
5. Cut green onion and green/red pepper into 2 cm–long and 0.2 cm–wide diagonally.

Recipe

1. Preheat the pot, put the beef and mushrooms, stir–fry for 2 min. on medium heat, then add rice washed water. 【Photo 4】
2. Dissolve soybean paste, and boil it for 4 min. on high heat. When it boils, lower the heat to medium, boil it for another 10 min. 【Photo 5】
3. When the paste soaked out fairly, add tofu and coarse red pepper powder, boil it for 2 min. Add green/red pepper and boil for another 1 min. 【Photo 6】

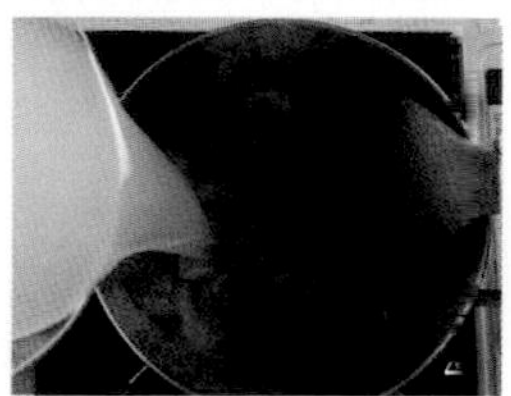

· After adding tofu, just boil it shortly to be soft.
· In summer season, young pumpkin slices in the stew may serve better taste.

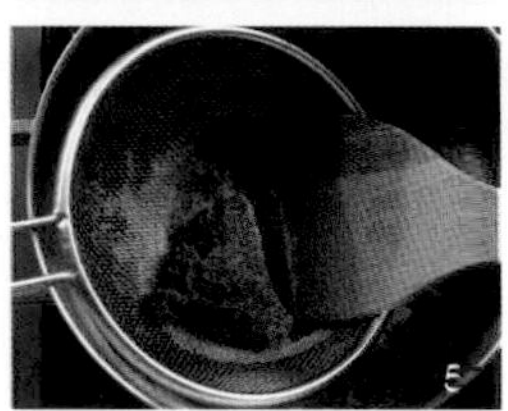

Heating Time	Process	Heat Control
Preparation	Preparing beef and vegetables	
0 min	Stir–frying beef and mushrooms	M–heat 2 min.
	Adding rice washed water and dissolving soybean paste	H–heat 4 min. M–heat 10 min.
10 min	Adding tofu and coarse red pepper powder	M–heat 2 min.
	Adding green onion and green/red pepper	M–heat 1 min.

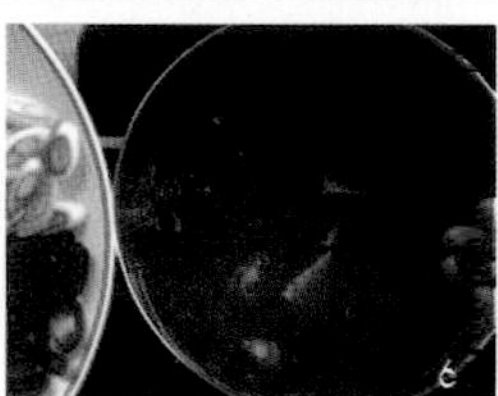

Gegamjeong 게감정

Crab Stew

Gegamjeong is a stew made of blue crab and red pepper paste. In olden days, it was often served on the king's dining table. The delicate crab flesh and spicy soup give *gegamjeong* a unique taste. The crab is tasty and nutritious, and there is a saying, 'Travelers should not look at the blue crab.'

Total weight after cooking	Weight for one serve	Service temperature	Total heating time	Total cooking time	Standard utensil
980 g (4 serves)	245 g	65~80 ℃	32 min.	1 hour	24 cm pot, 30 cm frying pan

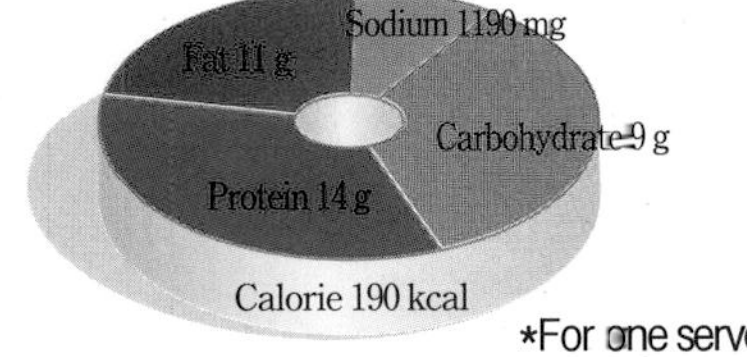

*For one serve

Ingredients & Quantity

600 g (2 bodies) blue crab (female)
120 g beef (minced top round)
seasoning sauce : 3 g (½ tsp) clear soy sauce, 2.3 g (½ tsp) minced green onion, 1.4 g (¼ tsp) minced garlic
1 g (½ tsp) sesame salt, 0.3 g (⅛ tsp) ground black pepper, 2 g (½ tsp) sesame oil
80 g tofu, 10 g (3 ea) brown oak mushrooms
80 g mung bean sprouts, 400 g (2 cups) water, 1 g (¼ tsp) salt
seasonings for filling stuffs : 4 g (1 tsp) salt, 0.3 g (⅛ tsp) ground black pepper, 1 g (½ tsp) sesame seeds,
4 g (1 tsp) sesame oil
150 g radish, 35 g (5 tbsp) wheat flour, 60 g (1 ea) egg
800 g (4 cups) water, 17 g (1 tbsp) soybean paste, 76 g (4 tbsp) red pepper paste
20 g (1 roots) green onion, 16 g (1 tbsp) minced garlic, 2.75 g (½ tsp) ginger juice, 2 g (½ tsp) salt
40 g crown daisy

1

Preparation

1. Clean crabs by brushing, cut the end part of legs. Split the crab shells from the bodies, scrape out the flesh (145 g), then drain water. 【Photo 2】
2. Clean blood of minced beef with cotton cloths, season with seasoning sauce.
3. Wrap tofu with cotton cloths, mash by squeezing. Remove the heads of mung bean sprouts.
4. Soak mushrooms in water for 1 hour, remove the stems, wipe water out, then chop finely.
5. Cut the radish into 2.5 cm-wide, 2 cm-long and 0.5 cm-thick. Trim and wash green onion, cut into 2 cm-long and 0.3 cm-thick diagonally.

3

Recipe

1. Pour water in the pot, heat it up for 2 min. on high heat. When it boils, put salt and mung bean sprouts, scald it for 2 min. cut them into 0.5 cm-long, and squeeze water out.
2. Pour water in the pot, put soybean paste and red pepper paste in the water through a strainer. Add crab legs and radish, heat it up for 2 min. on high heat. When it boils, lower the heat to medium, boil it for 10 min. to blend crab soup, then take the legs out.
3. Provide filling stuffs with seasoned crab flesh and all prepared stuffs with seasonings. 【Photo 3】
4. Coat inside of the crab shell with wheat flour, place filling stuffs on it evenly. 【Photo 4】
5. Coat the surface of filling stuffs with wheat flour again, then coat it with egg water over. Panfry it for 1 min. on medium heat, and another 1 min. after egg water coating again. 【Photo 5】
6. Put the fried crabs into the boiled crab soup, heat it up for 2 min. on high heat. When it boils, lower the heat to medium, boil for 10 min. Add green onion, garlic, ginger juice, salt and crown daisy, then bring it to a boil. 【Photo 6】

4

5

· Use alive crab for this dish.

Heating Time	Process	Heat Control
Preparation	Cleaning and trimming blue crab. Preparing beef tofu, mushrooms and vegetables	
0 min	Scalding mung bean sprouts. Boiling crab soup	H-heat 4 min. H-heat 2 min. M-heat 10 min.
	Preparing filling stuffs	
	Stuffing fillings into the crab shell and frying	M-heat 2 min.
20 min	Boiling crab stew	H-heat 2 min. M-heat 12 min.

6

Sundubu-jjigae 순두부찌개

Spicy Soft Tofu Stew

Sundubu-jjigae is a stew of soft tofu and clams in a spicy broth. Soft tofu is made with soaked soybeans which are called 'beef from the garden.' It is soft and sweet in taste. From olden days, Koreans developed tofu making skills and various dishes with tofu.

Total weight after cooking	Weight for one serve	Service temperature	Total heating time	Total cooking time	Standard utensil
1.04 kg(4 serves)	260 g	65~80 ℃	11 min.	30 min.	20 cm pot

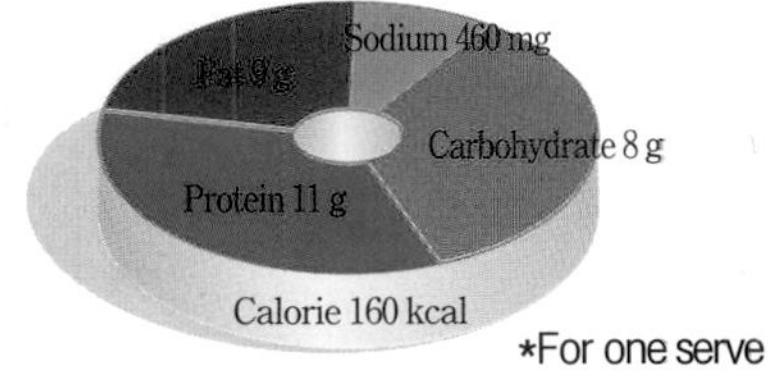

*For one serve

Ingredients & Quantity

600 g soft tofu : 300 g (1½ cups) water
200 g clam flesh : 4 g (1 tsp) salt, 1 kg (5 cups) water
seasoning sauce: 18 g (1 tbsp) clear soy sauce, 2 g (½ tsp) salt, 10 g (1½ tbsp) ground red pepper
28 g (2 tbsp) minced green onion, 16 g (1 tbsp) minced garlic, 20 g (1½ tbsp) sesame oil
10 g (½ root) green onion, 15 g (1 ea) green pepper, 10 g (½ ea) red pepper

Preparation

1. Slice the soft tofu into 5 cm–cubes.
2. Rinse the clam flesh in salt water and drain water on a strainer. 【Photo 2】
3. Blend seasoning sauce. 【Photo 3】
4. Cut the green onion and green/red pepper into 2 cm–long and 0.3 cm–thick diagonally. 【Photo 4】

Recipe

1. Season clam flesh with half of the seasoning sauce.
2. Put the soft tofu and water in the pot, boil it on high heat for 2 min. When it boils, lower the heat to medium and boil it for 5 min.
3. Add seasoned clam flesh and remained half of the seasoning sauce, then boil it another 2 min. 【Photo 5】
4. Add the green onion and green/red pepper, then bring it to a boil. 【Photo 6】

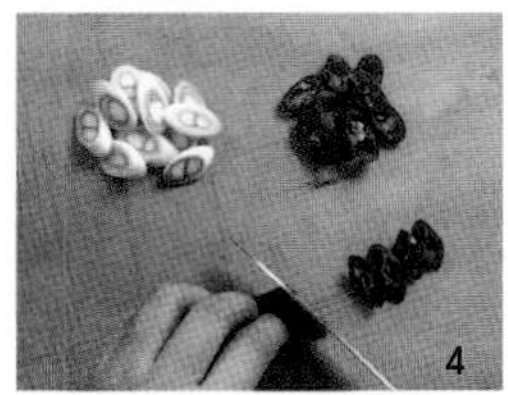

- Clam flesh may be replaced by oyster or pork in the stew.
- Soft tofu should be boiled shortly for soft taste, if too long, untasty.

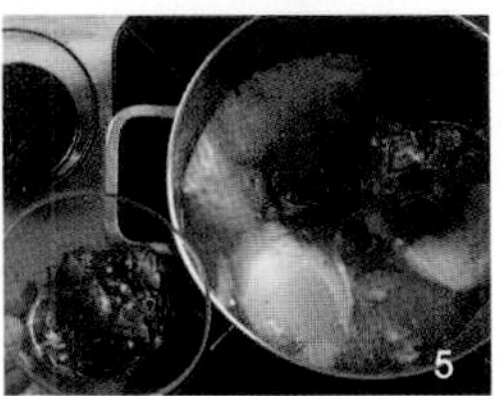

Heating Time	Process	Heat Control
Preparation	Washing clam flesh. Seasoning clam flesh. Cutting vegetables	
0 min	Boiling soft tofu stew. Boiling after adding clam flesh	H–heat 2 min. M–heat 7 min.
10 min	Boiling after adding green onion and green/red pepper	M–heat 2 min.

Guldubu-jjigae 굴두부찌개

Tofu Stew with Oysters

Guldubu-jjigae is a clear stew made of oysters, tofu and salted anchovy juice. Among seafood, the oyster contains the highest amount of nutrition and plenty of protein, so it is called 'milk from the sea.' Oysters have been widely enjoyed in Korea since it is surrounded by sea on three sides.

Total weight after cooking	Weight for one serve	Service temperature	Total heating time	Total cooking time	Standard utensil
880 g (4 serves)	220 g	65~80 ℃	9 min.	30 min.	18 cm pot

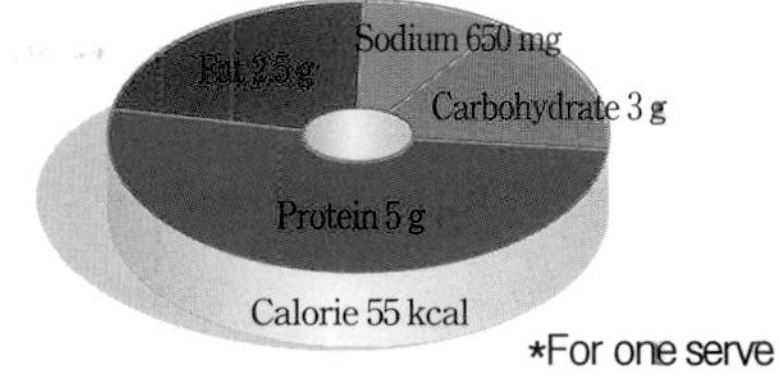

*For one serve

Ingredients & Quantity

100 g oyster, 200 g (1 cup) water, 4 g (1 tsp) salt
150 g (1/3 cake) tofu
20 g small green onion, 10 g (1/2 ea) red pepper, 5.5 g (1 tsp) minced garlic
700 g (3 1/2 cups) water, 15 g (1 tbsp) salted shrimp juice, 2 g (1/2 tsp) salt, 1 g (1/4 tsp) sesame oil

Preparation

1. Rinse the oyster softly in salt water and drain water on a strainer (98 g). 【Photo 2】
2. Cut the tofu into 2 cm–wide, 3 cm–long and 0.8 cm–thick (120 g). 【Photo 3】
3. Trim & wash small green onion and cut it into 3 cm–long (12 g). Halve the red pepper and seed, then shred it at intervals of 2 cm–long and 0.3 cm–wide (6 g). 【Photo 4】

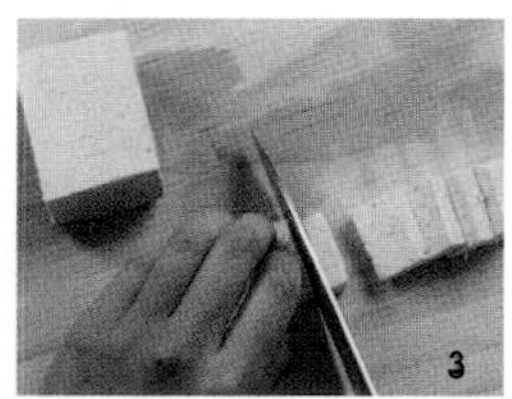

Recipe

1. Pour water in the pot and boil it for 4 min. on high heat. When it boils, season it with salted shrimp juice, add oyster, tofu and minced garlic, boil it for another 3 min. 【Photo 5】
2. When the oyster and tofu float up as well–done, add small green onion and red pepper, season with salt, bring it to a boil, then add sesame oil. 【Photo 6】

· To make clean and clear soup, do not boil too long after adding oyster.
· Adjust the salt quantity according to the saltiness of shrimp juice.
· Oyster may be replaced by salted pollack roe.

Heating Time	Process	Heat Control
Preparation 0 min	Preparing oyster, tofu and vegetables Boiling water Boiling after adding shrimp juice, oyster, tofu and minced garlic Seasoning with small green onion and red pepper	 H–heat 4 min. H–heat 3 min. H–heat 2 min.

Kimchi-jjigae 김치찌개

Kimchi Stew

Kimchi-jjigae is a stew made of well-fermented Kimchi and pork. Along with *doenjang-jjigae*, it is a typical stew that may be cooked with pork, beef and/or seafood to provide a variety of flavors. Kimchi is always served on the table as a side dish, but it may also be cooked in other dishes, such as *kimchi-bap* and *kimchi-jjim*.

Total weight after cooking	Weight for one serve	Service temperature	Total heating time	Total cooking time	Standard utensil
1.2 kg (4 serves)	300 g	65~80 ℃	1 hour 9 min.	2 hours	20 cm pot

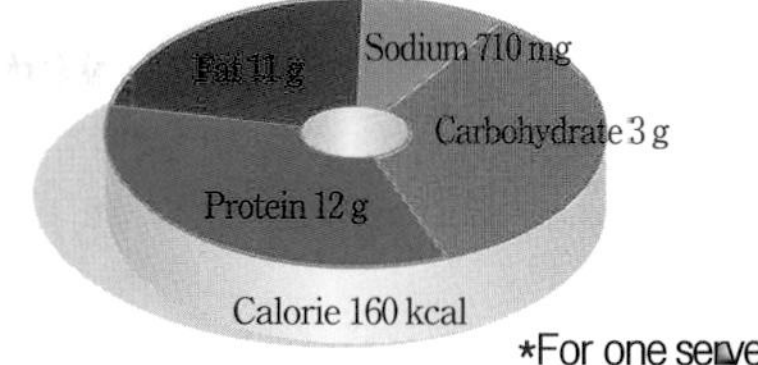

*For one serve

Ingredients & Quantity

280 g (¼ head) Cabbage Kimchi
150 g pork (neck fillet)
seasoning : 16 g (1 tbsp) minced garlic, 16 g (1 tbsp) ginger juice, 15 g (1 tbsp) refined rice wine
13 g (1 tbsp) sesame oil
1.2 kg (6 cups) stew water : 1.6 kg (8 cups) water, 100 g radish, 100 g (⅔ heads) onion, 20 g kelps
2.2 g (1 tsp) ground red pepper
2 g (½ tsp) salt
150 g (⅓ cake) tofu, 20 g green onion, 0.3 g (⅛ tsp) ground black pepper

1

Preparation

1. Remove the inside stuffs of the cabbage Kimchi, and cut the Kimchi into 2 cm–long (250 g).
2. Clean blood of the pork with cotton cloths, cut it into 2.5 cm–square and 0.2 cm–thick, and season. 【Photo 2】
3. Trim & clean the radish, skin, and cut it into 5 cm–square and 2 cm–thick (95 g). Shred the onion at intervals of 1 cm–wide (95 g).
4. Clean the kelps with damp cotton cloths.
5. Cut the tofu into 2.5 cm–wide, 3 cm–long and 0.8 cm–thick (130 g).
6. Trim & clean the green onion, and cut it into 2 cm–long diagonally (18 g).

2

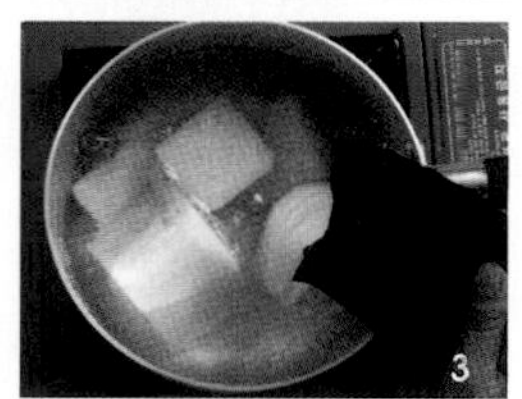
3

Recipe

1. Put water, radish and onion in the pot, heat it up for 8 min. on high heat. When it boils, reduce the heat to medium and boil it for 20 min. Add the kelps, turn off the heat and let it sit for 1 min. Filter it for stew soup. 【Photo 3】
2. Preheat the pot and oil. Put the pork and stir–fry it for 2 min. on medium heat. Add the cabbage Kimchi and stir–fry together for another 2 min. 【Photo 4】
3. Pour the stew soup and ground red pepper over the fried pork and Kimchi, boil it for 5 min. on high heat. Then reduce the heat to medium and boil it for 30 min.
4. Season it with salt, add tofu, green onion, ground black pepper, bring it to a boil. 【Photos 5 & 6】

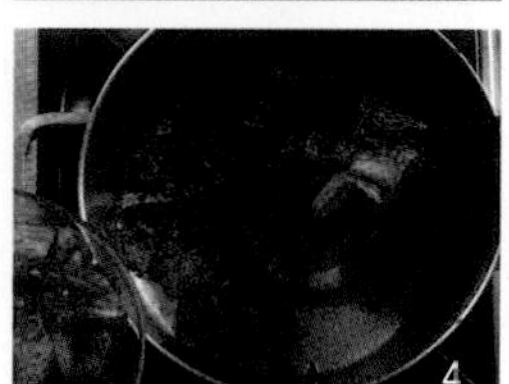
4

· Well–fermented Kimchi may make better taste.
· Salted anchovy juice may be used for seasonings.
· Do not squeeze Kimchi juice out too much.
· Ground red pepper or Kimchi juice may be added more upon taste.

5

Heating Time	Process	Heat Control
Preparation	Preparing Kimchi and pork. Preparing vegetables, kelps and tofu	
0 min	Boiling stew soup. Adding kelps	H–heat 8 min. M–heat 20 min.
30 min	Stir–frying pork and cabbage Kimchi	M–heat 4 min.
	Boiling stew	H–heat 5 min. M–heat 30 min.
70 min	Seasoning with salt. Adding tofu, green onion and ground black pepper	M–heat 2 min.

6

Domimyeon 도미면

Stuffed Sea-bream Casserole with Vegetables

Domimyeon is a casserole made of fried sea bream fillets, vegetables, and potato starch noodles in boiling broth. This dish is served and eaten while it is simmering. *Domimyeon* is unique in taste, luxurious-looking, and easy to eat since it uses boneless fish fillets.

Total weight after cooking	Weight for one serve	Service temperature	Total heating time	Total cooking time	Standard utensil
1.4 kg(4 serves)	350 g	65~80 ℃	52 min.	2 hours	20 cm pot, 28 cm simmering pot, 30 cm frying pan

Fat 19 g
Sodium 820 mg
Carbohydrate 9 g
Protein 25 g
Calorie 300 kcal

*For one serve

Ingredients & Quantity

500 g (small 1 body) sea-bream : 0.8 g (1/5 tsp) salt, 0.1 g ground white pepper
broth : 150 g beef(brisket, shank), 1.2 kg (6 cups) water
seasoning sauce① : 3 g (1/2 tsp) clear soy sauce, 1 g (1/4 tsp) sesame oil
60 g beef (top round, sirloin)
seasoning sauce② : 6 g (1 tsp) clear soy sauce, 4.5 g (1 tsp) minced green onion
2.8 g (1/2 tsp) minced garlic, 0.1 g ground black pepper, 1 g (1/4 tsp) sesame oil
dumpling : 20 g minced beef, 10 g tofu
seasoning sauce③ : 2 g (1/3 tsp) soy sauce, 2.3 g (1/2 tsp) minced green onion, 1.8 g (1/4 tsp) minced garlic
0.1 g ground black pepper, 2 g (1/2 tsp) sesame oil
10 g (2 ea) brown oak mushrooms, 1 g stone mushrooms, 2 g Jew's ear mushrooms
20 g (1 ea) red pepper, 40 g potato starch noodles, 20 g crown daisy
3.5 g (1 tsp) pine nuts, 8 g (4 ea) gingko, 10 g (2 ea) walnut
15 g watercress, 180 g (3 ea) egg, 21 g (3 tbsp) wheat flour, 26 g (2 tbsp) edible oil
800 g (4 cups) broth, 9 g (1/2 tbsp) clear soy sauce, 4 g (1 tsp) salt

1

Preparation

1. Remove the scales, fins and internal organs of the sea-bream and rinse (450 g). Slice fillet from both sides of the fish and cut it into 4 cm-wide and 5 cm-long (170 g). Sprinkle salt and ground white pepper, let it sit for 10 min. pad dry with cotton cloths. 【Photo 2】
2. Clean blood of the beef for broth with cotton cloths (145 g). Clean blood of top round with cotton cloths (50 g), and shred it at intervals of 0.3 cm-wide, season with seasoning sauce②.
3. Clean blood of the minced beef with cotton cloths (17 g). Wrap the tofu with dry cotton cloths, squeeze water out (9 g) and mash. Season the mixture of minced beef and tofu with seasoning sauce③, shape dumplings into 1.5 cm-diameter (4 g). 【Photo 3】
4. Soak the mushrooms in water for 1 hour, remove the stems of brown oak mushrooms and wipe water with cotton cloths, cut it into 2 cm-wide and 4~5 cm-long (20 g). Wash the stone mushrooms by rubbing, wipe water with cotton cloths (2 g), chop it finely and mix it with egg white. Trim the Jew's ear mushrooms and separate it sheet by sheet (24 g).
5. Trim & wash the crown daisy (15 g). Halve the red pepper lengthwise and cut it into 2 cm-wide and 4~5 cm-long (10 g). Soak the potato starch noodles in water for 1 hour (85 g). 【Photo 4】
6. Remove tops of the pine nuts and wipe the nuts with dry cotton cloths. Soak the walnuts in warm water and skin. Stir-fry the gingko and skin.
7. Panfry egg for garnish. Panfry the stone mushrooms and watercress with coatings of wheat flour liquid and beaten egg, cut them into same size of brown oak mushrooms. 【Photo 5】

2

3

4

Recipe

1. Put water and beef in the pot and heat it up for 7 min. on high heat. When it boils, reduce the heat to medium and simmer it for 30 min. Strain the broth through cotton cloths (800 g). Take out the beef, slice it into 2 cm-wide, 1.5 cm-long and 0.3 cm-thick, season it with 40 g of seasoning sauce①.
2. Coat the beef dumplings with wheat flour and beaten egg, panfry for about 3 min. on medium heat.
3. Coat the slices of sea-bream with wheat flour and beaten egg. Preheat the frying pan and oil, panfry it on medium heat for 2 min. and for another 2 min. after turn over (185 g).
4. Place the boiled and sliced beef, seasoned beef and potato starch noodles in the simmering pot, and put the sea-bream's head & bones on it. Then place the fried sea-bream, egg garnish, vegetables and nuts around the pot. Add broth and boil it for 4 min. on high heat. When it boils, season with diluted clear soy sauce and salt. Bring it to a boil and finally put the crown daisy on top. 【Photo 6】

· The head and bone of sea-bream may be used after slight steaming before adding to the pot.

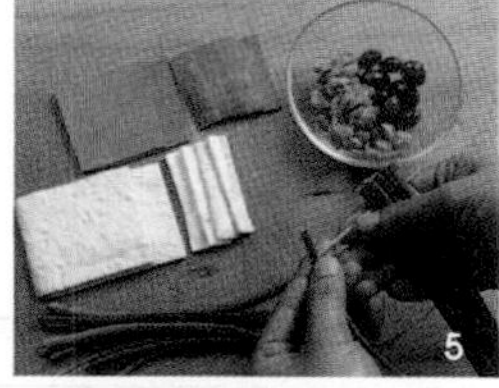
5

6

Heating Time	Process	Heat Control
Preparation	Trimming and cleaning sea-bream, beef, vegetables and nuts Soaking mushrooms and potato starch noodles	
0 min	Simmering broth. Seasoning the pressed meat	H-heat 7 min. M-heat 30 min.
40 min	Pan-frying beef dumplings. Pan-frying slices of sea-bream	M-heat 3 min. M-heat 4 min.
50 min	Simmering soup	H-heat 6 min.

Dubu-jeongol 두부전골

Tofu Hot Pot

Dubu-jeongol is a hot pot of tofu stuffed with beef, and vegetables in broth. This dish is served and eaten while it is simmering. *Dubu-jeongol* is rich in protein and soft in texture. It is enjoyed by men and women of all ages. *Jeongol* (hot pot) is a communal dish that is suitable for Korean dining culture that several people around the table enjoy food together.

Total weight after cooking	Weight for one serve	Service temperature	Total heating time	Total cooking time	Standard utensil
1.2 kg(4 serves)	300 g	65~80 ℃	1 hour 31 min.	2 hours	18 cm pot, 28 cm simmering pot, 30 cm frying pan

Fat 13 g
Sodium 310 mg
Carbohydrate 4 g
Protein 22 g
Calorie 220 kcal
*For one serve

Ingredients & Quantity

250 g (½ cake) tofu, 1 g (¼ tsp) salt, 12 g (2 tbsp) starch, 26 g (2 tbsp) edible oil
150 g beef (top round · sirloin) for broth : 300 g beef (brisket), 1.2 kg (6 cups) water
fragrant seasoning : 20 g green onion, 10 g garlic
seasoning sauce : 13 g (⅔ tbsp) soy sauce, 4 g (1 tsp) sugar, 4.5 g (1 tsp) minced green onion
2.8 g (½ tsp) minced garlic, 1 g (½ tsp) sesame salt
0.3 g (⅛ tsp) ground black pepper, 4 g (1 tsp) sesame oil
3 g (½ tsp) clear soy sauce, 4 g (1 tsp) salt
10 g (3 sheets) brown oak mushrooms, 60 g (5 ea) agaric mushrooms, 400 g (2 cups) water, 4 g (1 tsp) salt
30 g watercress, 200 g (1 cup) water, 2 g (½ tsp) salt
60 g bamboo shoot, 100 g mung bean sprouts, 30 g carrot, 120 g (2 ea) egg

Preparation

1. Cut the tofu into 2 cm−wide, 4 cm−long and 0.5 cm−thick, sprinkle salt on it (240 g).
2. Clean blood of broth beef with cotton cloths. Put water and beef in the pot, heat it up for 6 min. on high heat, when it boils, lower the heat to medium, simmer it for 30 min. Add fragrant seasoning, simmer it for 25 min to make broth (800 g). 【Photo 2】
3. Clean blood of beef with cotton cloths, shred 2/3 of the beef into 6 cm−long, 0.3 cm−wide/thick, season with ⅔ of seasoning sauce. Chop the rest of the beef (⅓) and season with the remained ⅓ of seasoning sauce.
4. Soak brown oak mushrooms in water for 1 hour, remove the stems, wipe water off. Cut them into 1.5 cm−wide, 5 cm−long and 0.5 cm−thick. Remove the heads and tails of mung bean sprouts (85 g).
5. Trim and wash carrot, cut into 1.5 cm−wide, 5 cm−long and 0.3 cm−thick. Cut the bamboo shoot into same size of carrot, maintaining comb shape. Trim and wash watercress (20 g). 【Photo 3】
6. Panfry eggs for yellow/white garnish and cut into 1.5 cm−wide, 5 cm−long.

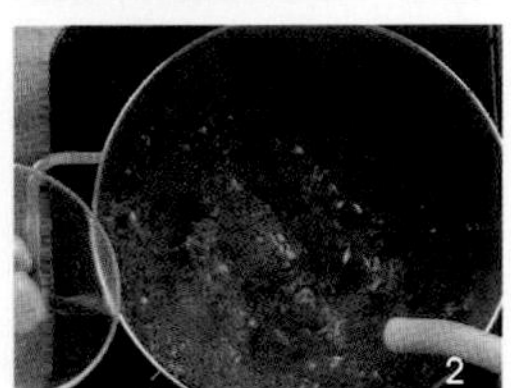
2

3

Recipe

1. Coat tofu with starch. Preheat the frying pan and oil, panfry coated tofu for 5 min. on medium heat (211 g). 【Photo 4】
2. Pour water in the pot, heat it up for 2 min. on high heat. When it boils, scald agaric mushrooms with salt for 1 min. then rip up into 1 cm of width (46 g)
3. Pour water in the pot, heat it up for 1 min. on high heat. When it boils, scald watercress with salt for 1 min. rinse in cold water, wipe water with cotton cloths, and rip up thinly.
4. Place chopped beef on the fried tofu evenly, fold one side of tofu over, then bind it in the middle with watercress. 【Photo 5】
5. Put the seasoned beef on the bottom of pot, and place tofu and other vegetables over the beef, matching color. Pour broth over it, heat it up for 3 min. on high heat. When it boils, lower the heat to medium, boil for another 15 min. Season with clear soy sauce and salt, bring it to a boil. 【Photo 6】

4

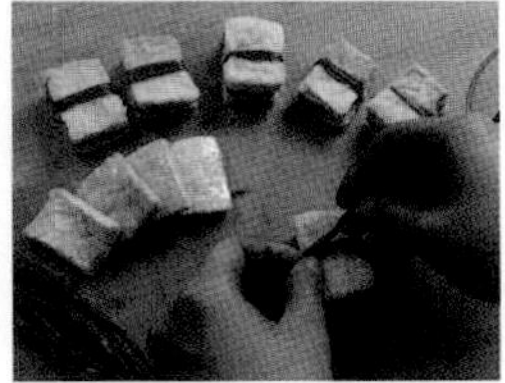

- Tofu may be coated with wheat flour instead of starch.
- Do not boil this stew too long. Serve as soon as the meat slightly cooked.

6

Heating Time	Process	Heat Control
Preparation	Preparing tofu, beef, mushrooms and vegetables Pan−frying egg for garnish	
0 min	Boiling broth. Adding fragrant seasonings	H−heat 6 min. M−heat 30 min. M−heat 25 min.
60 min	Pan−frying tofu. Scalding mushrooms and watercress	M−heat 5 min. H−heat 5 min.
70 min	Boiling stew	H−heat 3 min. M−heat 17 min.

Beoseot-jeongol 버섯전골

Mixed Mushroom Hot Pot

Beoseot-jeongol is a hot pot made of various mushrooms and vegetables. This dish is clear, light in taste and has a wonderful aroma of mushrooms. It is a stew for the autumn season when the cold wind starts to blow. From olden days, people believed that mushrooms have a medicinal effect and used them in various fried or grilled dishes.

Total weight after cooking	Weight for one serve	Service temperature	Total heating time	Total cooking time	Standard utensil
1.36 kg(4 serves)	340 g	65~80 ℃	16 min.	1 hour	28 cm simmering pot

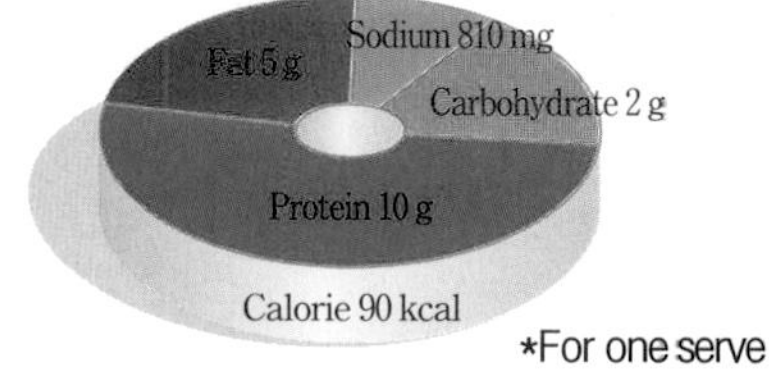

*For one serve

Ingredients & Quantity

60 g (5 ea) oyster mushrooms
120 g (3 ea) fresh pine mushrooms
60 g fresh brown oak mushrooms
150 g beef(top round)
seasoning sauce : 3 g (½ tsp) clear soy sauce, 2 g (½ tsp) sugar, 2.3 g (½ tsp) minced green onion
1.4 g (¼ tsp) minced garlic, 1 g (½ tsp) sesame salt, 0.1 g ground black pepper
2 g (½ tsp) sesame oil
20 g small green onion, 50 g watercress, 20 g (1 ea) red pepper
1 kg (5 cups) water
18 g (1 tbsp) clear soy sauce
4 g (1 tsp) salt

1

2

Preparation

1. Wash the mushrooms in water softly, drain water, and shred them into 5 cm-long and 0.5 cm-wide/thick. 【Photo 2】
2. Clean blood of beef with cotton cloths, shred it into 5 cm-long and 0.3 cm-wide/thick, season with seasoning sauce.
3. Wash small green onion and watercress cleanly, cut them into 5 cm-long(small green onion 18 g, watercress 30 g). 【Photo 3】
4. Shred red pepper into 4 cm-long and 0.3 cm-wide/thick. 【Photo 4】

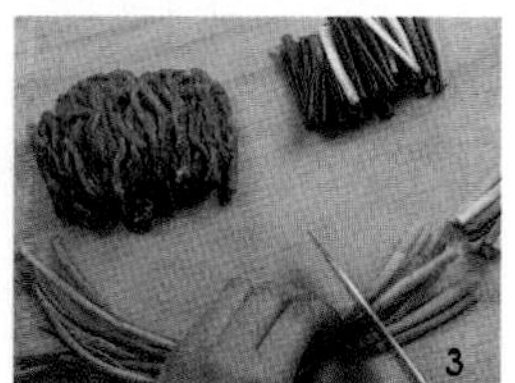
3

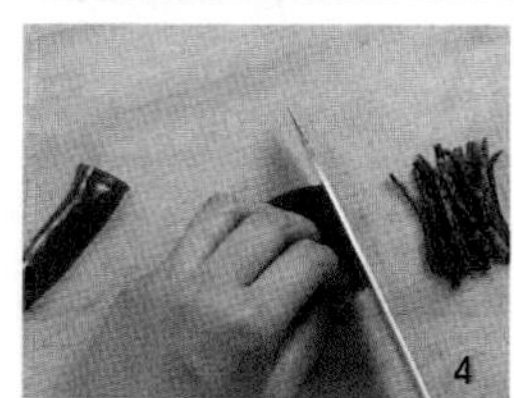
4

Recipe

1. Put all prepared stuffs in the simmering pot, place them roundly matching color, add water. 【Photo 5】
2. Heat it up for 4 min. on high heat. When it boils, lower the heat to medium, boil it for another 10 min. When it boils again, season with clear soy sauce and salt, bring it to a boil. 【Photo 6】

· Broth may be replaced by water.
· To keep the fragrance of mushrooms, do not boil mushroom hot pot too long.

5

Heating Time	Process	Heat Control
Preparation 0 min 10 min	Preparing mushrooms, beef and vegetables Placing in the simmering pot. Simmering mushroom hot pot Seasoning with salt	H-heat 4 min. M-heat 10 min. M-heat 2 min.

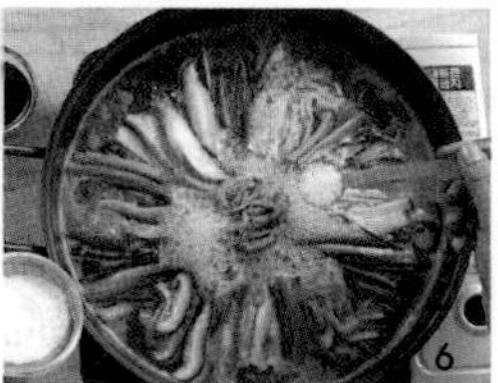
6

Sinseollo 신선로

Royal Casserole

Sinseollo is a casserole containing various meats, fish and vegetables in broth. The ingredients are placed around the pot according to color. Nuts and other delicacies accompany the meat, fish and vegetables in one pot. It provides an array of flavors and nutrients.

Total weight after cooking	Weight for one serve	Service temperature	Total heating time	Total cooking time	Standard utensil
2kg(4 serves)	500g	65~80℃	1 hour 13 min.	3 hours	18 cm Sinseollo pot, 18 cm pot, 30 cm frying pan

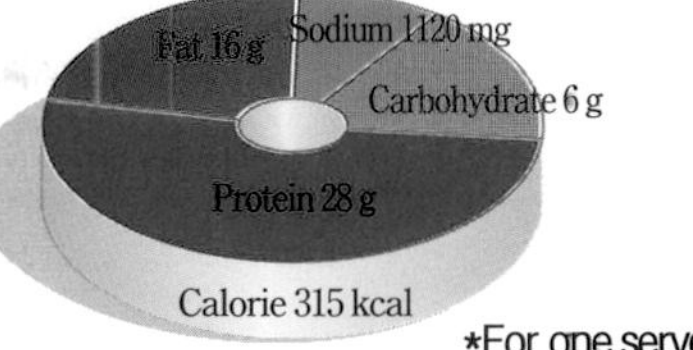

*For one serve

Ingredients & Quantity

broth : 200 g beef (brisket, shank), 100 g radish, 1.6 kg (8 cups) water
seasoning sauce ① : 6 g (1 tsp) clear soy sauce, 2.3 g (½ tsp) minced green onion, 1.4 g (¼ tsp) minced garlic
3 g (1 tsp) clear soy sauce, 6 g (½ tbsp) salt
100 g beef (top round)
for dumplings : 50 g minced beef(top round), 20 g tofu
seasoning sauce ② : 3 g (½ tsp) clear soy sauce, 2.3 g (½ tsp) minced green onion
1.4 g (¼ tsp) minced garlic, 1 g (½ tsp) sesame salt, 0.1 g ground black pepper
4 g (1 tsp) sesame oil
30 g tripe, 4 g (1 tsp) salt, 21 g (3 tbsp) wheat flour, 30 g liver, 100 g (½ cups) milk
50 g spinal cord, 50 g white flesh fish
seasoning tripe · liver · spinal cord · white flesh fish : 4 g (1 tsp) salt, 1.3 g (⅛ tsp) ground black pepper
30 g soaked sea slug, 10 g (2 sheets) brown oak mushrooms
30 g carrot, 400 g (2 cups) water, 4 g (1 tsp) salt
20 g watercress, 240 g (4 ea) egg, 50 g (½ cup) wheat flour, 65 g (5 tbsp) edible oil
10 g (2 ea) walnut, 8 g (4 ea) gingko, 3.5 g (1 tsp) pine nuts

1

Preparation

1. Clean blood of broth beef with cotton cloths. Put the beef and water into the pot, heat it up for 9 min. on high heat. Lower the heat to medium, simmer it for 20 min. Add radish and continue to simmer for 20 min. Take out the beef and radish, cut them into 2 cm-wide, 3 cm-long and 0.5 cm-thick. Season with seasoning sauce ① (radish 80 g, beef 130 g). Filter the broth through cotton cloths and season with clear soy sauce and salt (1.2 kg).
2. Clean blood of beef with cotton cloths, shred it into 5 cm-long and 0.3 cm-wide/thick, season with 2/3 of seasoning ②.
3. Clean blood of minced beef. Wrap the tofu with cotton cloths and mash by squeezing. Season the beef and tofu together with remained 1/3 of seasoning sauce ②, knead it, shape dumplings into 1.5 cm-diameter. Add salt and wheat flour to the tripe, clean it by fumbling, put some knife slits on it. Peel thin skin of the liver, slice it into 5 cm-wide, 6 cm-long and 0.3 cm-thick, marinate in the milk for 10 min. Uncoil the spinal cord and cut into 15 cm-long. Slice the white flesh of the fish into 5 cm-wide, 6 cm-long and 0.3 cm-thick. 【Photo 3】
4. Season the tripe, liver, spinal cord and fish flesh with salt and ground black pepper.
5. Cut the soaked sea slug into 2 cm-wide and 6 cm-long.
6. Soak the dried brown oak mushrooms in water for 1 hour. remove stems, wipe water off with cotton cloths. Shred them into same size of sea slug. Trim and wash carrot, cut into 2 cm-wide, 6 cm-long and 0.4 cm-thick.
7. Panfry egg for garnish, and panfry watercress after coating with wheat flour and beaten egg. Cut them into 2 cm-wide and 6 cm-long. 【Photo 4】
8. Soak the walnut in hot water, and skin. Preheat the frying pan and oil. Stir-fry gingko for 2 min. on medium heat, then skin. Remove tops of the pine nuts and wipe the nuts with dry cotton cloths.

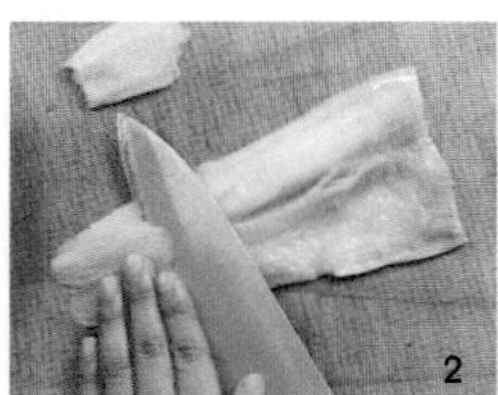
2

3

Recipe

1. Coat the dumplings with wheat flour and beaten egg. Preheat the frying pan and oil, panfry the dumplings for 2 min. on medium heat with rolling over.
2. Coat the tripe, liver, spinal cord and fish flesh with wheat flour and beaten egg. Preheat the frying pan, oil, panfry them on medium heat for 2 min. for each side. Cut them into 2 cm-wide and 6 cm-long. 【Photo 5】
3. Pour water into the pot, heat it up for 2 min. on high heat. When it boils, put the carrot and salt, scald for 20 sec.
4. Place the seasoned beef, shred radish and beef on the bottom of the Sinseollo pot. Decorate with prepared stuffs on the pot, and put the dumplings, walnuts, gingko and pine nuts on it. 【Photo 6】
5. Pour the broth into the Sinseollo pot, cover the lid. Place blazing charcoal under the funnel, boil it for 3 min.

4

- Adjust the length of the stuffs to the diameter of the pot.
- It is an another choice to place the excess fried stuffs on the bottom of the pot.
- Solidified alcohol can be substitute for charcoal.

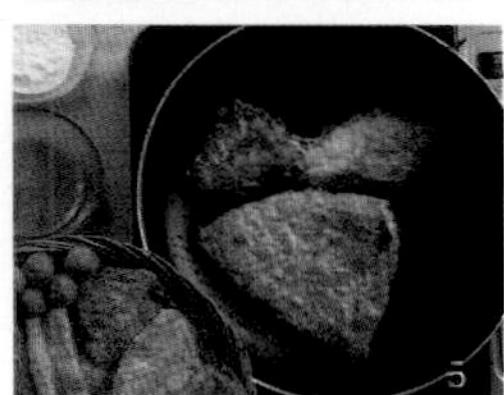
5

Heating Time	Process	Heat Control
Preparation	Preparing beef. Shaping dumplings	
	Preparing frying stuffs. Preparing garnish	
0 min	Simmering broth	H-heat 9 min. M-heat 20 min.
	Seasoning beef and radish. Seasoning broth	
50 min	Pan-frying dumplings	M-heat 2 min.
	Pan-frying stuffs. Scalding carrot	M-heat 16 min. H-heat 2 min. and 20 sec.
70 min	Placing in the Sinseollo pot and boiling	H-heat 3 min..

6

Eobok-jaengban 어복쟁반

Boiled Meat Platter

Eobok-jaengban is a dish made of clear beef broth with pressed brisket, ox tongue, vegetables such as mushrooms, and buckwheat noodles on a brass platter. This dish is served and eaten while it is simmering. Originally, *eobok-jaengban* used cheap cuts of meat instead of lean meat in the northern area of Korea.

Total weight after cooking	Weight for one serve	Service temperature	Total heating time	Total cooking time	Standard utensil
2 kg(4 serves)	500 g	65~80 ℃	4 hours 59 min.	over 5 hours	18 cm pot, 28 cm simmering pot, 32 cm pot

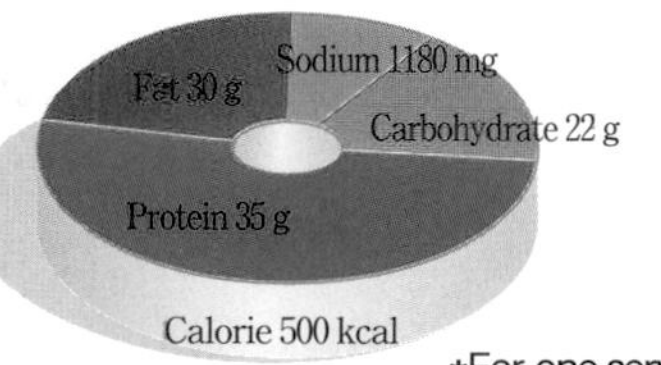

*For one serve

Ingredients & Quantity

600 g (½ part) gristle (from knee bone of cattle), 200 g ox-tongue , 800 g (4 cups) precleaning water
200 g beef (brisket)
3.4 kg (17 cups) boiling water
fragrant seasoning : 50 g (1 head) green onion, 100 g (1 head) garlic
15 g (⅔ tbsp) clear soy sauce, 2 g (½ tsp) salt
25 g (5 sheets) brown oak mushrooms
150 g agaric mushrooms : 500 g (2½ cup) water, 2 g (½ tsp) salt
seasoning : 4 g (1 tsp) salt, 8 g (2 tsp) sesame oil
120 g (2 ea) egg, 1 kg (5 cups) boiling water, 4 g (1 tsp) salt
125 g (¼ ea) pear, 10 g (1 tbsp) pine nuts
100 g buckwheat noodles, 800 g (4 cups) boiling water, 200 g (1 cup) additional boiling water
seasoning sauce : 45 g (2½ tbsp) clear soy sauce, 2.2 g (1 tsp) coarse red pepper powder
14 g (1 tbsp) minced green onion, 8 g (½ tbsp) minced garlic
2 g (1 tsp) sesame salt, 6 g (½ tbsp) sesame oil

Preparation

1. Soak the gristle and ox-tongue in water for 3~4 hours to draw out the blood.
2. Clean blood of beef with cotton cloths. Trim green onion and garlic, wash cleanly and make fragrant seasoning.
3. Soak brown oak mushrooms in water for 1 hour, remove the stems, wipe water with cotton cloths and shred at intervals of 0.5 cm-wide/thick.
4. Remove tops of the pine nuts and wipe the nuts with dry cotton cloths.
5. Blending seasoning and seasoning sauce.

Recipe

1. Pour precleaning water in the pot and heat it up for 5 min. on high heat. When it boils, put the gristle and ox-tongue, boil them for 5 min. Discard the boiling water and pour water again in the pot. Heat it up for 10 min. on high heat. When it boils, lower the heat to medium and simmer for 3 hours While simmering, skim off floated foam and fats. Add fragrant seasoning and beef, simmer it for another 1 hour. 【Photo 2】
2. Take out the beef from the pot, shred it into 3 cm-wide, 4 cm-long and 0.3 cm-thick, season with half of seasoning. Cool down the broth, filter through cotton cloths, skim fats (800 g), season with diluted clear soy sauce and salt to provide broth. 【Photo 3】
3. Pour water in the pot and heat it up for 2 min. on high heat. When it boils, put the agaric mushrooms and scald for 1 min. rip up into 1cm-wide, and season with remained seasoning. 【Photo 4】
4. Put water, salt and eggs in the pot, heat it up for 5 min. on high heat. When it boils, lower the heat to medium, boil for another 12 min. Put the eggs into cold water, and then peel off the shell, cut into 1 cm-thick round. Peel the pear, shred it into 0.5 cm-thick. 【Photo 5】
5. Pour water in the pot and heat it up for 4 min. on high heat. When it boils, put the noodles, boil for 1 min. When it boils again, add 100 g (½ cup) of water, wait for 1 min. When it boils again, add 100 g of water. After additional boiling for 30 sec. take the noodles out, rinse them in cold water by rubbing with hands, and drain water (210 g).
6. Place seasoned meat, mushrooms, eggs, pear, pine nuts and noodles in the simmering pot, add the broth. Heat it up for 3 min. on high heat. When it boils, lower the heat to medium, simmer it for 10 min. Serve with seasoning sauce. 【Photo 6】

· This is a dish to enjoy while boiling on the heat.

1

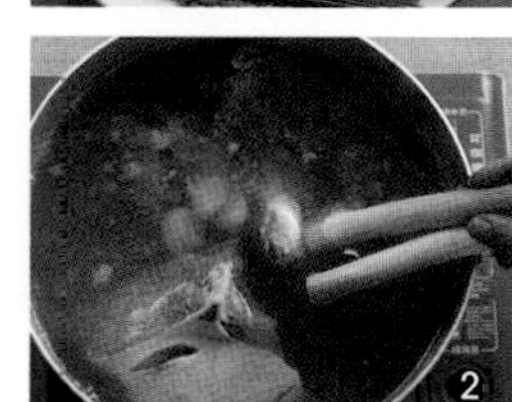
2

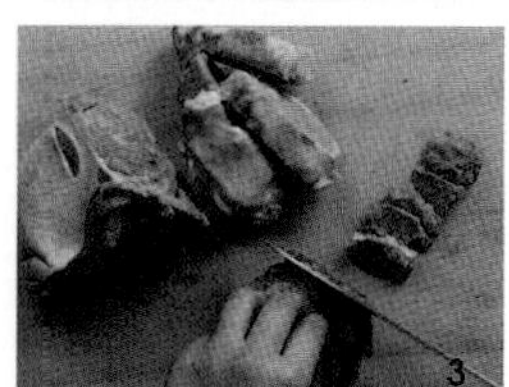
3

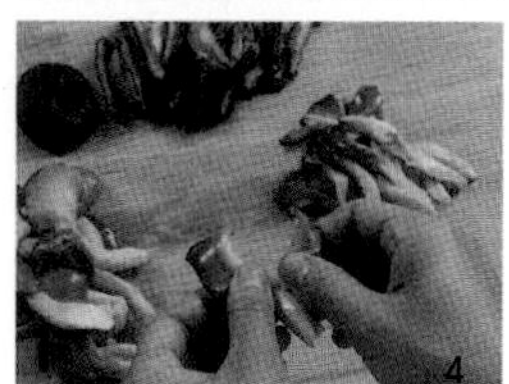
4

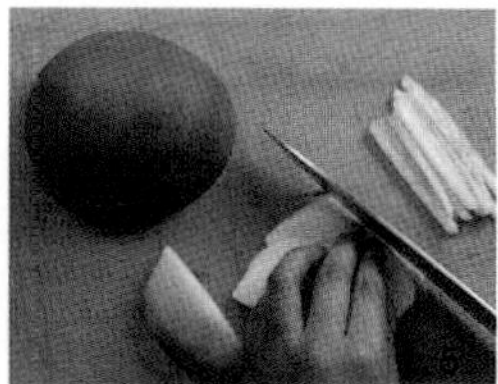

6

Heating Time	Process	Heat Control
Preparation	Preparing gristle, beef, brown oak mushrooms and pine nuts, Blending seasoning sauce	
0 min	Pre-cleaning gristle and ox-tongue by quick boiling	H-heat 10 min.
10 min	Simmering gristle and ox-tongue	H-heat 10 min. M-heat 180 min.
	Adding fragrant seasoning and beef	M-heat 60 min.
260 min	Taking out beef and cutting. Seasoning broth	
	Scalding agaric mushrooms	H-heat 3 min.
270 min	Boiling egg	H-heat 5 min. M-heat 12 min.
280 min	Boiling noodles	H-heat 6 min.
290 min	Boiling meat platter	H-heat 3 min. M-heat 10 min.

Soe-galbijjim 쇠갈비찜

Braised Beef Ribs

Soe-galbijjim is braised beef ribs with Korean radish or brown oak mushrooms, vegetables and seasonings. This is a typical Korean dish, loved by men and women of all ages. *Jjim* is a popular cooking method that simmers or braises seasoned ingredients with water.

Total weight after cooking	Weight for one serve	Service temperature	Total heating time	Total cooking time	Standard utensil
500 g(4 serves)	125 g	70~75 ℃	1 hour 14 min.	4 hours	20 cm pot, 30 cm frying pan

Sodium 385 mg
Fat 15 g
Carbohydrate 12 g
Protein 19 g
Calorie 255 kcal
*For one serve

Ingredients & Quantity

400 g beef ribs, 3 cups precleaning water
800 g (4 cups) water
seasoning sauce : 36 g (2 tbsp) soy sauce, 12 g (1 tbsp) sugar, 6 g (1 tsp) honey
50 g (pear 100 g) pear juice 14 g (1 tbsp) minced green onion
8 g (½ tbsp) minced garlic, 3 g (½ tbsp) sesame salt, 3 g (⅛ tsp) ground black pepper
5 g (1 tsp) refined rice wine, 13 g (1 tbsp) sesame oil
10 g (2 sheets) brown oak mushrooms, 100 g radish, 70 g carrot
60 g (4 ea) chestnut , 16 g (4 ea) jujube, 16 g (8 ea) gingko, 3.5 g (1 tsp) pine nuts
60 g (1 ea) egg, 13 g (1 tbsp) edible oil
13 g (1 tbsp) sesame oil

1

Preparation

1. Cut the beef ribs into 5 cm–long, remove excess fats and tendons (350 g). Soak it in water for a total 3 hours, changing the water every hour to draw out the blood. Put knife slits on the meat at intervals of 1.5 cm–wide. 【Photo 2】
2. Soak the brown oak mushrooms in water for 1 hour, remove stems, wipe water off with cotton cloths, cut into 2~4 pieces.
3. Cut the radish and carrot into 3 cm–square and 2.5 cm–thick, trim the edges. 【Photo 3】
4. Skin the chestnuts. Wipe the jujube with damp cotton cloths, cut the flesh round, and roll up.
5. Preheat the frying pan and oil, stir–fry the gingko for 2 min. on medium heat, maintaining green color, and skin.
6. Remove tops of the pine nuts, wipe the nuts with dry cotton cloths.
7. Panfry the egg for garnish, cut into 2 cm diaper shape.
8. Blend seasoning sauce.

2

3

Recipe

1. Pour water into the pot, heat it up for 3 min. on hight heat. When it boils, boil the beef ribs for 2 min. to clean the beef ribs, rinse the beef ribs in water. 【Photo 4】
2. Put the beef ribs and water into pot, heat it up for 4 min. When it boils, lower the heat to medium, simmer it for 20 min. Take out the beef ribs from the broth, and filter the broth after cooling down.
3. Put the beef ribs and half of the seasoning sauce into the pot, marinate it for 10 min. Add 500 g (2½ cups) of broth, heat it up for 3 min. When it boils, lower the heat to medium, boil it for 20 min. more. 【Photo 5】
4. When the beef ribs is well–done and the broth is reduced into half, add the mushrooms, radish, chestnuts and the remained half of the seasoning sauce. Boil it for 12 min. add carrot, boil for another 7 min. Then add jujube, gingko and pine nuts, boil for 3 min. with sprinkling broth onto the beef ribs to set a gloss on. 【Photo 6】
5. When the broth is dragged, take out the radish. Mix the ribs with sesame oil together. Serve with egg garnish.

4

5

· Boil the beef ribs slowly on medium heat to get soft and tasteful beef ribs.
· To set a gloss on the beef ribs, braze it with sprinkling seasoning sauce after the meat is well–done.

Heating Time	Process	Heat Control
Preparation	Preparing beef ribs, vegetables and garnish. Blending seasoning sauce	
0 min	Boiling beef ribs for precleaning. Simmering beef ribs broth Marinating beef ribs in seasoning sauce	H–heat 5 min. H–heat 4 min. M–heat 20 min.
30 min	Boiling beef ribs	H–heat 3 min. M–heat 20 min.
50 min	Adding vegetables and seasoning sauce	M–heat 19 min.
70 min	Adding garnish	M–heat 3 min.

6

Dakjjim 닭찜

Simmered Chicken

Dakjjim is a dish of chicken pieces simmered with seasonings along with various vegetables such as onions, carrots, and potatoes. Chicken is often favored over other meats because it is low in price and calories, and high in protein.

Total weight after cooking	Weight for one serve	Service temperature	Total heating time	Total cooking time	Standard utensil
560 g(4 serves)	140 g	70~75 ℃	48 min.	2 hours	20 ㎝ pot, 30 ㎝ frying pan

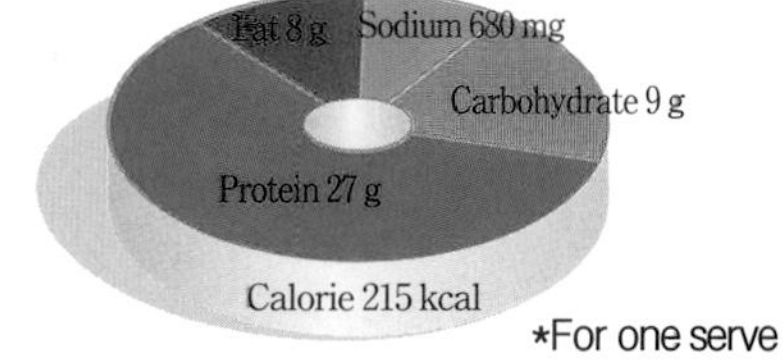

*For one serve

Ingredients & Quantity

700 g chicken, 1 ㎏ (5 cups) water
70 g carrot
10 g (2 sheets) brown oak mushrooms, 80 g onion, 16 g (8 ea) gingko
60 g (1 ea) egg
13 g (1 tbsp) edible oil
seasoning sauce : 45 g (2½ tbsp) soy sauce, 18 g (1½ tbsp) sugar, 14 g (1 tbsp) minced green onion
8 g (½ tbsp) minced garlic, 5.5 g (1 tsp) ginger juice, 3 g (½ tbsp) sesame salt
13 g (1 tbsp) sesame oil
300 g (1½ cups) water

1

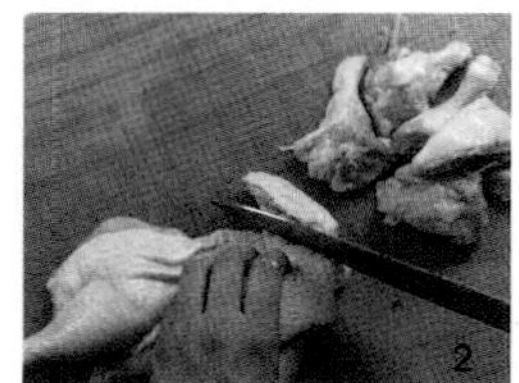

2

3

Preparation

1. Remove intestines and fats from the chicken, trim and wash cleanly. Cut it into 4~5 cm–wide and long (600 g). 【Photo 2】
2. Wash the carrot, cut it into 3 cm–wide, 2.5 cm–long and 2.5 cm–thick and trim the edges (53 g).
3. Soak the brown oak mushrooms in water for 1 hour, remove stems, wipe water with cotton cloths, and cut it into 2~4 pieces.
4. Cut the onion into 3 cm–wide and 4 cm–long (65 g). 【Photo 3】
5. Preheat the frying pan and oil. On medium heat, stir–fry gingko for 2 min. with rolling, maintaining green color, then skin.
6. Panfry egg for garnish, cut it into 2 cm–long diaper shape.
7. Blend seasoning sauce.

4

Recipe

1. Pour water into the pot, heat it up for 5 min. on high heat. When it boils, clean the chicken by quick boiling for 2 min. (550 g). 【Photo 4】
2. Put the chicken into the pot, add half of the seasoning sauce and water. Boil it for 3 min. on high heat. When it boils, lower the heat to medium, simmer it for 20 min. slowly. Add remained half of the seasoning sauce, simmer for 10 min. more. Add carrot and boil it for another 5 min. 【Photo 5】
3. When the broth is dragged, put the gingko, braise it for 3 min. with sprinkling broth to set a gloss on. 【Photo 6】
4. Place on a dish and top with egg garnish.

· Do not add vegetables in early step, or it may become soften.

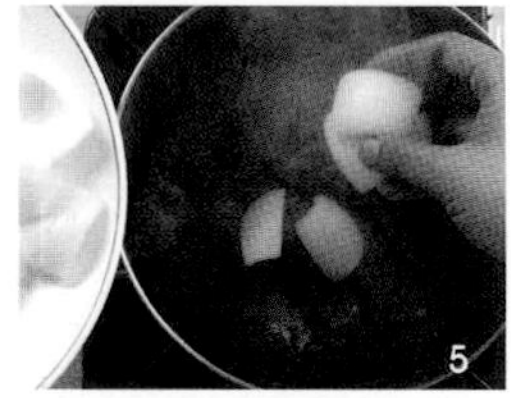

5

6

Heating Time	Process	Heat Control
Preparation	Preparing chicken, vegetables and garnish. Blending seasoning sauce	
0 min	Precleaning chicken by quick boiling	H–heat 7 min.
	Simmering chicken after seasoning	H–heat 3 min. M–heat 30 min.
40 min	Adding carrot, brown oak mushrooms and onion	M–heat 5 min.
	Adding gingko	M–heat 3 min.
	Topping with egg garnish	

Daehajjim 대하찜

Steamed Prawn

Daehajjim is a dish of large prawns steamed with seasoning. It has a light and clean taste. *Daeha* are large prawns that can be up to 25 cm long. Prawns are considered to be a healthy food that strengthens the kidney and provides vitality. Prawns contain a fair amount of good quality protein, calcium, phosphorus, iodine and iron.

Total weight after cooking	Weight for one serve	Service temperature	Total heating time	Total cooking time	Standard utensil
200 g (4 serves)	50 g	50~65 ℃	10 min.	30 min.	26 cm steamer, 30 cm frying pan

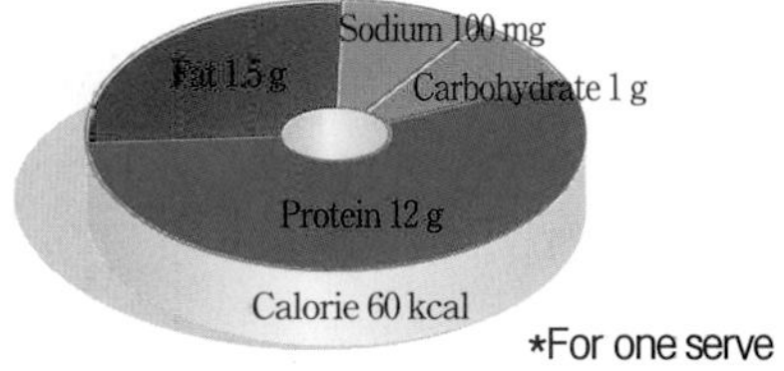

*For one serve

Ingredients & Quantity

260 g (large 4 bodies) shrimps : 1 kg (5 cups) shrimp boiling water
seasonings : 15 g (1 tbsp) refined rice wine, 1 g (1/4 tsp) salt, 0.3 g (1/8 tsp) ground black pepper
fragrant seasonings : 20 g green onion, 20 g garlic
7 g (1/2 ea) green pepper, 10 g (1/2 ea) red pepper, 1 g stone mushrooms, 60 g (1 ea) egg
13 g (1 tbsp) sesame oil
8 pieces skewer

1

Preparation

1. Peel prawn shell off, remaining heads and tails (250 g), score the back with a knife, remove intestines. Spread the flesh flat out and put many slits on it. Season with seasonings and skewer the flesh through not to be twisted. 【Photos 2 & 3】
2. Clean small green onion and garlic. Cut the green onion into 5 cm−long and 0.5 cm−wide, and garlic into 0.5 cm−thick.
3. Wash green/red pepper, shred them into 2 cm−long and 0.2 cm−wide and thick.
4. Soak stone mushrooms in water for 1 hour, remove the belly buttons and wash. Wipe water with cotton cloths and shred into 2 cm−long and 0.1 cm−wide.
5. Panfry egg for yellow/white garnish and shred into 2 cm−long and 0.2 cm−wide. 【Photo 4】

2

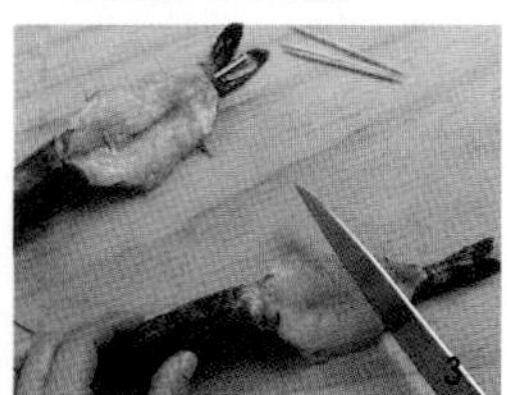

3

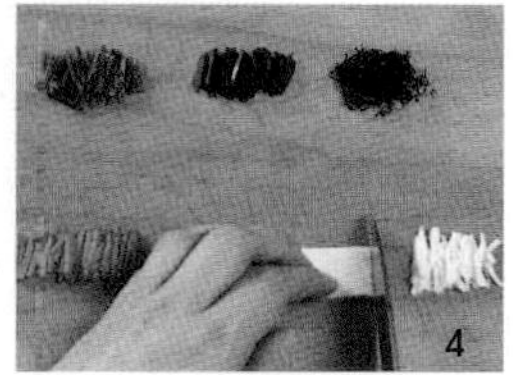

4

Recipe

1. Pour water in the steaming pot and heat it up on high heat for 5 min. When it gives off steam, layer the fragrant seasoning on the bottom and put the shrimps, then steam it for 5 min. 【Photo 5】
2. Take the steamed shrimps out, remove the skewers, and coat with sesame oil.
3. Garnish shrimps with green/red pepper, yellow/white egg garnish and stone mushrooms. 【Photo 6】

· Skewer the shrimps through from tail to the head entirely not to be twisted.
· Remove the skewer with twisting it.

5

Heating Time	Process	Heat Control
Preparation	Trimming prawn. Preparing garnish	
0 min	Boiling water in the steaming pot	H−heat 5 min.
5 min	Steaming shrimps	H−heat 5 min.
10 min	Coating sesame oil and garnishing	

6

Tteokjjim 떡찜

Braised Rice Cake Rod Stuffs

Tteokjjim is a dish of rice cake rods, beef, and vegetables braised with seasonings. It is said that in olden days, the court kitchen ladies prepared *tteokjjim* for the king, who lacked physical exercise and sometimes suffered from indigestion, because it was thought to ease stomach troubles.

Total weight after cooking	Weight for one serve	Service temperature	Total heating time	Total cooking time	Standard utensil
600 g(4 serves)	150 g	70~75 ℃	57 min.	2 hours	20 cm pot, 30 cm frying pan

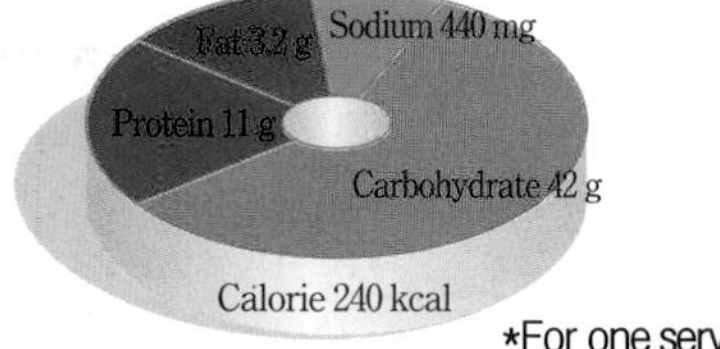

*For one serve

Ingredients & Quantity

300 g white rice cake rod, sesame soy sauce : 3 g (½ tsp) soy sauce, 4 g (1 tsp) sesame oil
40 g beef (top round)
100 g beef (shank), 800 g (4 cups) water
seasoning sauce① : 6 g (1 tsp) soy sauce, 2 g (½ tsp) sugar, 2.3 g (½ tsp) minced green onion
1.4 g (¼ tsp) minced garlic, 1 g (½ tsp) sesame salt, 0.1 g ground black pepper
4 g (1 tsp) sesame oil
60 g carrot, 400 g (2 cups) water, 1 g (¼ tsp) salt
60 g (4 ea) chestnut, 5 g (1 sheet) brown oak mushrooms
3.5 g (1 tsp) pine nuts, 16 g (4 ea) jujube, 25 g (12 ea) gingko
60 g (1 ea) egg, 15 g watercress, 2.3 g (1 tsp) wheat flour, 4 g (1 tsp) edible oil
seasoning sauce② : 27 g (1½ tbsp) soy sauce, 12 g (1 tbsp) sugar, 7 g (½ tbsp) minced green onion
5.5 g (1 tsp) minced garlic, 2 g (1 tsp) sesame salt, 6.5 g (½ tbsp) sesame oil

1

Preparation

1. Cut the white rice cake rod into 6 cm−long, and put knife slits on 4 places, taking care not to apart both ends. Season them with sesame soy sauce (280 g). 【Photo 2】
2. Clean blood of beef (top round, shank) with cotton cloths. Mince the top round finely and season with half of the seasoning sauce ①.
3. Cut the carrot into 2.5 cm−square and trim the edges (46 g). Skin the chestnuts (40 g). Stir−fry the gingko and skin. Soak brown oak mushrooms in water for about 1 hour, remove stems, wipe water with cotton cloths and cut it into 2~4 pieces (12 g). 【Photo 3】
4. Remove tops of the pine nuts, wipe the nuts with dry cotton cloths. Wipe the jujube with damp cotton cloths, cut the flesh and roll up (14 g).
5. Panfry egg for yellow/white garnish. Pan−fry watercress after coating with wheat flour liquid and beaten egg, then cut into 2 cm−long of diaper shape. 【Photo 4】

2

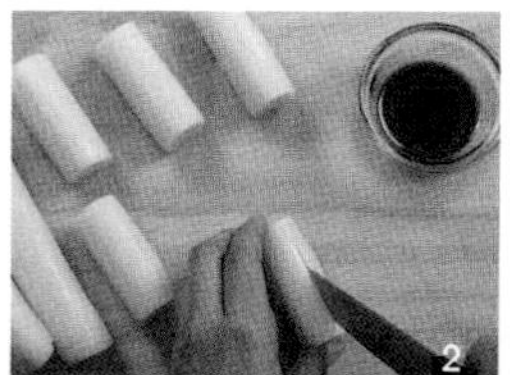
3

4

Recipe

1. Insert the seasoned beef into the slits of the rice cake rods. 【Photo 5】
2. Put the shank and water in the pot and heat it up on high heat. When it boils, reduce the heat to medium, simmer it for 30 min. Take out the meat and cut then into 2 cm−wide, 3 cm−long and 0.7 cm−thick. Mix them with remained half of the seasoning sauce ①. Strain the broth through cotton cloths (300 g, 1½ cup).
3. Pour water in the pot and heat it up for 2 min. on high heat. When it boils, scald the carrot with salt for 2 min.
4. Put the shank, carrot, chestnuts, brown oak mushrooms, broth and half of the seasoning sauce ② in the pot. Boil it for 5 min. on high heat, add the rice cake rods, jujube and remained seasoning sauce ②, reduce the heat to medium and boil it for 13 min. Put the gingko and pine nuts. 【Photo 6】
5. Place in a dish, garnish with yellow/white egg strips and fried watercress.

5

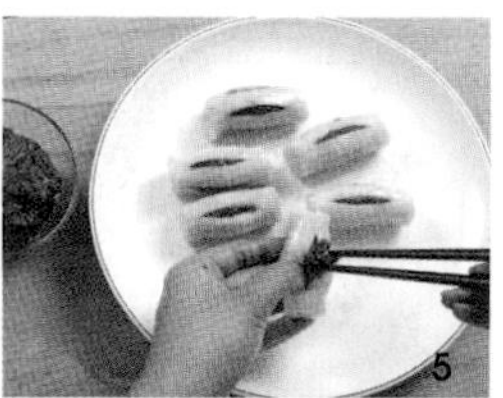
6

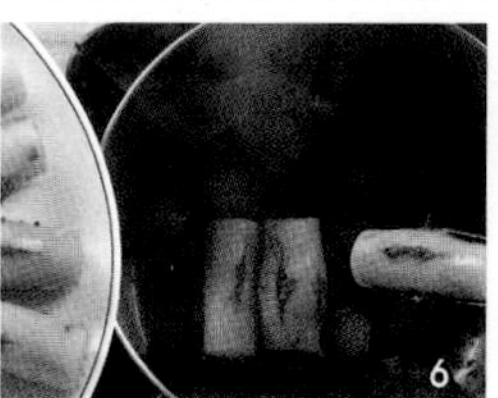

· If the rice rod is dried hard, scald it in boiled water to be soft.
· Do not put the rice rods in the pot from the beginning, or it may be burst.

Heating Time	Process	Heat Control
Preparation	Soaking brown oak mushrooms. Preparing white rice rods and beef Trimming vegetables and nuts.	
0 min	Inserting beef fillings into rice rods. Simmering beef (shank) Scalding carrot	H−heat 5 min. M−heat 30 min. H−heat 4 min.
40 min	steaming rice cake rod stuffed with beef and vegetables	H−heat 5 min. M−heat 13 min.
60 min	Placing on a dish and garnishing	

Oiseon 오이선

Stuffed Cucumber

Oiseon is a dish of cucumbers stuffed with beef, brown oak mushrooms, and egg white and yolk garnish. The cucumbers are slit with a knife and the filling is tucked into the slits. They are then sprinkled with sweet vinegar sauce. It has a tantalizing sweet and sour taste and a pretty color. This dish stimulates the appetite and is usually served as an appetizer.

Total weight after cooking	Weight for one serve	Service temperature	Total heating time	Total cooking time	Standard utensil
320 g(4 serves)	80 g(5 ea)	4~10 ℃	5 min.	2 hours	30 cm frying pan

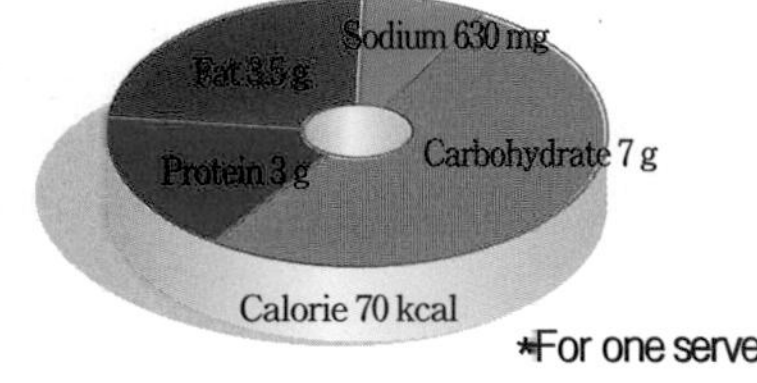

*For one serve

Ingredients & Quantity

200 g (1 ea) cucumber, 200 g (1 cup) water, 4 g (1 tbsp) salt

30 g beef, 10 g (2 sheets) brown oak mushrooms

seasoning sauce : 6 g (1 tsp) soy sauce, 4 g (1tsp) sugar, 2.3 g (½ tsp) minced green onion
1.1 g (1/5 tsp) minced garlic, 1 g (½ tsp) sesame salt, 0.1 g ground black pepper
2 g (½ tsp) sesame oil

60 g (1 ea) egg, 8 g (2 tsp) edible oil, 0.1 g shred red pepper

sweet vinegar : 4 g (1 tsp) salt, 24 g (2 tbsp) sugar, 60 g (4 tbsp) vinegar, 15 g (1 tbsp) water

Preparation

1. Wash the cucumber by rubbing, halve it lengthwise, put 3 diagonal slits at intervals of 0.5 cm−wide on the skin side and cut off at the 4th slit. 【Photo 2】
2. Marinate cucumber in salt water for 15 min, wipe water by dry cotton cloths (160 g). 【Photo 3】
3. Clean blood of beef with cotton cloths, shred it into 2.5 cm−long and 0.2 cm−wide/thick.
4. Soak the brown oak mushrooms in water for about 1 hour, remove stems and shred it into same size of beef (30 g), season the beef and mushrooms together with seasoning sauce. 【Photo 4】
5. Panfry egg for yellow/white garnish and cut it finely into same size of beef.
6. Cut the shred red pepper into 1 cm of length.
7. Blend sweet vinegar.

Recipe

1. Preheat the frying pan and oil. Stir−fry the cucumber for 1 min. on high heat, then cool it down (150 g). 【Photo 5】
2. Preheat the frying pan and oil. Stir−fry the beef and mushrooms for 2 min. respectively on medium heat.
3. Insert the fried beef and mushrooms into the slits together and add the yellow/white garnish. 【Photo 6】
4. Top the shred red pepper on the garnished cucumber. Place it on a dish and sprinkle sweet vinegar. Sweet vinegar may be served in a side bowl instead of sprinkling.

· Select thin, straight and soft cucumber.
· Sweet vinegar should be sprinkled just before serving for better taste and better color.

Heating Time	Process	Heat Control
Preparation	Marinating cucumber. Preparing beef and mushrooms Pan−frying yellow/white garnish. Blending sweet vinegar	
0 min	Stir−frying cucumber Stir−frying beef and mushrooms	H−heat 1 min. M−heat 4 min.
5 min	Inserting filling stuffs into the cucumber Topping with shred red pepper. Sprinkling sweet vinegar	

Sigeumchi-namul 시금치나물

Blanched and Seasoned Spinach

Sigeumchi-namul is blanched spinach with seasoning. Spinach is a typical green vegetable in Korea. It was described as an important vegetable in the book *Hunmongjahoe* written by *Choe Sejin* during the *Joseon* Dynasty (1527). Spinach was probably used in cooking since then.

Total weight after cooking	Weight for one serve	Service temperature	Total heating time	Total cooking time	Standard utensil
260 g (4 serves)	65 g	15~25 ℃	15 min.	30 min.	24 ㎝ pot

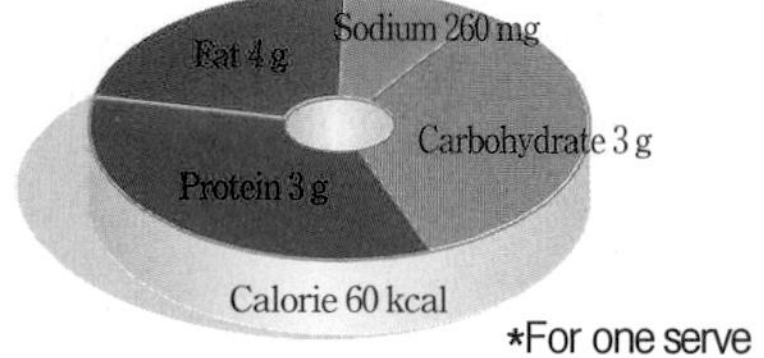

*For one serve

Ingredients & Quantity

400 g spinach, 3 ㎏ (15 cups) water, 4 g (1 tsp) salt

seasoning sauce : 3 g (½ tsp) clear soy sauce, 2 g (½ tsp) salt, 4.5 g (1 tsp) minced green onion
2.8 g (½ tsp) minced garlic, 3.5 g (½ tbsp) sesame seed, 8 g (2 tsp) sesame oil

0.2 g shred red pepper

Preparation

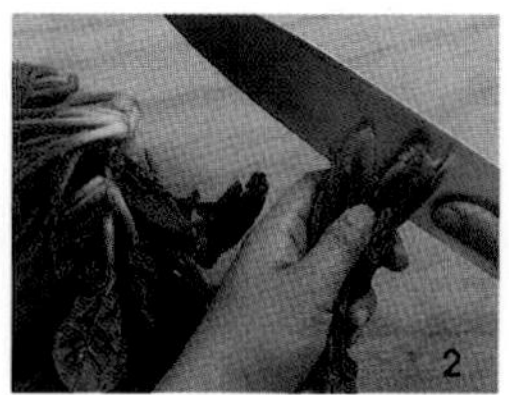

1. Trim spinach and cut off the roots. Put a crisscross slit on the root side, rinse it under running water 3~4 times. 【Photo 2】
2. Blend seasoning sauce 【Photo 3】
3. Cut the shred red pepper into 1 ㎝−long.

Recipe

1. Pour water into the pot, heat it up for 13 min. on high heat. When it boils, scald spinach with salt for 2 min. maintaining green color. Rinse in water, drain water by squeezing, and cut into 5~6 ㎝−long (230 g). 【Photo 4】
2. Mix the spinach with seasoning sauce thoroughly until seasoning soaked evenly. Place it on a dish and top with shred red pepper. 【Photos 5 & 6】

· Squeeze water out from spinach softly, or it may become untasty due to lack of water.
· 'Pohangcho' spinach is a little harder than normal. So, scald it for 1~2 min. more.

Heating Time	Process	Heat Control
Preparation	Trimming spinach and shred red pepper. Blending seasoning sauce	H−heat 15 min.
0 min	Scalding spinach	
10 min	Seasoning spinach. Topping with shred red pepper	

Beoseot-namul 버섯나물

Assorted Mushrooms

Beoseot-namul is an assorted fried mushrooms dish with brown oak, snow puff and oyster mushrooms. The mushrooms are stir-fried or sauted, or marinated with sauce. It has a unique taste and fragrance. Mushrooms have been enjoyed since olden days because it was believed that they have various benefits such as enhancing vision and balancing the nerves.

Total weight after cooking	Weight for one serve	Service temperature	Total heating time	Total cooking time	Standard utensil
280 g (4 serves)	70 g	15~25 ℃	9 min.	1 hour	30 cm pot, 30 cm frying pan

Fat 3.5 g
Sodium 480 mg
Carbohydrate 5 g
Protein 2 g
Calorie 65 kcal
*For one serve

Ingredients & Quantity

100 g agaric mushrooms : 1 kg (5 cups) water, 2 g (½ tsp) salt
10 g (4 sheets) brown oak mushrooms
100 g cultivated pine mushrooms
5 g Jew's ear mushrooms
50 g snow puff mushrooms
seasoning sauce : 9 g (½ tbsp) soy sauce , 4 g (1 tsp) salt , 4 g (1 tsp) sugar
13 g (1 tbsp) edible oil
4 g (1 tsp) sesame oil, 2 g (1 tsp) sesame seeds

Preparation

1. Clean the agaric mushrooms. 【Photo 2】
2. Soak the brown oak mushrooms in water for 1 hour, remove the belly buttons, wipe water with cotton cloths and cut it into 2~4 pieces (53 g).
3. Wash and peel the cultivated pine mushrooms, shred it at intervals of 0.5 cm−thick, maintaining mushroom shape. 【Photo 3】
4. Soak Jew's ear mushrooms in water for 1 hour (40 g) and wash, rip up into the same size of brown oak mushrooms.
5. Wash snow puff mushrooms and cut into 5 cm−long.
6. Blend seasoning sauce.

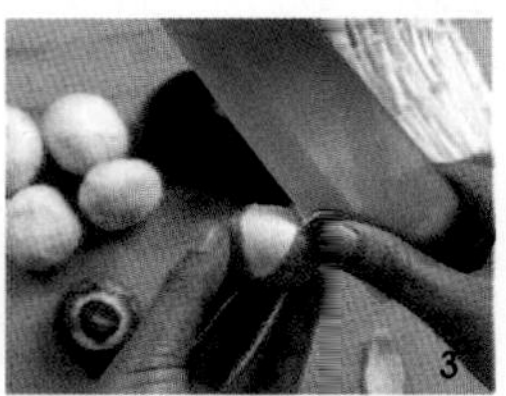

Recipe

1. Pour water in the pot, heat it up on high heat for 5 min. When it boils, add salt and agaric mushrooms, scald for 1 min. then rip up into 0.5 cm−thick (85 g). 【Photo 4】
2. Mix each mushrooms with divided portion of seasoning sauce respectively. 【Photo 5】
3. Preheat the frying pan and oil, stir−fry all mushrooms together except snow puff mushrooms on high heat for 2 min. Then add snow puff mushrooms, sesame oil and sesame seeds, stir−fry on medium heat for another 1 min. 【Photo 6】

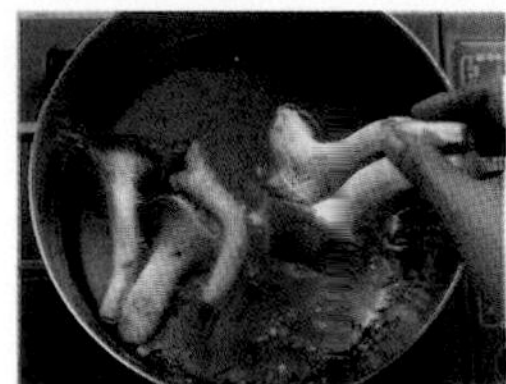

· **Do not put green onion and/or garlic into the mushroom salad for maintaining original mushroom fragrance.**
· **To display good color, red pepper or shred red pepper may be added.**

Heating Time	Process	Heat Control
Preparation 0 min	Trimming mushrooms. Blending seasoning sauce Scalding agaric mushrooms Seasoning mushrooms Stir−frying brown oak mushrooms cultivated pine mushrooms and Jew's ear mushrooms Stir−frying after putting snow puff mushrooms sesame oil and sesame seeds	H−heat 6 min. H−heat 2 min. M−heat 1 min.

Gujeolpan 구절판

Platter of Nine Delicacies

Gujeolpan is the name of nine sectioned platter in which eight different vegetables and meats are placed in each compartment and wheat flour pancakes in the center. *Gujeolpan* was originally the name of the platter but it later became the name of the food. *Gujeolpan* is a good dish for the travel or picnic because it can serve several foods at the same time.

Total weight after cooking	Weight for one serve	Service temperature	Total heating time	Total cooking time	Standard utensil
400 g (4 serves)	100 g	15~25 ℃	15 min.	2 hours	18 cm pot, 30 cm frying pan

Sodium 450 mg
Fat 6 g
Protein 6 g
Carbohydrate 13 g
Calorie 130 kcal
*For one serve

Ingredients & Quantity

50 g beef (top round), 10 g (2 sheets) brown oak mushrooms
seasoning sauce : 9 g (½ tbsp) soy sauce, 2 g (½ tsp) sugar, 2.3 g (½ tsp) minced green onion
1.4 g (¼ tsp) minced garlic, 1 g (½ tsp) sesame salt, 0.1 g ground black pepper
2 g (½ tsp) sesame oil
10 g stone mushrooms
100 g (½ ea) cucumber, 0.5 g (⅛ tsp) salt
30 g (⅛ ea) carrot, 0.5 g (⅛ tsp) salt
100 g mung bean sprouts, 400 g (2 cups) water, 1 g (¼ tsp) salt
mung bean sprouts seasoning : 1 g (¼ tsp) salt, 2 g (½ tsp) sesame oil
60 g (1 ea) egg, 0.5 g (⅛ tsp) salt
wheat flour pancake : 56 g (8 tbsp) wheat flour, 135 g (9 tbsp) water, 1 g (¼ tsp) salt
39 g (3 tbsp) edible oil
mustard juice : 6 g (½ tbsp) fermented mustard, 15 g (1 tbsp) vinegar, 4 g (1 tsp) sugar, 2 g (½ tsp) salt
9.5 g (½ tbsp) honey, 15 g broth (or 1 tbsp water)

1

Preparation

1. Clean blood of the beef with cotton cloths (45 g). Shred it into 5~6 cm-long, 0.2 cm-wide and thick. Season it with half of the seasoning sauce①.
2. Soak the mushrooms in water for about 1 hour, remove stems of brown oak mushrooms, wipe water, shred it at intervals of 0.1 cm-wide/thick and season it with the remained seasoning sauce① (30 g). Wash the stone mushrooms by rubbing, remove belly buttons, roll it up and shred it at intervals of 0.1 cm-wide (7 g). 【Photo 2】
3. Wash the cucumber by rubbing, cut into 5 cm-long and 0.1 cm-thick roundly, and shred them into 0.1 cm-wide (25 g). Wash the carrot, skin, cut into 5 cm-long and shred into 0.1 cm-wide/thick (25 g), marinate them with salt for 5 min. respectively, wipe water with cotton cloths. Remove the heads and tails of mung bean sprouts (76 g). 【Photo 3】
4. Panfry the egg for yellow/white garnish and cut it into same size of the cucumber.
5. Mix wheat flour, salt and water evenly, sieve and knead it to make pancake dough.
6. Prepare mustard juice.

3

4

Recipe

1. Preheat the frying pan and oil. Stir-fry the beef and brown oak mushrooms for 2 min. respectively on medium heat.
2. Preheat the frying pan and oil. Stir-fry the stone mushrooms for 10 sec. on low heat. Preheat the frying pan and oil. Stir-fry the cucumber and carrot for 30 sec. respectively on high heat, spread them out and cool down. 【Photo 4】
3. Pour water in the pot and heat it up for 2 min. on high heat. When it boils, scald mung bean sprouts with salt for 2 min. (68 g) and mix it with seasonings together.
4. Preheat the frying pan and oil. Panfry wheat flour pancakes with 6 g of the dough into 0.2 cm-thick, 6 cm-diameter (20 sheets). 【Photo 5】
5. Place the pancake in the middle of the platter and decorate with prepared stuffs around the platter, matching colors. Serve with mustard juice. 【Photo 6】

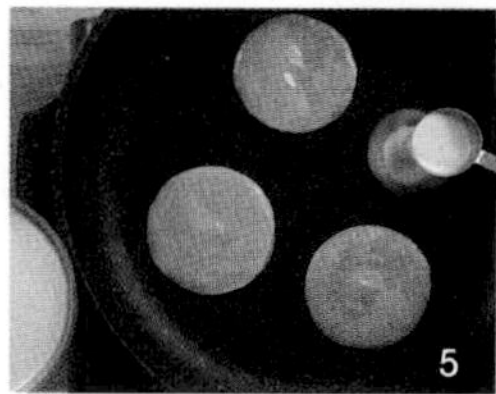
5

· 6~8 g may be proper for the weight of one sheet of wheat flour pancake.
· Bamboo shoots, shrimps, sea slugs and abalones may be used for this dish.

6

Heating Time	Process	Heat Control
Preparation	Preparing beef. Trimming vegetables. Soaking mushrooms Pan-frying egg. Blending mustard juice	
0 min	Stir-frying beef, brown oak mushrooms and stone mushrooms Stir-frying cucumber and carrot. Scalding mung bean sprouts	M-heat 4 min. L-heat 10 sec. H-heat 1 min. H-heat 4 min.
10 min	Pan-frying wheat flour pancakes Decorating stuffs on the platter	M-heat 5 min.

Japchae 잡채

Potato Starch Noodles Stir-fried with Vegetables

Japchae is a dish mixed of potato starch noodles with various stir-fried vegetables. *Japchae* is served without fail on holidays and traditional ceremonial days. The name "*japchae*" (sundried vegetables) came about because it is mixed with various vegetables.

Total weight after cooking	Weight for one serve	Service temperature	Total heating time	Total cooking time	Standard utensil
400 g(4 serves)	100 g	15~25 ℃	27 min.	2 hours	18 cm pot, 30 cm frying pan

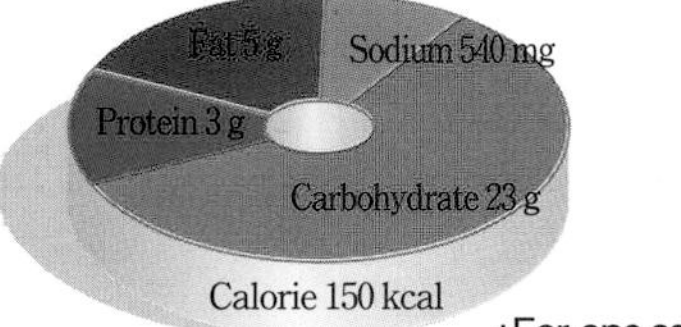

*For one serve

Ingredients & Quantity

50 g beef (top round), 10 g (2 sheets) brown oak mushrooms, 3 g Jew's ear mushrooms
seasoning sauce① : 9 g (½ tbsp) soy sauce, 2 g (½ tsp) sugar, 2.3 g (½ tsp) minced green onion
1.4 g (¼ tsp) minced garlic, 1 g (½ tsp) sesame salt, 2 g (½ tsp) sesame oil
0.1 g ground black pepper
70 g (⅓ ea) cucumber, 0.5 g (⅛ tsp) salt, 30 g Carrot, 0.5 g (⅛ tsp) salt
30 g skinned bellflower roots, 2 g (½ tsp) salt, 150 g (1 head) onion
30 g mung bean sprouts, 400 g (2 cups) water, 1 g (¼ tsp) salt
mung bean sprout seasoning : 0.5 g (⅛ tsp) salt,2 g (½ tsp) sesame oil
60 g (1 ea) egg, 0.5 g (⅛ tsp) salt
60 g potato starch noodles, 400 g (2 cups) boiling water
seasoning sauce② : 18 g (1 tbsp) soy sauce, 12 g (1 tbsp) sugar, 6.5 g (½ tbsp) sesame oil
3.5 g (½ tbsp) sesame seeds, 1 g (¼ tsp) salt
26 g (2 tbsp) edible oil

1

Preparation

1. Clean blood of the beef with cotton cloths, shred it into 6 cm–long, 0.3 cm–wide and thick (45 g), then season them with half of the seasoning sauce①.
2. Soak the mushrooms in water for about 1 hour, remove stems of brown oak mushrooms and shred it at intervals of 0.3 cm–wide and thick (28 g). Separate Jew's ear mushrooms by sheet (18 g), season them with remained half of the seasoning sauce① respectively.
3. Wash the cucumber by rubbing, cut into 5~6 cm–long and 0.3 cm–thick roundly, shred them into 0.3 cm–wide (23 g). Wash the carrot and skin. Cut and slice them into 5~6 cm–long and 0.3 cm–wide and thick (20 g), marinate them with salt for 5 min. respectively, and wipe water with cotton cloths.
4. Cut the bellflower roots into same size of the cucumber (26 g), wash it with salt by fumbling for 1 min. to draw out bitter taste. Skin and wash the onion, and shred it into same size of the cucumber (100 g). Remove the heads and tails of mung bean sprouts (26 g). 【Photo 2】
5. Panfry egg as yellow/white garnish, cut it into 4 cm–long and 0.3 cm–wide/thick.

2

3

Recipe

1. Preheat the frying pan and oil. Stir–fry the beef, brown oak mushrooms and Jew's ear mushrooms respectively for about 2 min. on medium heat.
2. Preheat the frying pan and oil. Stir–fry the cucumber and carrot respectively for 30 sec. on high heat. Stir–fry the bellflower roots and onion respectively for 2 min. on medium heat. 【Photo 3】
3. Pour water in the pot, heat it up for 2 min. on high heat. When it boils, scald mung bean sprouts with salt for 2 min., drain water through a strainer (24 g), mix it with mung bean sprout seasoning.
4. Pour water in the pot and heat it up for 2 min. on high heat. When it boils, add potato starch noodles and boil it for 8 min. Take the noodles out and drain water, cut it into 20 cm–long and mix it with seasoning sauce②. 【Photo 4】
5. Preheat the frying pan and oil. Stir–fry the noodles for 2 min. on medium heat. 【Photo 5】
6. Mix the noodles and prepared stuffs together and top with yellow/white garnish. 【Photo 6】

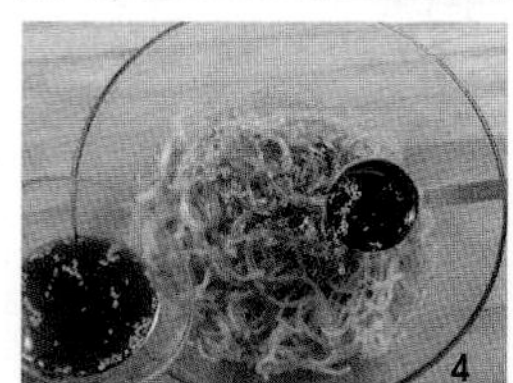
4

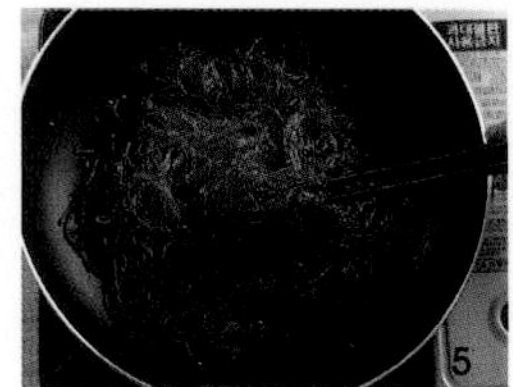
5

- To get the better quality and better color, all stuffs for this dish should be fried quickly on high heat.
- Pork, spinach and oyster mushrooms may be used as ingredients for this dish.

Heating Time	Process	Heat Control
Preparation	Preparing beef. Soaking mushrooms. Preparing vegetables	
0 min	Stir–frying beef and mushrooms	M–heat 6 min.
	Stir–frying cucumber, carrot, bellflower roots and onion	H–heat 1 min. M–heat 4 min.
	Scalding mung bean sprouts	H–heat 4 min.
15 min	Boiling noodles and seasoning	H–heat 10 min.
25 min	Stir–frying noodles. Mixing stir–fried noodles and vegetables together	M–heat 2 min.

6

Tangpyeongchae 탕평채

Mung Bean Jelly Mixed with Vegetables and Beef

Tangpyeongchae is a dish made of jellied mung beans, sprouts, beef, watercress, and eggs. It is sweet and sour in taste, rich in nutrition and harmonized with colors from the meat and vegetables. The name '*tangpyeongchae*' came about when the dish appeared on the table for the first time, during discussions of *tangpeongchaek* (unbiased policy) in the *Yeongjo* era of the *Joseon* Dynasty.

Total weight after cooking	Weight for one serve	Service temperature	Total heating time	Total cooking time	Standard utensil
400 g (4 serves)	100 g	4~10 ℃	12 min.	1 hour	18 cm pot, 30 cm frying pan

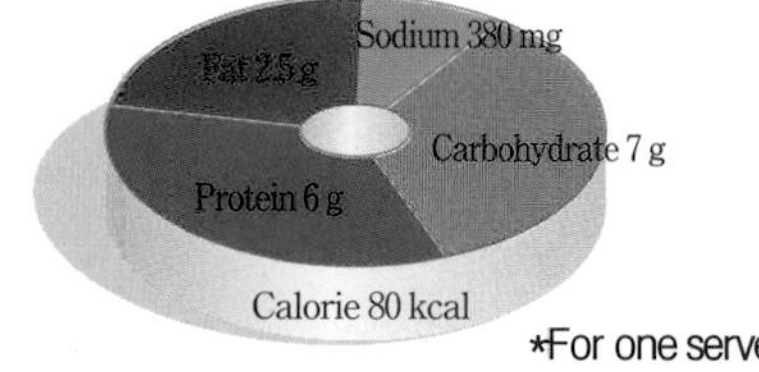

*For one serve

Ingredients & Quantity

300 g (1 cake) mung bean jelly, 600 g (3 cups) water
seasoning : 2 g (1 tsp) salt, 2 g (½ tsp) sesame oil
100 g beef (top round)
seasoning sauce : 13 g (⅔ tbsp) soy sauce, 6 g (½ tbsp) sugar, 4.5 g (1 tsp) minced green onion
2.5 g (½ tsp) minced garlic, 1 g (½ tsp) sesame salt
0.3 g (⅛ tsp) ground black pepper, 2 g (½ tsp) sesame oil
100 g mung bean sprouts, 50 g watercress, 400 g (2 cups) water, 1 g (¼ tsp) salt
2 g (¼ ea) red pepper, 2 g (1 sheet) laver
60 g (1 ea) egg, 4 g (1 tsp) edible oil
vinegar soy sauce : 13 g (⅔ tbsp) soy sauce, 30 g (2 tbsp) vinegar, 12 g (1 tbsp) sugar
2 g (1 tsp) sesame salt

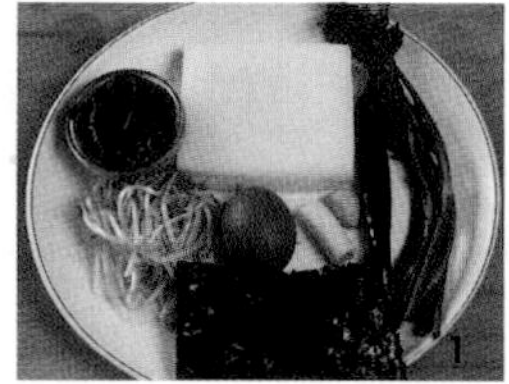
1

Preparation

1. Shred mung bean jelly into 7 cm–long and 0.5 cm–wide/thick. 【Photo 2】
2. Clean blood of beef with cotton cloths, shred into 5 cm–long and 0.3 cm–wide/thick (70 g), mix with seasoning sauce together (100 g). 【Photo 3】
3. Remove heads and tails of mung bean sprouts (80 g). Trim watercress stalks cleanly (25 g) and wash under running water. Shred red pepper at intervals of 3 cm–long. 【Photo 4】
4. Panfry egg for yellow/white garnish, and cut into 4 cm–long and 0.3 cm–wide.
5. Blend vinegar soy sauce.

2

3

Recipe

1. Put water in to a pot, heat it up for 3 min. on high heat. When it boils, scald mung bean jelly for 1 min. (250 g), take out the jelly from the pot and drain water. Mix with seasoning together. 【Photo 5】
2. When the frying pan heated up, put the beef and pan–fry it for 2 min. on medium heat.
3. Pour water in the pot and heat it up for 2 min. on high heat. When it boils, scald mung bean sprouts with salt for 2 min. (70 g). Scald watercress for 1 min. (27 g) and rinse in water, cut into 4 cm–long.
4. Toast laver for 1 min. on low heat and crush up.
5. Mix mung bean jelly with beef, mung bean sprouts, watercress and vinegar soy sauce together. Garnish with red pepper, laver and egg garnish. 【Photo 6】

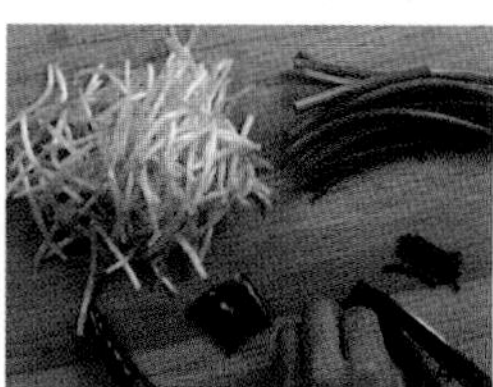

5

- Thinly shred mung bean jelly may serve different taste.
- Mix the salad just before serving, not to be watery.
- Small vinegar soy sauce bowl may be served with main dish, instead of mixing together with jelly.

6

Heating Time	Process	Heat Control
Preparation	Cutting mung bean jelly. Preparing beef and vegetables. Blending vinegar soy sauce	
0 min	Scalding mung bean jelly. Pan–frying beef	M–heat 2 min. H–heat 4 min.
	Scalding watercress and mung bean sprouts	H–heat 3 min.
10 min	Toasting laver. Mixing with vinegar soy sauce	L–heat 1 min.

Deodeok-saengchae 더덕생채

Deodeok Salad

Deodeok-saengchae is thinly ripped *deodeok* roots mixed with spicy and sour seasonings. *Deodeok* is referred to as *sasam* (ginseng from sand). It is high in saponin like ginseng and bellflower roots. In Oriental medicine, it is considered a health food that is good for the stomach, and strengthens the lungs, intestines and kidney.

Total weight after cooking	Weight for one serve	Service temperature	Total heating time	Total cooking time	Standard utensil
260 g(4 serves)	65 g	4~10 ℃	0 min.	1 hour	

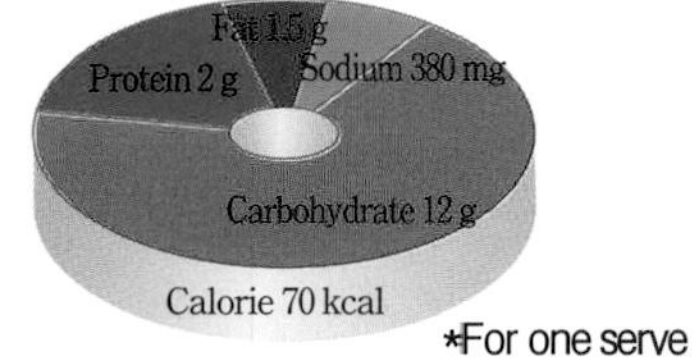

*For one serve

Ingredients & Quantity

300 g deodeok roots, 400 g (2 cups) water, 6 g (½ tbsp) salt

seasoning sauce : 12 g (1 tbsp) sugar, 15 g (2½ tsp) red pepper paste, 4.4 g (2 tsp) ground red pepper
2 g (½ tsp) salt, 14 g (1 tbsp) minced green onion, 5.5 g (1 tsp) minced garlic
2 g (1 tsp) sesame salt, 15 g (1 tbsp) vinegar

1

Preparation

1. Trim and wash the deodeok roots, skin, and slice them into 0.5 cm–thick (210 g).
2. Soak the sliced roots in salt water for 20 min. to get rid of bitter taste. pot dry with cotton cloths. 【Photo 2】
3. Press and roll the roots with wooden roller and rip up around 6 cm–long and 0.3 cm–wide and thick (205 g). 【Photos 3 & 4】
4. Blend seasoned red pepper paste. 【Photo 5】

2

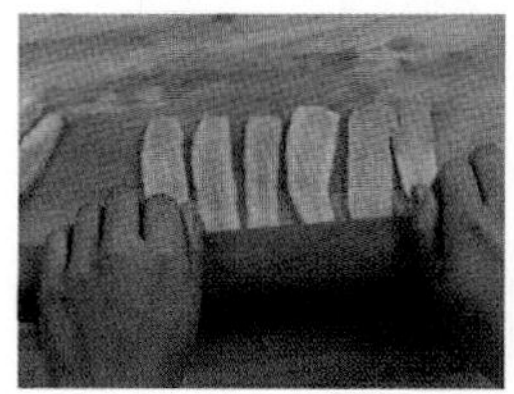

Recipe

1. Mix the doedoek roots with seasoning sauce together. 【Photo 6】

· Doedoek roots may be slightly pounded with wooden mallet after pad drying.

5

Cooking Time	Process	Heat Control
0 min	Trimming doedoek roots	
10 min	Soaking in salt water	
30 min	Tearing doedoek roots	
40 min	Mixing with seasoning sauce	

6

Chamnamul-saengchae 참나물생채

Chamnamul Fresh Vegetable Salad

Chamnamul-saengchae is a salad dish made of fresh *chamnamul* (wild greens) and seasonings. '*Cham*' means true and *chamnamul* means 'true *namul*.' It has a unique taste and flavor, and is served as a raw salad or leaves for stuffing. In the northern part of Korea, people make Kimchi with *chamnamul* as a specialty dish.

Total weight after cooking	Weight for one serve	Service temperature	Total heating time	Total cooking time	Standard utensil
140 g(4 serves)	35 g	4~10 ℃	0 min.	30 min.	

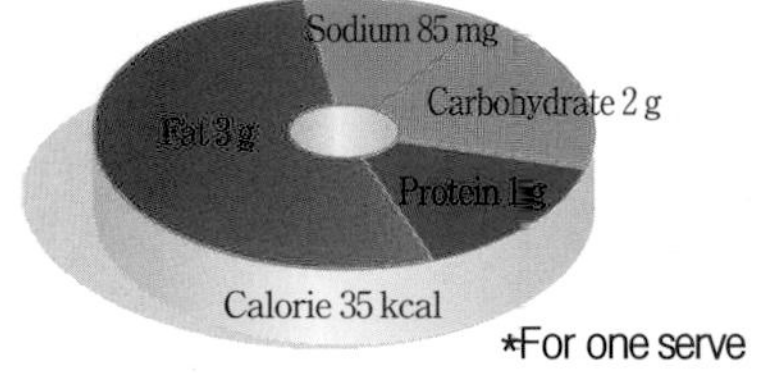

Ingredients & Quantity

110 g chamnamul (wild herbs)

seasoning sauce : 9 g (½ tbsp) soybean paste, 6 g (1 tsp) red pepper paste, 14 g (1 tbsp) minced green onion
5.5 g (1 tsp) minced garlic, 1.8 g (1 tsp) sesame seeds, 13 g (1 tbsp) sesame oil
15 g (1 tbsp) vinegar

Preparation

1. Select soft chamnamul (wild herbs).
2. Trim and wash the wild herbs, rinse again under running water and drain water.
3. Cut them into 6 cm−long (95 g). 【Photo 2】
4. Blend seasoning sauce. 【Photo 3】

Recipe

1. Mix wild herbs with seasoning sauce together softly. 【Photos 4 & 5】
2. Place on a dish. 【Photo 6】

· To provide fresh salad, mix the wild herbs just before serving.

Cooking Time	Process	Heat Control
0 min 10 min	Trimming and washing chamnamul (wild herbs) Blending seasoning sauce Mixing wild herbs with seasoning sauce	

Gyeojachae 겨자채

Assorted Cold Plate with Mustard Sauce

Gyeojachae is a fresh salad dish made of various vegetables, Korean pear, chestnuts, and sliced pressed meat in a mustard dressing. *Gyeojachae* stimulates the appetite with its hot, sweet and sour taste. It is usually served as an appetizer. It should be assembled just before serving to keep its taste fresh and prevent it from becoming watery.

Total weight after cooking	Weight for one serve	Service temperature	Total heating time	Total cooking time	Standard utensil
400 g(4 serves)	100 g	4~10 ℃	43 min.	1 hour	20 cm pot, 30 cm frying pan

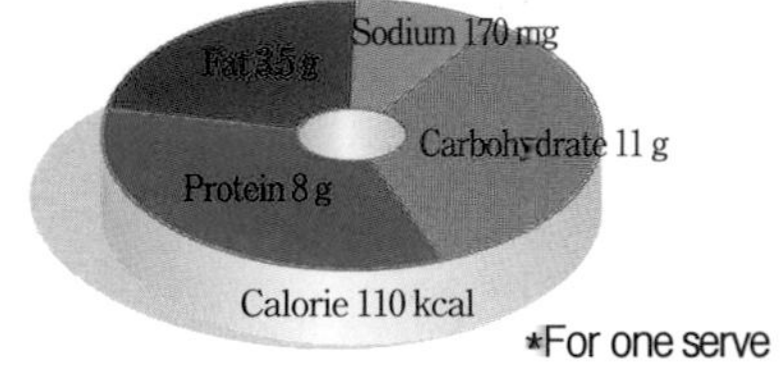

*For one serve

Ingredients & Quantity

200 g beef (brisket), 600 g (3 cups) water
fragrant seasoning : 20 g green onion, 10 g garlic
80 g (1/2 ea) cucumber, 50 g (1/3 ea) carrot, 90 g cabbage
125 g (medium 1/4 ea) pear, 100 g (1/2 cup) water, 2 g (1/2 tsp) sugar
50 g (3 ea) chestnut, 60 g (1 ea) egg, 5 g (1/2 tbsp) pine nuts
mustard juice : 39 g (3 tbsp) fermented mustard, 4 g (1 tsp) salt, 45 g (3 tbsp) vinegar
24 g (2 tbsp) sugar, 45 g (3 tbsp) broth

1

Preparation

1. Clean blood of beef with cotton cloths. Wash fragrant seasoning cleanly.
2. Put the beef and water in the pot, boil it for 3 min. on high heat. When it boils, skim off foam and residue and continue to boil it for another 5 min. Add fragrant seasoning, lower the heat to medium and simmer it for 35 min. 【Photo 2】
3. Take out the beef from the broth, wrap it with cotton cloths, press it with heavy weight for 30 min. Slice it into 1.5 cm–wide, 5 cm–long and 0.3 cm–thick (100 g). 【Photo 3】
4. Wash cucumber, carrot and cabbage, cut them into 5 cm–long, 1.5 cm–wide and 0.3 cm–thick. Dip them in cold water (cucumber 60 g, carrot 35 g, cabbage 80 g).
5. Peel the pear and cut into same size of carrot, dip in sugar water (pear 80 g). Skin the chestnuts, and slice it into 0.5 cm–thick, maintaining chestnut shape (35 g). 【Photo 4】
6. Remove tops of the pine nuts and wipe the nuts with dry cotton cloths.
7. Pan–fry eggs for yellow/white garnish (20 g) and cut it into same size of carrot.
8. Blend mustard juice. 【Photo 5】

2

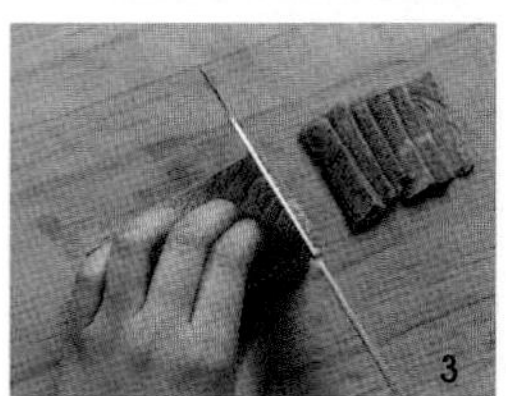
3

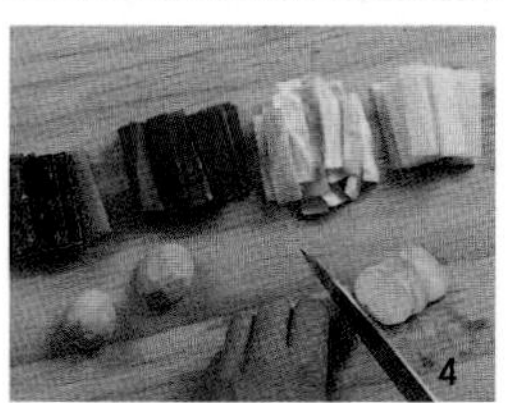
4

Recipe

1. Place the pressed beef, vegetables and egg garnish on a dish roundly. Put the chestnuts and pine nuts in the center, then serve with mustard juice. 【Photo 6】

· Seafoods such as shrimps and abalones may be added to this dish.
· Dip the vegetables in iced water shortly, then it may be crispy.

5

6

Heating Time	Process	Heat Control
Preparation	Preparing beef, vegetables and pine nuts Making mustard juice. Pan–frying egg garnish	
0 min	Boiling beef	H–heat 8 min. M–heat 35 min.
40 min	Slicing meet. Placing stuffs on a dish	

Dotorimuk-muchim 도토리묵무침

Seasoned Acorn Starch Jelly

Dotorimuk-muchim is a dish made of jellied acorn starch, vegetables and seasoning sauce. *Dotorimuk-muchim* was considered a specialty or a dish for the relief of the famine victims in olden days when provisions were scarce. Recently, it has become a popular diet food because it is in low calories.

Total weight after cooking	Weight for one serve	Service temperature	Total heating time	Total cooking time	Standard utensil
400 g(4 serves)	100 g	4~10 ℃	0 min.	30 min.	

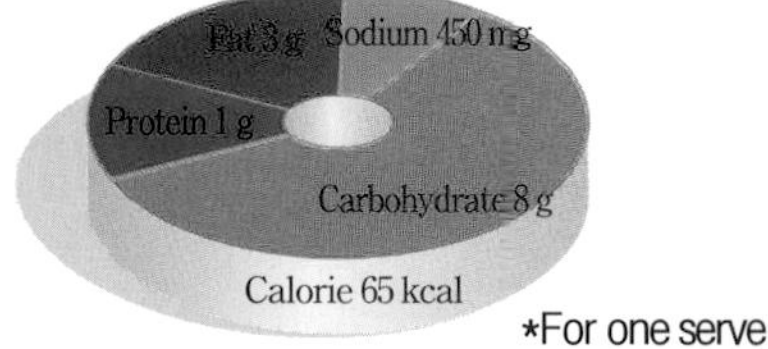

*For one serve

Ingredients & Quantity

300 g (1 cake) acorn starch jelly

70 g (⅓ ea) cucumber, 30 g carrot, 30 g crown daisy, 15 g (1 ea) green pepper, 10 g (½ ea) red pepper

seasoning sauce : 24 g (1⅓ tbsp) soy sauce, 2 g (½ tsp) sugar, 1.1 g (½ tsp) ground red pepper
4.5 g (1 tsp) minced green onion, 2.7 g (½ tsp) minced garlic, 2 g (1 tsp) sesame seeds
13 g (1 tbsp) sesame oil

Preparation

1. Cut and slice the acorn starch jelly into 3 cm-wide, 4 cm-long and 1 cm-thick (260 g). 【Photo 2】
2. Wash the cucumber by rubbing with salt, cut it into 4 cm-long and 1.5 cm-wide, slice them at intervals of 0.3 cm diagonally (60 g). Cut and slice the carrots into same size of the cucumber (20 g).
3. Cut the green/red pepper into 2 cm-long and 0.5 cm-thick diagonally and seed. (green pepper 10 g, red pepper 7 g).
4. Trim and wash the crown daisy and cut it into 5 cm-long (20 g). 【Photo 3】
5. Blend seasoning sauce. 【Photo 4】

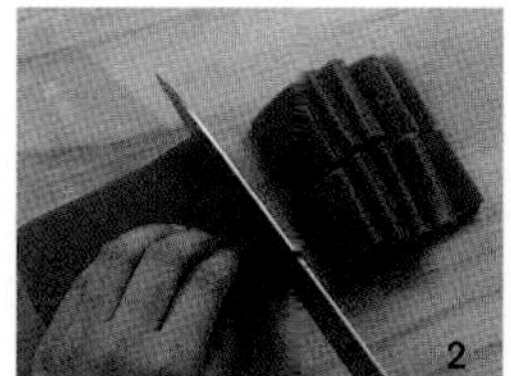

Recipe

1. Add the vegetables and seasoning sauce to the acorn starch jelly. 【Photo 5】
2. Mix altogether softly. 【Photo 6】

· When making acorn starch jelly, soak the acorn in the water to get rid of bitter taste.
· Instead of sesame oil, green perilla oil may be added to the jelly upon taste.

Cooking Time	Process	Heat Control
0 min	Preparing acorn starch jelly Trimming and cleaning cucumber, carrot, crown daisy and green/red pepper	
20 min	Mixing with seasoning sauce	

Soegogi-jangjorim 쇠고기장조림

Beef Chunks Braised in Soy Sauce

Soegogi-jangjorim is a dish of beef (rib eye round, shank or top round) braised in soy sauce. The beef is usually ripped or cut into thin slices. This is a fairly salty dish so it is storable and suitable as a basic side dish.

Total weight after cooking	Weight for one serve	Service temperature	Total heating time	Total cooking time	Standard utensil
280 g(4 serves)	70 g	15~25 ℃	1 hour 16 min.	2 hours	18 cm pot

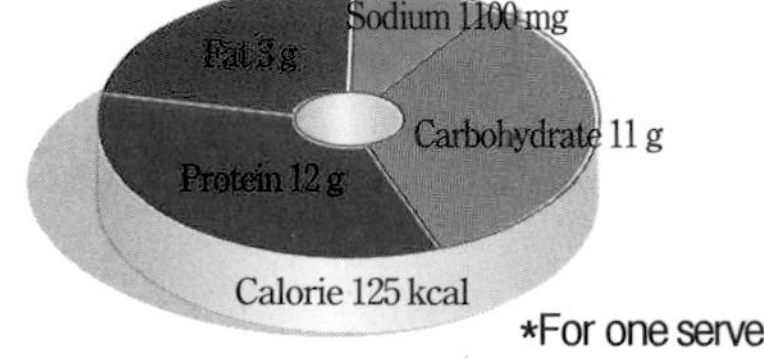

*For one serve

Ingredients & Quantity

200 g beef (top round), 600 g (3 cups) water
fragrant seasoning, 10 g green onion, 20 g garlic
100 g (5½ tbsp) soy sauce, 24 g (2 tbsp) sugar
30 g garlic, 50 g ground cherry pepper

1

Preparation

1. Clean blood of beef with cotton cloths. 【Photo 2】
2. Cut the beef into 5 cm-wide, 6 cm-long and 5 cm-thick. 【Photo 3】
3. Trim and wash garlic. Remove tops of the ground cherry pepper and wash cleanly.

2

3

Recipe

1. Put water and beef in the pot. Heat it up for 3 min. on high heat. When it boils, lower the heat to medium, add the fragrant seasoning, simmer it for 30 min. Then take out the fragrant seasoning. 【Photo 4】
2. When the meat is well-done, add soy sauce and sugar, boil it for another 30 min. until the soy sauce soup reduced into half. 【Photo 5】
3. Add garlic into the soy sauce, boil it for 10 min. Add ground cherry pepper, boil it for 3 min. more. 【Photo 6】
4. Rip up the meat into 1 cm-thick, place the meat on a dish, decorate with garlic and ground cherry pepper on the side. Spread soy sauce soup over the meat.

· **Add soy sauce and sugar after the meat well-done, then the meat would not be tough.**

5

Heating Time	Process	Heat Control
Preparation	Drawing out blood from the beef	
0 min	Boiling beef. Adding fragrant seasoning	H-heat 3 min. M-heat 30 min.
30 min	Additional boiling after adding soy sauce and sugar	M-heat 30 min.
60 min	Boiling after adding garlic	M-heat 10 min.
70 min	Boiling after adding ground cherry pepper	M-heat 3 min.

6

Nakji-bokkeum 낙지볶음

Stir-fried Baby Octopus

Nakji-bokkeum is a stir-fry of baby octopus with various vegetables and seasonings. There is a saying, "If you feed 3 to 4 octopi to a scraggy cow, it will soon have strength." Octopus has been enjoyed as a health food since olden days. It tastes best in the autumn and winter. Octopus can also be grilled, or served raw and sliced.

Total weight after cooking	Weight for one serve	Service temperature	Total heating time	Total cooking time	Standard utensil
480 g(4 serves)	120 g	65~70 ℃	3 min.	30 min.	30 cm frying pan

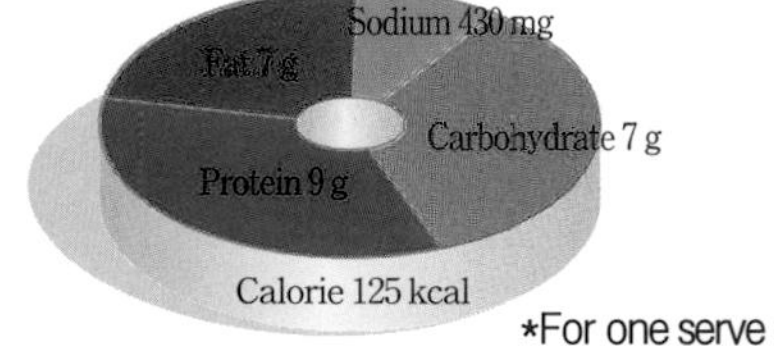

*For one serve

Ingredients & Quantity

450 g ($2\frac{1}{4}$ bodies) baby octopus, 12 g (1 tbsp) salt, 14 g (2 tbsp) wheat flour
100 g ($\frac{1}{2}$ heads) onion, 25 g ($1\frac{1}{2}$ ea) green pepper, 20 g (1 ea) red pepper, 13 g (1 tbsp) edible oil, 4 g (1 tsp) sesame oil
seasoning sauce : 6 g (1 tsp) soy sauce, 19 g (1 tbsp) red pepper paste, 14 g (2 tbsp) ground red pepper
4 g (1 tsp) sugar, 14 g (1 tbsp) minced green onion, 8 g ($\frac{1}{2}$ tbsp) minced garlic
2 g ($\frac{1}{2}$ tsp) minced ginger, 0.3 g ($\frac{1}{8}$ tsp) ground white pepper, 8 g (2 tsp) sesame oil

Preparation

1. Turn out the inside of the head of octopus, remove internal organs and eyes, put salt and wheat flour into it and clean it by fumbling. 【Photo 2】
2. Cut the head into 6 cm-long, 1.5 cm-wide and cut the legs into 6 cm-long (350 g). 【Photo 3】
3. Trim & clean the onion and shred it at intervals of 1 cm-wide (80 g).
4. Wash the green/red pepper, cut it into 2 cm-long and 0.3 cm-thick diagonally and seed (green pepper 14 g,red pepper 16 g). 【Photo 4】
5. Blend seasoning sauce. 【Photo 5】

Recipe

1. Preheat the frying pan and oil. Stir-fry the onion for 1 min. on high heat. Add octopus and seasoning and fry for 1 min. more. 【Photo 6】
2. Add green/red pepper and sesame oil, panfry for 20 sec. on high heat.

· Carrot and/or other vegetables may be added more upon taste.
· Quick frying on high heat will serve better color and less watery.

Heating Time	Process	Heat Control
Preparation 0 min	Preparing octopus and vegetables. Blending seasoning sauce Stir-frying onion Stir-frying after adding octopus and seasoning Stir-frying after adding green/red pepper and sesame oil	 H-heat 1 min. H-heat 1 min. H-heat 20 sec.

Gungjung-tteokbokki 궁중떡볶이

Rice Cake Pasta and Vegetables, Royal Style

Gungjung-tteokbokki is a dish made of white rice cakes, beef and various dried and raw vegetables stir-fried with soy sauce for seasoning. *Tteokbokki* was not spicy and only made with soy sauce until the 18th century. But nowadays, it is cooked with a spicy red bean paste, which had been seen in recipes since the 1950s.

Total weight after cooking	Weight for one serve	Service temperature	Total heating time	Total cooking time	Standard utensil
600 g (4 serves)	150 g	65~70 ℃	15 min.	2 hours	18 cm pot, 30 cm frying pan

Fat 5 g
Protein 9 g
Sodium 460 mg
Carbohydrate 41 g
Calorie 250 kcal
*For one serve

Ingredients & Quantity

300 g white steamed rice cake, 13 g (1 tbsp) sesame oil
100 g beef (top round)
15 g (3 sheets) brown oak mushrooms
20 g dried pumpkin strips
seasoning sauce ① : 9 g (½ tbsp) soy sauce, 6 g (½ tbsp) sugar, 4.5 g (1 tsp) minced green onion
2.8 g (½ tsp) minced garlic, 0.3 g (⅛ tsp) ground black pepper, 4 g (1 tsp) sesame oil
50 g (⅓ ea) onion, 15 g (1 ea) green pepper, 20 g (1 ea) red pepper
60 g mung bean sprouts, 400 g (2 cups) water, 4 g (1 tsp) salt
60 g (1 ea) egg, 13 g (1 tbsp) edible oil
seasoning sauce ② : 18 g (1 tbsp) soy sauce, 6 g (½ tbsp) sugar, 6 g (1 tsp) honey
4.5 g (1 tsp) minced green onion, 2.8 g (½ tsp) minced garlic, 4 g (1 tsp) sesame oil
50 g (¼ cups) water

1

Preparation

1. Cut the white rice cake into 4~5 cm−long, shred them into 4 pieces lengthwise, mix them with sesame oil together (250 g). **[Photo 2]**
2. Clean blood of beef with cotton cloths, cut into 5 cm−long, 0.3 cm−wide/thick. Soak the brown oak mushrooms and dried pumpkin strips in water for 1 hour. Cut them into 5 cm−long, 0.7 cm−wide and 0.3 cm−thick (beef 80 g, brown oak mushrooms 45 g, pumpkin strips 80 g). **[Photo 3]**
3. Shred the onion, green/red pepper into 5 cm−long and 0.7 cm−wide.
4. Remove the heads and tails of mung bean sprouts, wash in water. **[Photo 4]**
5. Panfry egg for garnish, shred into 5 cm−long and 0.7 cm−wide.
6. Blend seasoning sauce ① and ②.

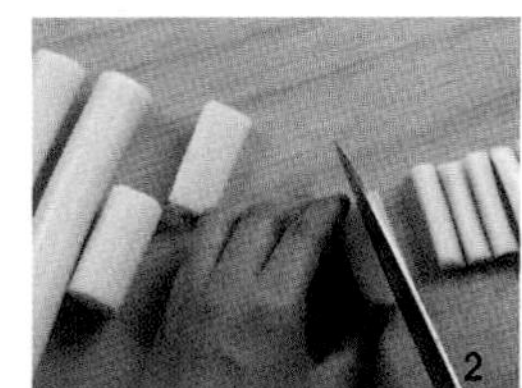
2

3

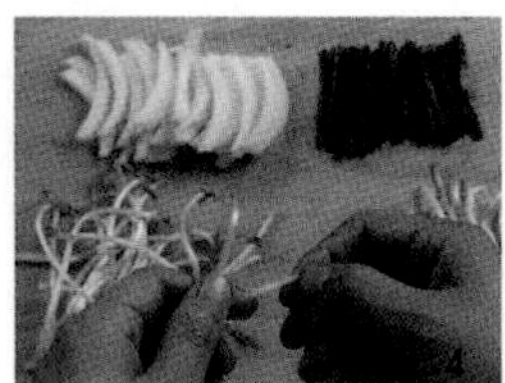

Recipe

1. Pour water into the pot, heat it up for 2 min. on high heat. When it boils, scald the mung bean sprouts with salt for 2 min. drain water (43 g).
2. Preheat the frying pan and oil, stir−fry the onion and pumpkin strips for 2 min. respectively on medium heat. Stir−fry the green/red pepper for 20 sec. Season the beef and mushrooms with seasoning sauce ①, and stir−fry for 2 min. on medium heat.
3. Preheat the frying pan, stir−fry white rice cake with seasoning sauce ② for 3 min. on medium heat. Add the beef, mushrooms, pumpkin strips, onion, green/red pepper and mung bean sprouts, then stir−fry for 30 sec. Turn the heat off, mix them with egg garnish thoroughly. **[Photos 5 & 6]**

· Pumpkin strips may be replaced by gourd strips and/or carrot.
· If white rice cake is dried hard, scald slightly in boiling water.

5

6

Heating Time	Process	Heat Control
Preparation	Preparing white rice cake, beef and vegetables Pan−frying egg garnish. Blending seasoning sauce	
0 min	Scalding mung bean sprouts. Stir−frying vegetables	H−heat 4 min. M−heat 5 min.
10 min	Stir−frying beef and brown oak mushrooms	M−heat 2 min.
	Stir−frying white rice cake	M−heat 3 min.
	Stir−frying after putting all stuffs. Mixing with egg garnish	M−heat 30 sec.

Neobiani 너비아니

Grilled Slice Beef

Neobiani is thinly sliced grilled beef with soy sauce seasoning. *Neobiani* means that the beef is sliced into broad sections. It is tender with a lot of knife slits in it.

Total weight after cooking	Weight for one serve	Service temperature	Total heating time	Total cooking time	Standard utensil
480 g (4 serves)	120 g (5 sheets)	70~75 ℃	5 min.	1 hour	iron grill

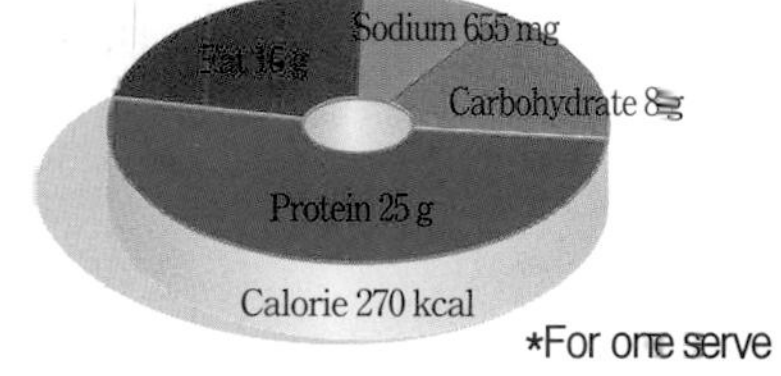

*For one serve

Ingredients & Quantity

600 g beef (sirloin), 70 g (pear 140 g) pear juice
seasoning sauce : 90 g (5 tbsp) soy sauce, 36 g (3 tbsp) sugar, 21 g (1 tbsp) honey
28 g (2 tbsp) minced green onion, 16 g (1 tbsp) minced garlic, 16 g (1 tbsp) ginger juice
6 g (1 tbsp) sesame salt, 0.5 g (1/5 tsp) ground black pepper, 26 g (2 tbsp) sesame oil
2 g (1 tsp) pine nuts powder
50 g lettuce
13 g (1 tbsp) edible oil

1

Preparation

1. Clean blood of beef with cotton cloths, remove fats and tendons (500 g), cut into 5 cm−wide, 7 cm−long and 0.3~0.5 cm thick along with opposite direction of the texture. Chop them slightly and marinate in pear juice for 10 min. 【Photos 2 & 3】
2. Blend seasoning sauce.
3. Trim and wash lettuce under running water cleanly.
4. Remove tops of the pine nuts, wipe the pine nuts with dry cotton cloths, pound it finely to make pine nuts powder (2 g).

2

3

Recipe

1. Add seasoning sauce to the beef, mix thoroughly until seasoning sauce permeated evenly into the beef. Let it sit for 30 min. (827 g). 【Photo 4】
2. Preheat the grill and oil. Put the beef piece by piece on it, and grill them for 3 min. for front side, and 2 min. for back side, at about 15 cm above the heat not to be burnt. 【Photos 5 & 6】
3. Sprinkle pine nuts powder and serve with lettuce.

4

· Cut the beef along with opposite direction of the texture, or the meat would be tough after grill.

5

Heating Time	Process	Heat Control
Preparation	Preparing beef. Blending seasoning sauce. Trimming and washing lettuce. Making pine nuts powder Marinating beef in seasoning sauce	
0 min	Grilling beef Sprinkling pine nuts powder	H−heat 5 min.

6

Bulgogi 불고기

Korean Barbecue

Bulgogi is a dish barbecued of thinly sliced beef that is pre–marinated with various seasonings on a hot barbecue pan. *Bulgogi* has been popular since the 1950s when the beef was served in thin slices to make it more tender and cut down the waiting time for diners.

Total weight after cooking	Weight for one serve	Service temperature	Total heating time	Total cooking time	Standard utensil
400 g (4 serves)	100 g	70~75 ℃	8 min.	1 hour	30 cm barbecue pan

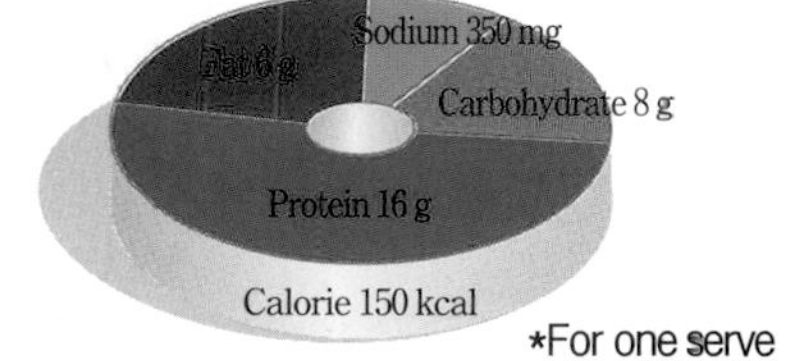

*For one serve

Ingredients & Quantity

300 g beef (sirloin)

seasoning sauce : 36 g (2 tbsp) soy sauce, 12 g (1 tbsp) sugar, 10 g (½ tbsp) honey
14 g (1 tbsp) minced green onion, 16 g (1 tbsp) minced garlic, 3 g (½ tbsp) sesame salt
0.5 g (1/5 tsp) ground black pepper, 50 g (pear 100 g) pear juice, 13 g (1 tbsp) sesame oil

200 g (medium 1 ea) onion

100 g lettuce

1

Preparation

1. Clean blood of beef with cotton cloths, remove fats and tendons, and cut into 5 cm–wide, 4 cm–long and 0.3 cm–thick along with opposite direction of the texture. 【Photo 2】
2. Skin onion and wash, shred at intervals of 0.5 cm–wide (190 g).
3. Blend seasoning sauce. 【Photo 3】
4. Wash lettuce under running water.

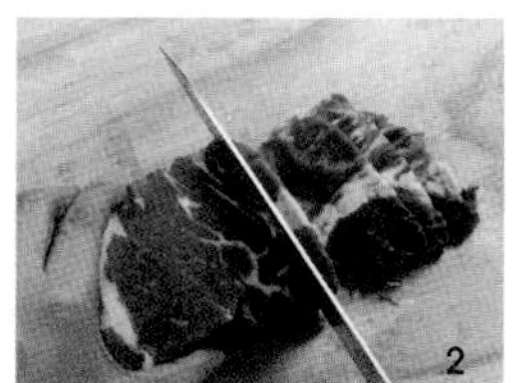
2

3

Recipe

1. Add seasoning sauce to the beef and fumble with hands, then add onion, marinate it for 30 min. 【Photos 4 & 5】
2. Heat the barbecue pan, pan–fry the beef on high heat for 3 min. then turn over the beef, lower the heat to medium, fry it another 5 min. 【Photo 6】
3. Serve with lettuce.

4

· Mushrooms and/or carrot may be added upon the taste.

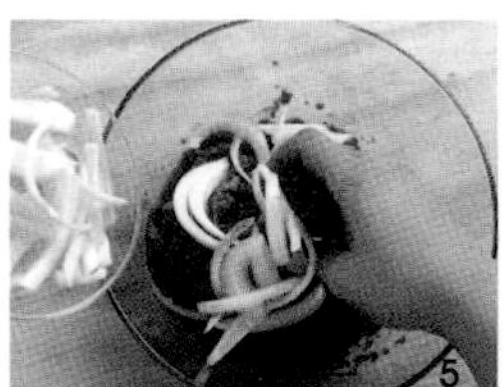
5

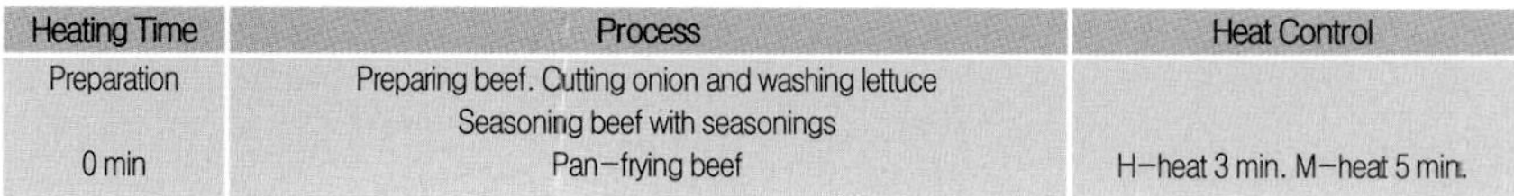

Heating Time	Process	Heat Control
Preparation	Preparing beef. Cutting onion and washing lettuce Seasoning beef with seasonings	
0 min	Pan–frying beef	H–heat 3 min. M–heat 5 min.

Soe-galbigui 쇠갈비구이

Marinated and Grilled Beef Ribs

Soe-galbigui is a dish of beef ribs that are pre-marinated with soy sauce seasoning, then grilled over a charcoal fire. This is a favorite dish for many Koreans. *Soe-galbigui* may have originated from *maejeok* which was a method of barbecuing skewered pre-seasoned beef over a charcoal fire.

Total weight after cooking	Weight for one serve	Service temperature	Total heating time	Total cooking time	Standard utensil
400g(4 serves)	100g(1 ea)	70~75℃	5 min.	4 hours	iron grill

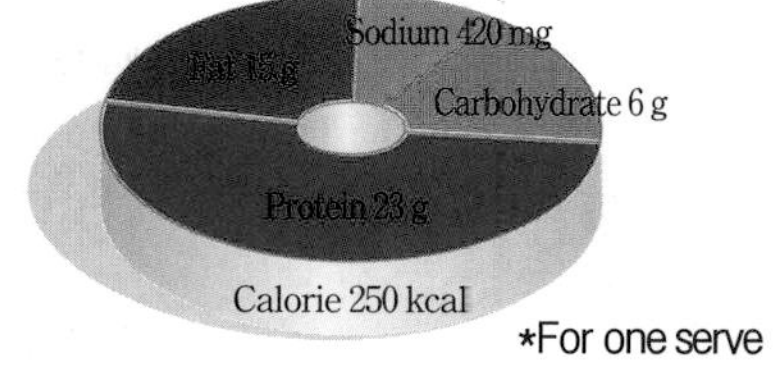

*For one serve

Ingredients & Quantity

660 g (4 ea) beef short ribs (on the bone)

seasoning① : 40 g (pear 100 g, 1/5 ea) pear juice, 15 g (1 tbsp) refined rice wine

seasoning sauce② : 36 g (2 tbsp) soy sauce, 12 g (1 tbsp) sugar, 15 g (onion 50 g, ⅓ head) onion juice
9.5 g (½ tbsp) honey, 14 g (1 tbsp) minced green onion, 8 g (½ tbsp) minced garlic
0.3 g (⅛ tsp) ground black pepper, 3 g (½ tbsp) sesame salt, 13 g (1 tbsp) sesame oil

13 g (1 tbsp) edible oil

10 g (1 tbsp) pine nuts

1

Preparation

1. Cut the beef ribs into 6~7 cm−long, remove excess fats and tendons from bone (500 g), soak it in plentiful water for a total 3 hours, changing the water every hour to draw out the blood.
2. Slice the meat of ribs into 0.5 cm−thick, taking care not to separate the meat from the bone edges. Put narrow slits on both sides of the meat. 【Photo 2】
3. Blend seasoning ① and seasoning sauce ②. 【Photo 3】
4. Prepare pine nuts powder (6 g).

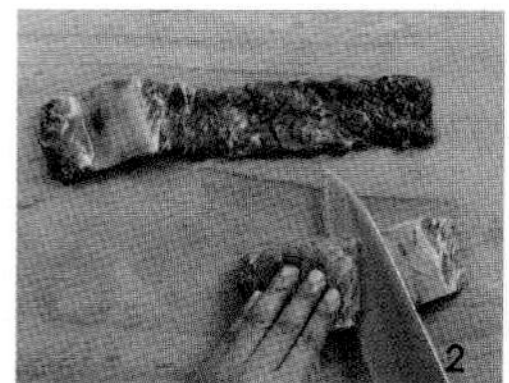

2

3

Recipe

1. Marinate the beef ribs with seasoning ① for 10 min. 【Photo 4】
2. Marinate the beef ribs again for 30 min.~1 hour after adding seasoning sauce ②, mix by fumbling with hands to soak the meat with sauce evenly. 【Photo 5】
3. Preheat the grill and oil. Grill the beef ribs on high heat at about 15 cm above the heat, for 2 min. for each side taking care not to be burnt. 【Photo 6】
4. Coat the beef ribs with seasoning sauce ② again and grill it for another 1 min. then sprinkle pine nuts powder on it.

4

· When the heat is too low, meat juice may be streamed and untasty. Grill it on over medium heat.
· Adjust the grilling time according to the thickness of the meat.

5

Heating Time	Process	Heat Control
Preparation	Preparing beef ribs after drawing out the blood. Preparing seasoning sauce and pine nuts powder Marinating beef ribs in seasoning	
0 min	Grilling beef ribs Sprinkling pine nuts powder	H−heat 5 min.

6

Jeyuk-gui 제육구이

Spicy Broiled Pork

Jeyuk-gui is pork seasoned with red pepper paste then broiled on a grill. Koreans have been breeding pigs in large numbers since olden days, and have developed various pork dishes. an An old cookbook *Eumsikdimibang* (1670) introduced the method of marinating pork with seasonings, coating it with wheat flour then frying it.

Total weight after cooking	Weight for one serve	Service temperature	Total heating time	Total cooking time	Standard utensil
480 g (4 serves)	120 g(6 pieces)	70~75 ℃	9 min.	1 hour	iron grill

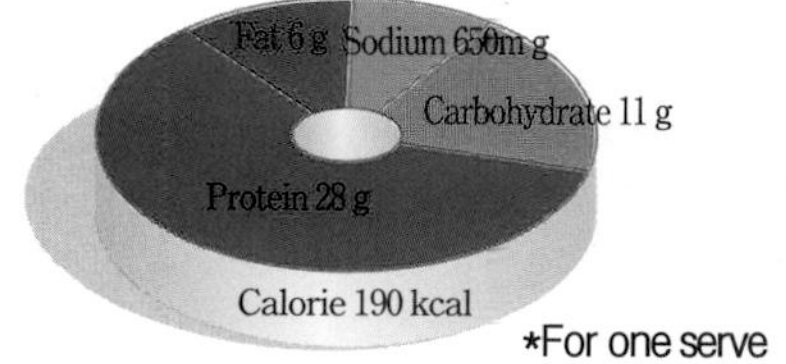

*For one serve

Ingredients & Quantity

550 g pork (fillet)

seasoning① : 8 g (½ tbsp) ginger juice, 15 g (1 tbsp) refined rice wine

seasoning sauce② : 49.5 g (2¾ tbsp) soy sauce, 19 g (1 tbsp) red pepper paste, 14 g (2 tbsp) ground red pepper 24 g (2 tbsp) sugar, 15 g (1 tbsp) refined rice wine, 14 g (2 tbsp) minced green onion 5.5 g (1 tbsp) minced garlic, 0.3 g (⅛ tsp) ground black pepper, 26 g (2 tbsp) sesame oil

13 g (1 tbsp) edible oil

50 g lettuce, 50 g crown daisy

1

Preparation

2

1. Clean blood of the pork with cotton cloths, cut it into 6 cm–wide, 4 cm–long and 0.4 cm–thick (480 g), put narrow slits on both sides. 【Photo 2】
2. Blend seasoning ① and seasoning sauce ②.
3. Trim and wash lettuce and crown daisy (lettuce 45 g, crown daisy 40 g).

3

Recipe

1. Add seasoning ① to the pork, marinate it for 10 min. 【Photo 3】
2. Add ⅔ of seasoning sauce ② to the pork, fumble them by hands to be soaked deeply, and then marinate for 30 min. 【Photo 4】
3. Preheat the grill and oil. Broil the marinated pork on high heat at about 15 cm above the heat for 3 min. for each side. 【Photo 5】
4. Broil it again for 3 min. with over–coating of the seasoning sauce, taking care not to be burnt. 【Photo 6】
5. Layer the lettuce and crown daisy on a dish and place broiled pork.

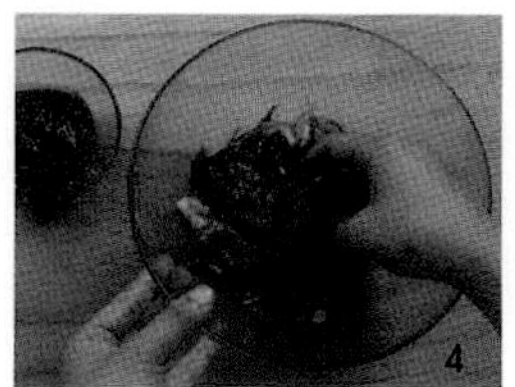
4

5

· Increasing the number of narrow slits would prevent the meat curling up.

· If the pork broiled on too high heat, the surface would be burnt, but inside be rare. Take care adjusting heat level.

Heating Time	Process	Heat Control
Preparation	Preparing pork and vegetables. Blending seasoning sauce	
0 min	Marinating in seasoning sauce Broiling pork Placing broiled pork with vegetables	H–heat 9 min.

6

Bugeo-gui 북어구이

Grilled Dried Pollack

Bugeo-gui is dried pollack that has been soaked then grilled with red pepper paste seasoning. '*Bugeo*' refers to dried pollack. According to Oriental medicine, *bugeo* has a special ability to counteract snake venom and rabies, as well as environmental toxins, and thus, braised *bugeo* or boiled *bugeo* soup is good for the health.

Total weight after cooking	Weight for one serve	Service temperature	Total heating time	Total cooking time	Standard utensil
260 g(4 serves)	65 g	70~75 ℃	5 min.	1 hour	iron grill

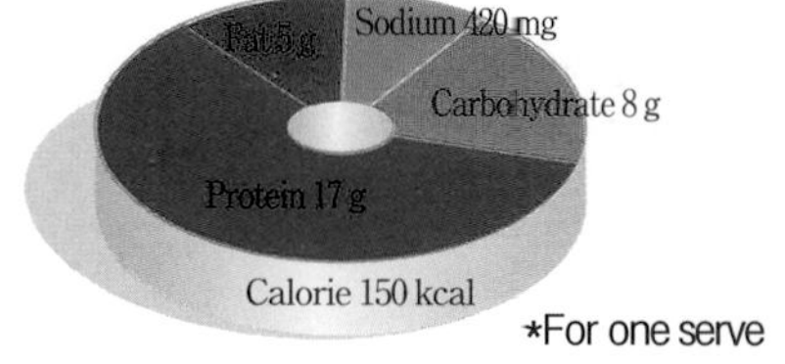

*For one serve

Ingredients & Quantity

140 g (2 bodies) dried pollack (skinned yellowish dried pollack)
sesame soy sauce : 9 g (½ tbsp) soy sauce, 8 g (⅔ tbsp) sesame oil
seasoning sauce : 38 g (2 tbsp) red pepper paste, 6 g (1 tsp) soy sauce, 6 g (½ tbsp) sugar
7 g (½ tbsp) minced green onion, 5.5 g (1 tsp) minced garlic, 2 g (1 tsp) sesame salt
0.3 g (⅛ tsp) ground black pepper, 13 g (1 tbsp) sesame oil
13 g (1 tbsp) edible oil

1

Preparation

1. Remove the head, tail and fins from dried pollack (100 g), soak it in water for 10 sec, wrap it with cotton cloths and let it sit for 30 min. Drain water by pressing, and take the bones and spines out (210 g). 【Photo 2】
2. Cut the soaked pollack into 6 cm-long. Put slits at intervals of 2 cm-wide on the skin side not to be curled up. 【Photo 3】
3. Blend sesame soy sauce and seasoning sauce. 【Photo 4】

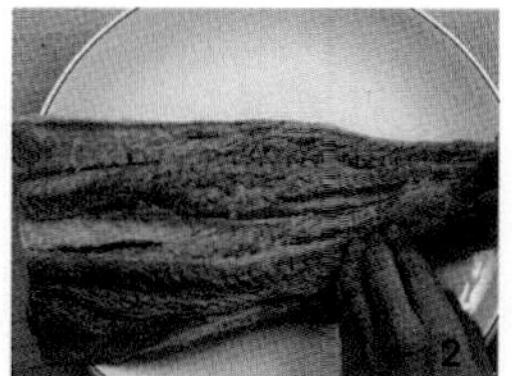
2

3

Recipe

1. Coat the dried pollack with sesame soy sauce.
2. Preheat the grill and oil. First-grill the coated pollack on high heat at about 15 cm above the heat for 1 min. for each side. 【Photo 5】
3. Coat the first-grilled pollack with seasoning sauce and grill on high heat at about 15 cm above the heat for 2 min. for front side and 1 min. after turning over. 【Photo 6】

4

· Red pepper paste seasoning may be replaced by soy sauce seasoning. Or add ground red pepper into the soy sauce.
· Unsplit pollack may be an option.
· Grilled pollack with minced beef or shrimps on one side may serve another good taste.
· Soaking time for dried pollack would be varied upon the dryness.

5

Heating Time	Process	Heat Control
Preparation	Soaking dried pollack and trimming Blending sesame soy sauce and seasoning sauce.	
0 min	First-grilling dried pollack Grilling after coating with seasoning sauce	H-heat 2 min. H-heat 3 min.

6

Jogiyangnyeom-gui 조기양념구이

Seasoned and Broiled Yellow Corvina

Jogiyangnyeom-gui is broiled *jogi* (yellow corvina) coated with red pepper paste seasoning. Dried *jogi* is called "*gulbi*" The taste of *gulbi* is so good that there is an old tale in which a miser, *Jaringobi,* hung one on the ceiling and enjoyed the taste only by glancing at it after every spoon of steamed rice.

Total weight after cooking	Weight for one serve	Service temperature	Total heating time	Total cooking time	Standard utensil
400 g (4 serves)	100 g	70~75 ℃	27 min.	1 hour	iron grill

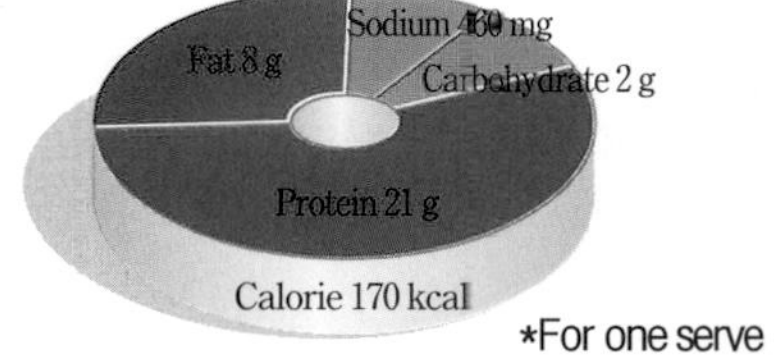

*For one serve

Ingredients & Quantity

500 g (small, 4 bodies) yellow corvina, 2 g (½ tsp) salt
sesame soy sauce : 9 g (½ tbsp) soy sauce, 6.5 g (½ tbsp) sesame oil
seasoning sauce : 6 g (1 tsp) soy sauce, 6 g (½ tbsp), sugar, 57 g (3 tbsp) red pepper paste
4.5 g (1 tsp) minced green onion, 2.8 g (½ tsp) minced garlic, 5.5 g (1 tsp) ginger juice
1 g (½ tsp) sesame salt, 0.1 g ground black pepper, 13 g (1 tbsp) sesame oil
13 g (1 tbsp) edible oil

Preparation

1. Scrape off the scales from yellow corvina and cut off the fins. Take out internal organs through the gill. Wash it cleanly, spread salt on both sides of the body, and marinate it for 30 min. 【Photo 2】
2. Blend sesame soy sauce and seasoning sauce.

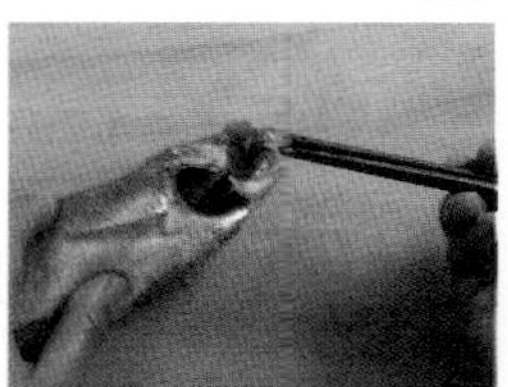

Recipe

1. Put knife slits on the yellow corvina body at intervals of 2 cm−wide. 【Photo 3】
2. Coat them with sesame soy sauce and marinate for 10 min. 【Photo 4】
3. Preheat the iron grill and oil. Broil the yellow corvina roughly, at about 15 cm above the heat, for 4 min. for one side and another 3 min. after turning over. 【Photo 5】
4. When the fish is broiled yellowish, coat them with seasoning sauce. On medium heat, broil it for 10 min. and another 10 min. after turning over, taking care not to be burnt. 【Photo 6】

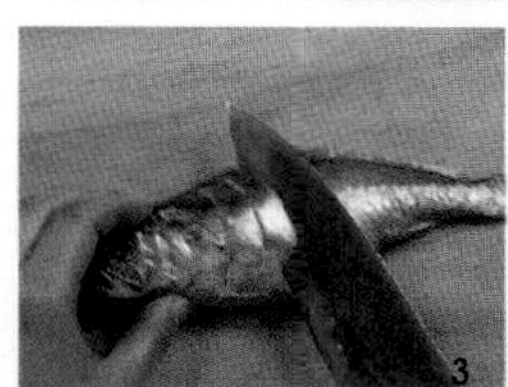

· Do not set the iron grill close to the heat source.

Heating Time	Process	Heat Control
Preparation	Preparing yellow corvina. Blending sesame soy sauce and seasoning sauce Putting slits on the yellow corvina. Marinating in sesame soy sauce	
0 min	First broiling	M−heat 7 min.
10 min	Broiling after coating with seasoned red pepper paste	M−heat 20 min.

Yukwonjeon 육원전

Pan–fried Beef Patties

Yukwonjeon is a dish of ground beef or pork and tofu, shaped into patties then pan–fried. There are two thoughts on how the dish got its name. One is that the name came from the round shape of meat, and the other is from the shape of the patties which is similar to that of an old brass coin.

Total weight after cooking	Weight for one serve	Service temperature	Total heating time	Total cooking time	Standard utensil
300g (4 serves)	75g	75~85℃	5 min.	30 min.	30cm frying pan

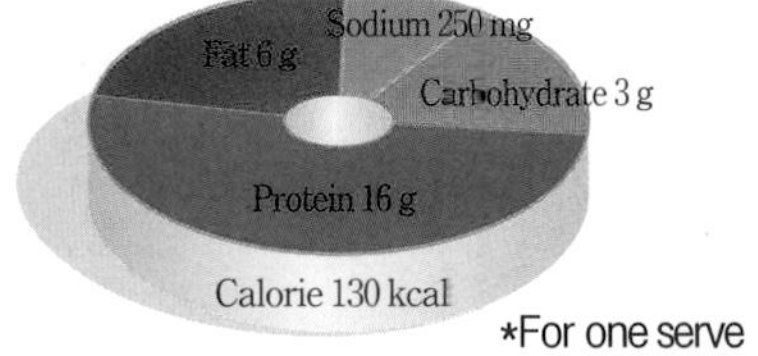

*For one serve

Ingredients & Quantity

200 g beef (top round), 50 g (1/6 cake) tofu

seasoning sauce : 2 g (⅓ tsp) soy sauce, 1 g (¼ tsp) salt, 2 g (½ tsp) sugar
4.5 g (1 tsp) minced green onion, 2.8 g (½ tsp) minced garlic

21 g (3 tbsp) wheat flour, 120 g (2 ea) egg

39 g (3 tbsp) edible oil

vinegar soy sauce: 18 g (1 tbsp) soy sauce, 15 g (1 tbsp) vinegar, 15 g (1 tbsp) water

Preparation

1. Clean blood of beef with cotton cloths and mince it.
2. Wrap the tofu with cotton cloths, squeeze water out and mash. 【Photo 2】
3. Put the beef and tofu together, add seasoning sauce, mix it by fumbling with hands (300 g). Then shape round and flat patties into 4 cm-diameter and 0.5 cm-thick. 【Photos 3 & 4】
4. Beat eggs.
5. Blend vinegar soy sauce.

Recipe

1. Coat patties with wheat flour and dip in beaten egg. 【Photo 5】
2. Preheat the frying pan, oil, and panfry patties on medium heat for 3 min. and another 2 min. after turn over. 【Photo 6】
3. Serve with vinegar soy sauce.

· When the meat and tofu kneaded together strongly, the surface of fried patties may be clean and smooth.
· Coat dumplings with plentiful flour, shake off the flour and dip in the egg water. Then the surface of the fried patties may be more clean and less-oily.

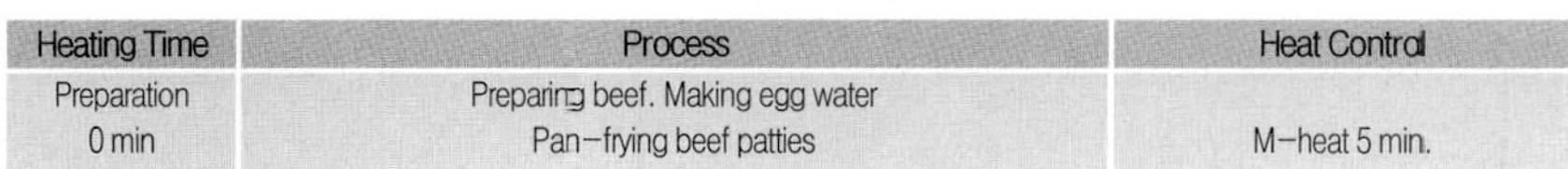

Heating Time	Process	Heat Control
Preparation 0 min	Preparing beef. Making egg water Pan-frying beef patties	 M-heat 5 min.

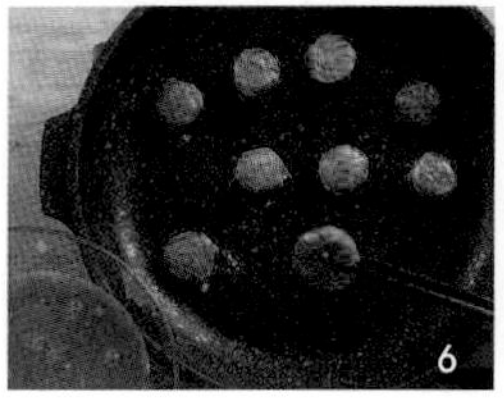

Saengseonjeon 생선전

Pan-fried Fish Fillet

Saengseonjeon is a dish of white fish fillets that are coated with wheat flour and egg wash then pan-fried. Fish used for *saengseonjeon* are white-flesh fish such as croaker, frozen pollack, sea bream and gray mullet. *Saengseonjeon* may also be called '*jeonyueo*', (oil-fried fish) or '*jeonyuhwa*' (oil-fried flower) for its beauty.

Total weight after cooking	Weight for one serve	Service temperature	Total heating time	Total cooking time	Standard utensil
300 g (4 serves)	75 g	75~85 ℃	4 min.	30 min.	30 cm frying pan

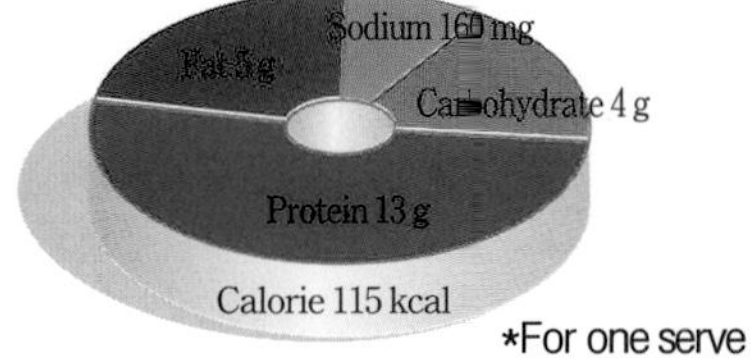

*For one serve

Ingredients & Quantity

300 g white fillet fish (frozen pollack), 1 g (¼ tsp) salt, 0.3 g (⅛ tsp) ground white pepper
21 g (3 tbsp) wheat flour, 120 g (2 ea) egg, 26 g (2 tbsp) edible oil
vinegar soy sauce : 18 g (1 tbsp) soy sauce, 15 g (1 tbsp) vinegar, 15 g (1 tbsp) water

Preparation

1. Trim and wash the fish, slice the flesh from both sides. Peel the skin and slice white fish flesh into 6 cm–wide, 5 cm–long and 0.5 cm–thick. 【Photo 2】
2. Sprinkle salt and ground white pepper on the fish fillet, let it sit for 10 min. and pot dry with cotton cloths (240 g). 【Photo 3】
3. Beat eggs.
4. Blend vinegar soy sauce.

Recipe

1. Coat sliced fish fillet with wheat flour and dip in beaten egg. 【Photos 4 & 5】
2. Preheat the frying pan and oil. Panfry the fish on medium heat for 2 min. and another 2 min. after turn over. 【Photo 6】
3. Serve with vinegar soy sauce.

· If the fish fillet is fried on too high heat, it will be burnt, if fried on too low heat, it will absorb too much oil, the coating will be easily off and mess the surface. Fry it on medium heat to be cooked into yellowish.
· The white flesh fish–such as croaker, flatfish and codfish may be cooked in same way.

Heating Time	Process	Heat Control
Preparation 0 min	Preparing fish. Making egg water Pan–frying fish fillet	 M–heat 4 min.

Haemul-pajeon 해물파전

Seafood Green Onion Pancake

Haemul-pajeon is a savory pancake with plenty of green onion and seafood coated with mushy dough and beaten egg on top. *Haemul-pajeon* is a well-harmonized dish that is studded with soft green onions and tasty seafood. *Dongnae-pajeon* is a famous dish from the city of *Busan*.

Total weight after cooking	Weight for one serve	Service temperature	Total heating time	Total cooking time	Standard utensil
400 g (4 serves)	100 g	75~85 ℃	8 min.	30 min.	30 cm frying pan

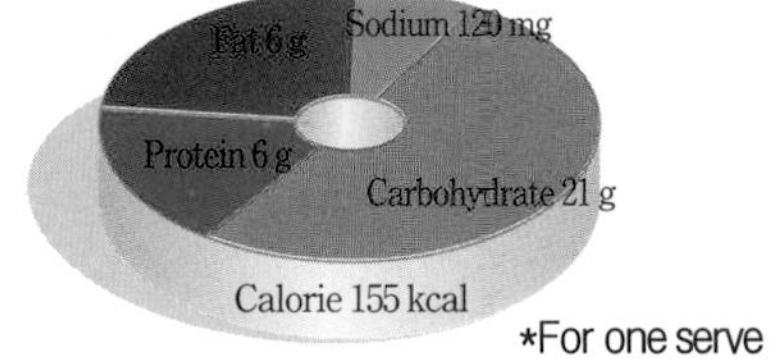

*For one serve

Ingredients & Quantity

100 g mussel flesh, 70 g clam flesh, 70 g oyster : 1 kg (5 cups) water, 2 g (½ tsp) salt
seasonings : 4 g (1 tsp) salt, 0.3 g (⅛ tsp) ground black pepper
200 g small green onion, 10 g (1 ea) green pepper, 15 g (1 ea) red pepper
dough : 95 g (1 cup) wheat flour, 30 g (⅓ cup) non–glutinous rice powder, 1 g (¼ tsp) salt, 200 g (1 cup) water
60 g (1 ea) egg
85 g (½ cup) edible oil
vinegar soy sauce : 18 g (1 tbsp) soy sauce, 15 g (1 tbsp) vinegar, 15 g (1 tbsp) water

1

Preparation

1. Wash seafoods in salt water softly and drain water on a strainer (190 g). Shred them into 1 cm–wide, season with salt and ground black pepper, then let it sit for 10 min. [Photo 2]
2. Cut the green/red pepper into 2 cm–long and 0.3 cm–thick diagonally and seed. Trim and wash small green onion, cut into 10 cm–long (150 g). [Photo 3]
3. Add non–glutinous rice powder, salt and water to the wheat flour, then mix thoroughly (270 g). [Photo 4]
4. Beat egg.
5. Blend vinegar soy sauce.

2

3

4

Recipe

1. Preheat the frying pan and oil. On medium heat, put half ladle of dough on the pan. [Photo 5]
2. Place small green onion on the dough and add prepared seafoods, green/red pepper on it. Spread out another half ladle of dough on it, and spread 2~3 tbsp of beaten egg over it. [Photo 6]
3. On medium heat, panfry for 5 min. When bottom is well–done, turn over, cover the lid, fry for another 3 min.
4. Serve with vinegar soy sauce.

5

6

· For 'Dongrae' green onion pancake, non–glutinous rice powder or glutinous rice powder with anchovies soup may be added into the dough.
· Beaten egg may be an option upon the taste.

Heating Time	Process	Heat Control
Preparation	Preparing seafoods. Trimming small green onion. Kneading wheat flour. Blending vinegar soy sauce	
0 min	Pan–frying seafood green onion pancake	M–heat 5 min. M–heat 3 min.

Bindaetteok 빈대떡

Mung Bean Pancake

Bindaetteok is a savory pancake made of ground mung beans, meat, vegetables and Kimchi. It was originally used as the supporter for the oil-fried meat on a large dining table. Later, it became a delicious-looking food for a *binja* (pauper), so it was named '*binjatteok*' (pauper's cake).

Total weight after cooking	Weight for one serve	Service temperature	Total heating time	Total cooking time	Standard utensil
340 g(4 serves)	85 g	75~85 ℃	11 min.	over 5 hours	18 cm pot, 30 cm frying pan

Fat 7 g
Sodium 35 mg
Protein 6 g
Carbohydrate 13 g
Calorie 140 kcal

*For one serve

Ingredients & Quantity

90 g (½ cups) thin skin mung bean (geopi-nokdu), 1 g (¼ tsp) salt, 110 g water
40 g cabbage Kimchi
20 g soaked bracken, 30 g minced pork
seasoning sauce : 3 g (½ tsp) soy sauce, 4.5 g (1 tsp) minced green onion, 2.8 g (½ tsp) minced garlic
0.1 g ground black pepper, 2 g (½ tsp) sesame oil
mung bean sprouts 50 g, 600 g (3 cups) water, 2 g (½ tsp) salt
mung bean seasoning : 0.5 g (⅛ tsp) salt, 2 g (½ tsp) sesame oil
5 g (⅓ ea) green pepper, 5 g (¼ ea) red pepper
26 g (2 tbsp) edible oil
vinegar soy sauce : 18 g (1 tbsp) soy sauce, 15 g (1 tbsp) vinegar, 15 g (1 tbsp) water

Preparation

1. Wash the thin skin mung bean (geopi-nokdu) cleanly, soak it in water for 8 hours, skin by rubbing with hands, drain water on a strainer (167 g).
2. Remove inside stuffs from the cabbage Kimchi, squeeze out Kimchi juice, cut the Kimchi into 1 cm-long (25 g).
3. Remove the tough area of the soaked bracken, cut into 2 cm-long, mix them with pork and season with seasoning sauce. Remove the tails of mung bean sprouts, wash cleanly. 【Photo 2】
4. Cut the green/red pepper into 1 cm-long and 0.2 cm-thick diagonally, and seed by shaking.
5. Blend vinegar soy sauce.

Recipe

1. Put the soaked mung bean and water into the grinder, grind them for 1 min., season with salt (270 g). 【Photo 3】
2. Pour water into the pot, heat it up for 3 min. on high heat. When it boils, scald mung bean sprouts with salt for 2 min. (35 g). Cut them into 2 cm-long, season with mung bean seasoning. Mix them with cabbage Kimchi, bracken and pork together (123 g). 【Photo 4】
3. Preheat the frying pan and oil. On medium heat, make a round disk with ground mung bean into 5~6 cm diameter, and put the seasoned vegetables and pork on it. 【Photo 5】
4. Add 18 g (1 tbsp) of ground mung bean over it, and top with green/red pepper. Panfry front side for 4 min. and 2 min. after turning over into yellowish pancake. Serve with vinegar soy sauce. 【Photo 6】

· Non-glutinous rice or glutinous rice may be add to the soaked mung bean during grinding.
· It is an option to fry all stuffs together after mixing
· The size of the pancake is an optional.

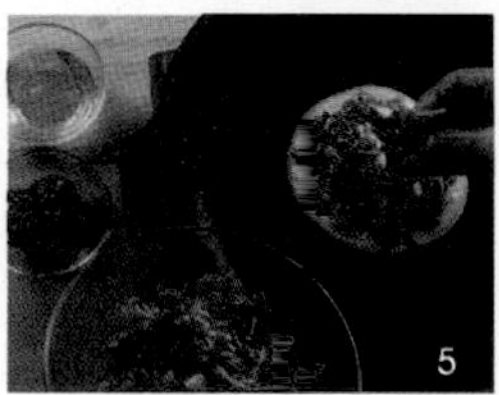

Heating Time	Process	Heat Control
Preparation	Soaking mung bean and cleaning. Preparing garnish. Blending vinegar soy sauce.	
0 min	Grinding mung bean. Scalding mung bean sprouts Mixing vegetables and pork	H-heat 5 min.
10 min	Pan-frying pancake	M-heat 6 min.

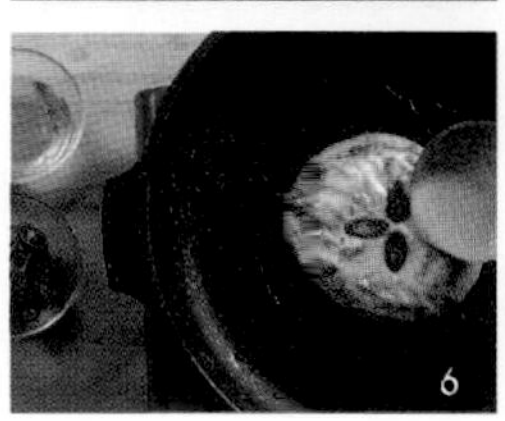

Hobakjeon 호박전

Pan-fried Summer Squash

Hobakjeon is a dish of pre-marinated summer squash that is coated with wheat flour and egg wash then pan-fried. It may also be fried with meat stuffing. In olden days, *hobakjeon* was fried with no coating or only wheat flour coating.

Total weight after cooking	Weight for one serve	Service temperature	Total heating time	Total cooking time	Standard utensil
280 g(4 serves)	70 g(5 ea)	75~85 ℃	3 min.	30 min.	30 cm frying pan

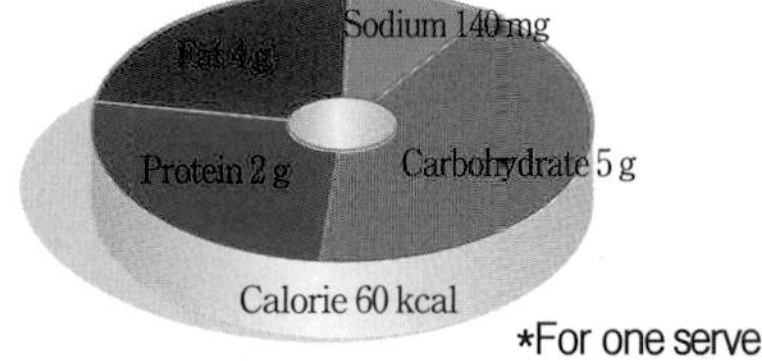

*For one serve

Ingredients & Quantity

300 g (medium 1 ea) summer squash, 2 g (½ tsp) salt
5 g (⅓ ea) green pepper, 5 g (¼ ea) red pepper
28 g (4 tbsp) wheat flour, 120 g (2 ea) egg, 0.5 g (⅛ tsp) salt
39 g (3 tbsp) edible oil
vinegar soy sauce :18 g (1 tbsp) soy sauce, 15 g (1 tbsp) vinegar, 15 g (1 tbsp) water

1

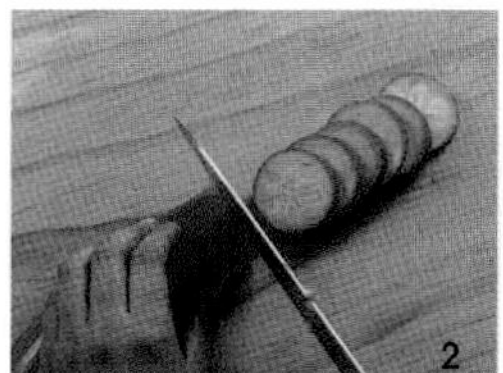
2

Preparation

1. Wash the summer squash cleanly, slice it into 0.6 cm–thick. 【Photo 2】
2. Marinate the squash with salt for 10 min. and pot dry (260 g). 【Photo 3】
3. Cut the green/red pepper into 0.1cm–thick roundly and seed by shaking (green pepper 4 g, red pepper 4 g).
4. Beat egg and mix with salt.
5. Blend vinegar soy sauce.

3

Recipe

1. Coat the squash slices with wheat flour and beaten egg. 【Photo 4】
2. Preheat the frying pan and oil, set the heat to medium and panfry the squash slices for 2 min. 【Photo 5】
3. When bottom side is well–done, turn over, garnish with the green/red pepper, fry for 1 min. 【Photo 6】
4. Serve with vinegar soy sauce.

· Pay attention to control the heat. If the heat is too high, squash may be burnt, but too low, absorb oil too much.

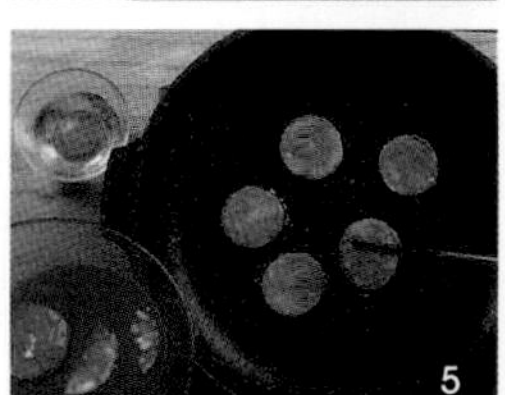
5

Heating Time	Process	Heat Control
Preparation 0 min	Marinating pumpkin. Trimming green/red pepper. Pan–frying summer squash Pan–frying after garnishing	 M–heat 2 min. M–heat 1 min.

6

Hwayangjeok 화양적

Beef and Vegetables Brochette

Hwayangjeok is a dish made of boiled beef and ingredients in five colors such as seasoned bellflower roots, brown oak mushrooms, carrots, cucumbers and eggs that are then skewered. There are many different kinds of *jeok* depending on the ingredients.

Total weight after cooking	Weight for one serve	Service temperature	Total heating time	Total cooking time	Standard utensil
220 g(4 serves)	55 g(2 ea)	75~85 ℃	13 min.	1 hour	18 cm pot, 30 cm frying pan

Fat 3.5 g
Sodium 2[illegible]0 mg
Carbohydrate 5 g
Protein 5 g
Calorie 70 kcal

*For one serve

Ingredients & Quantity

100 g beef (top round), 15 g (3 sheets) brown oak mushrooms
seasoning sauce : 18 g (1 tbsp) soy sauce, 6 g (½ tbsp) sugar, 2.3 g (½ tsp) minced green onion, 1.4 g (¼ tsp) minced garlic, 1 g (½ tsp) sesame salt, 0.3 g (⅛ tsp) ground black pepper, 6.5 g (½ tbsp) sesame oil
100 g skinned bellflower roots, 2 g (½ tsp) salt
50 g (½ ea) carrot, 2 g (½ tsp) salt, 200 g (1 cup) water
100 g (½ ea) cucumber, 1 g (¼ tsp) salt
180 g (3 ea) egg, 1 g (¼ tsp) salt
26 g (1 tbsp) edible oil
pine nuts juice : 9 g (1 tbsp) pine nuts powder, 23 g (1½ tbsp) broth, 1 g (¼ tsp) salt
8 pieces skewers

1

Preparation

1. Clean blood of beef with cotton cloths, slice it into 7 cm-wide/long and 0.5 cm-thick, chop them slightly, season with ⅔ of seasoning sauce.
2. Soak mushrooms in water for 1 hour, remove the stems, wipe water with cotton cloths (35 g). Shred into 1 cm-wide and season with the remained ⅓ of seasoning sauce. 【Photo 2】
3. Wash the bellflower roots cleanly and cut into 1 cm-wide, 0.6 cm-thick and 6 cm-long (38 g). Marinate with salt for 5 min.
4. Wash carrot and cucumber and cut them into same size of bellflower roots (carrot 30 g, cucumber 32 g). Marinate cucumber with salt for 2 min. wipe water off.
5. Panfry eggs into 0.5 cm-thick for yellow/white egg garnish, and cut into 1 cm-wide and 6 cm-long. 【Photo 3】
6. Blend pine nuts juice.

2

3

Recipe

1. Pour water in the pot and heat it up for 2 min. on high heat. When it boils, add salt, then scald bellflower roots and carrot respectively for 1 min. each. 【Photo 4】
2. Preheat the frying pan and oil, stir-fry bellflower roots, carrot and cucumber respectively for 1 min. each, on high heat. 【Photo 5】
3. Preheat the frying pan, lower the heat to medium, fry beef for 4 min. for each side, cut into 1 cm-wide and 6 cm-long.
4. Preheat the frying pan and oil, stir-fry brown oak mushrooms for 2 min. on medium heat.
5. Skewer prepared stuffs, matching color. Place them on a dish roundly and draw a line with pine nuts juice on it. 【Photo 6】

4

5

· After frying, vegetables should be spreaded out on a dish and cool to prevent discoloration.
· Pine nuts powder may be sprinkled instead of pine nuts juice.

Heating Time	Process	Heat Control
Preparation 0 min	Trimming beef, mushrooms and vegetables	
	Scalding bellflower roots and carrot	H-heat 4 min.
	Stir-frying bellflower roots, carrot and cucumber	H-heat 3 min.
	Pan-frying beef and brown oak mushrooms	M-heat 6 min.
10 min	Skewering and placing on a dish	

Minari-ganghoe 미나리강회

Minari Bundles with Meat

Minari-ganghoe is a dish of pressed meat, red pepper, and egg white and yolk garnish tied into bundles with blanched *minari* (Korean watercress). It is served with a vinegar red pepper paste sauce. *Minari-ganghoe* has a beautiful presentation. It best served in the spring when the *minari* is new and tender.

Total weight after cooking	Weight for one serve	Service temperature	Total heating time	Total cooking time	Standard utensil
120 g (4 serves)	30 g	4~10 ℃	50 min.	2 hours	20 ㎝ pot, 30 ㎝ frying pan

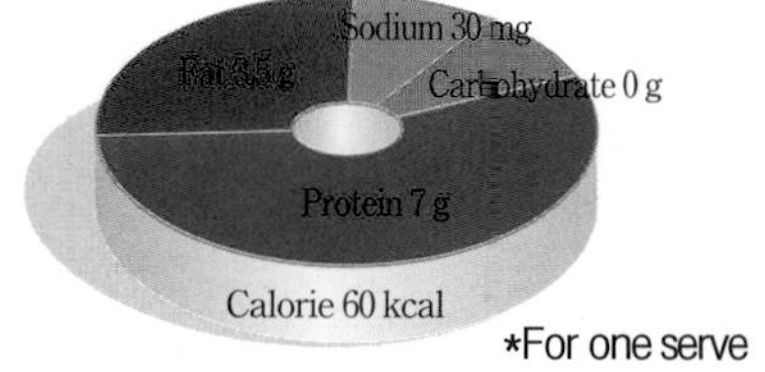

*For one serve

Ingredients & Quantity

120 g beef (top round), 1.2 ㎏ (6 cups) water
50 g watercress (minari), 600 g (3 cups) water, 6 g (½ tbsp) salt
10 g (½ ea) red pepper
120 g (2 ea) egg
13 g (1 tbsp) edible oil
vinegar red pepper paste : 38 g (2 tbsp) red pepper paste, 15 g (1 tbsp) vinegar, 6 g (½ tbsp) sugar

Preparation

1. Clean blood of beef with cotton cloths.
2. Pour water into the pot, heat it up for 6 min. on high heat. When it boils, lower the heat to medium, put the beef, simmer it for 40 min. Cool it down and slice it into 4 cm-long, 1.2 cm-wide and 0.5 cm-thick. (60 g). 【Photo 2】
3. Remove the leaves of the watercress, wash the stalks cleanly (26 g). 【Photo 3】
4. Panfry egg into 0.3 cm-thick for garnish, cut it into 1.2 cm-wide and 4 cm-long (27 g each).
5. Cut the red pepper into 3 cm-long and 0.3 cm-wide (8 g). 【Photo 4】
6. Blend vinegar red pepper paste.

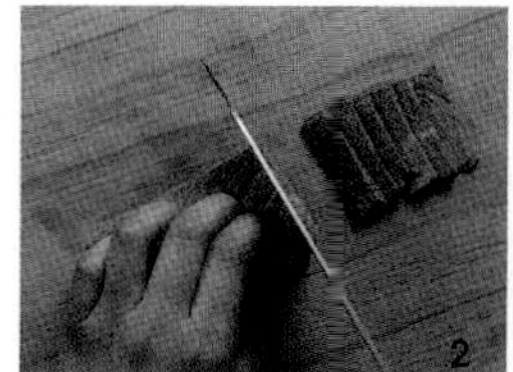

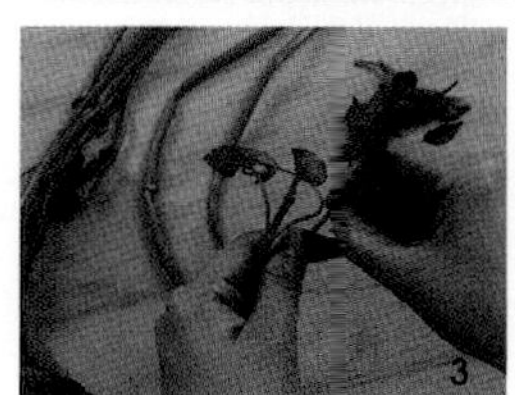

Recipe

1. Pour water into the pot, heat it up for 3 min on high heat. When it boils, scald watercress with salt for 30 sec. maintaining green color. Rinse in water, cut them into 15 cm-long. 【Photo 5】
2. Layer the beef slices, egg garnish and red pepper, bind them in the middle with two turns of watercress. 【Photo 6】
3. Serve with vinegar red pepper paste.

· Slice the boiled beef after cool down, or it may become brittle.
· If the scalded watercress stalks are large, halve them.

Heating Time	Process	Heat Control
Preparation	Preparing beef. Preparing watercress and red pepper Pan-frying egg garnish. Blending vinegar red pepper paste	
0 min	Simmering beef	H-heat 6 min. M-heat 40 min.
40 min	Scalding watercress. Making watercress (minari) bundles	H-heat 3 min. and 30 sec.

Eochae 어채

Parboiled Sliced Fish Fillet and Shell Fish

Eochae is a dish of parboiled white fish fillets and vegetables with starch coating that are color-coordinated and placed around a dish. It is served with a vinegar red pepper paste sauce. Because it is a chilled dish, milder white flesh fish, such as gray mullet or croaker, should be used.

Total weight after cooking	Weight for one serve	Service temperature	Total heating time	Total cooking time	Standard utensil
280 g (4 serves)	70 g	4~10 ℃	8 min.	2 hours	20 cm pot

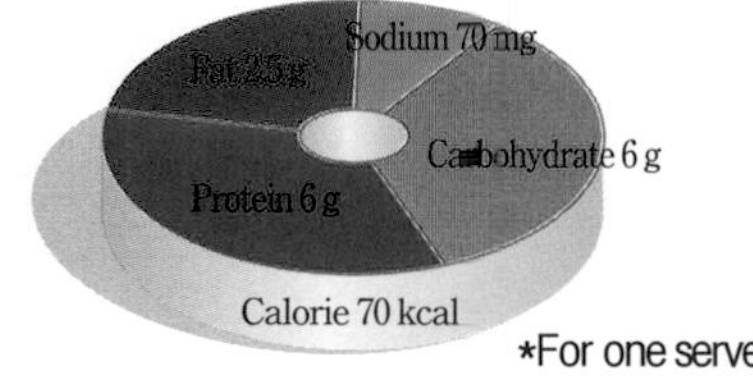

*For one serve

Ingredients & Quantity

300 g (½ body) croaker, 1 g (¼ tsp) salt, 0.3 g (⅛ tsp) ground white pepper
50 g (¼ ea) cucumber, 20 g (1 ea) red pepper, 15 g (3 sheets) brown oak mushrooms, 2 g stone mushrooms
30 g mung bean starch
60 g (1 ea) egg
5 g (½ tbsp) pine nuts
1 kg (5 cups) water
vinegar red pepper paste : 38 g (2 tbsp) red pepper paste, 15 g (1 tbsp) vinegar, 6 g (½ tbsp) sugar

Preparation

1. Remove the scales of croaker and wash. Slice fillets from both sides of the croaker, peel the skin off. Wipe water with cotton cloths, cut them into 3 cm-wide, 5 cm-long and 0.3 cm-thick (170 g). Marinate them with salt and ground white pepper for 10 min. 【Photo 2】
2. Wash cucumber cleanly and cut into 4 cm-long. Then cut them into 1.5~2 cm-wide, 4 cm-long and 0.5 cm-thick (35 g).
3. Wash the red pepper and halve it lengthwise. Seed and cut into same size of cucumber (10 g).
4. Soak mushrooms in water for 1 hour, remove stems of brown oak mushrooms, wipe water with cotton cloths (17 g). Wash stone mushrooms by rubbing, remove belly button, wipe water with cotton cloths, cut it into same size of cucumber.
5. Panfry egg for garnish strips, cut into same size of cucumber. 【Photo 3】
6. Remove tops of the pine nuts and wipe the nuts with dry cotton cloths.
7. Blend vinegar red pepper paste.

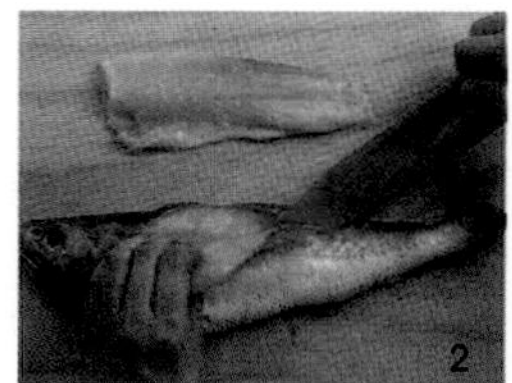

Recipe

1. Mix cucumber, red pepper, brown oak mushrooms, stone mushrooms and croaker slices with mung bean starch thoroughly. 【Photo 4】
2. Pour water into the pot, heat it up for 5 min. on high heat. When it boils, scald cucumber, red pepper, brown oak mushrooms and stone mushrooms for 30 sec. respectively. When the starch become clear, take them out, cool them down in water, and drain. Scald the slices of croaker for 1min. When the starch become clear, take them out, cool them down in water, and drain (190 g). 【Photo 5】
3. Place the croaker slices, cucumber, red pepper, brown oak mushrooms and stone mushrooms on a dish roundly, top with pine nuts in the center. 【Photo 6】
4. Serve with vinegar red pepper paste.

· White flesh, such as sea bream and flat fish are recommendable for this dish.

Heating Time	Process	Heat Control
Preparation	Preparing croaker, vegetables, pine nuts. Pan-frying egg for garnish. Blending vinegar red pepper paste	
0 min	Coating vegetables, croaker slices with starch Scalding vegetables and croaker slices	H-heat 8 min.
10 min	Placing on a dish and topping with pine nuts	

Yangjimeori-Pyeonyuk 양지머리편육

Pressed and Sliced Brisket

Yangjimeori-pyeonyuk is a dish of long-simmered brisket that has been pressed and cut into slices. '*Yangjimeori*' is the meat from ox chest, and "*pyeonyuk*" refers to thin slices of meat.

Total weight after cooking	Weight for one serve	Service temperature	Total heating time	Total cooking time	Standard utensil
280 g(4 serves)	70 g	15~25 ℃	1 hour 39 min.	4 hours	20 cm pot

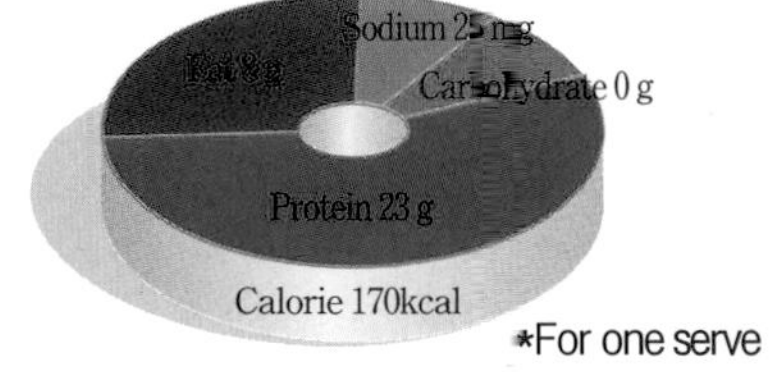

*For one serve

Ingredients & Quantity

600 g beef (brisket), 2 kg (10 cups) water
fragrant seasoning : 45 g green onion, 30 g (6 cloves) garlic, 2 g (½ tsp) salt
vinegar soy sauce : 18 g (1 tbsp) soy sauce, 22.5 g (1½ tbsp) vinegar, 15 g (1 tbsp) water
3 g (½ tbsp) pine nuts powder

Preparation

1. To draw out the blood from the beef, soak it in water for 1 hour, and cut it into 15 cm–wide, 9 cm–long. 【Photo 2】
2. Trim & clean the green onion and garlic.
3. Blend vinegar soy sauce.

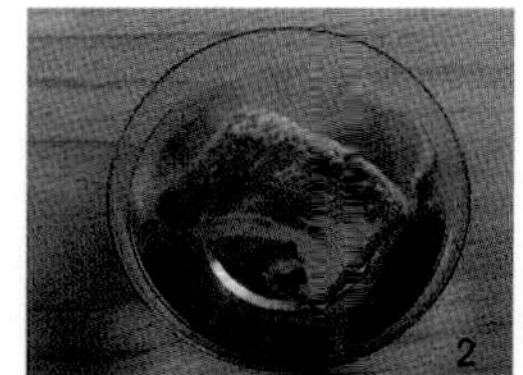

Recipe

1. Pour water in the pot and heat it up for 9 min. on high heat. When it boils, put the brisket, skim off the foam and other residue from the surface. 【Photo 3】
2. Reduce the heat to medium and boil it for 1 hour, add the fragrant seasoning and boil for another 30 min. (350 g). 【Photo 4】
3. When the meat is well–done, take out the meat, wrap it with cotton cloths and press with heavy weight for more than 1 hour to make flat. 【Photo 5】
4. When the meat flatten, cut and slice it into 3 cm–wide, 5 cm–long and 0.3 cm–thick along with the opposite direction of the texture (280 g). Serve it with vinegar soy sauce. 【Photo 6】

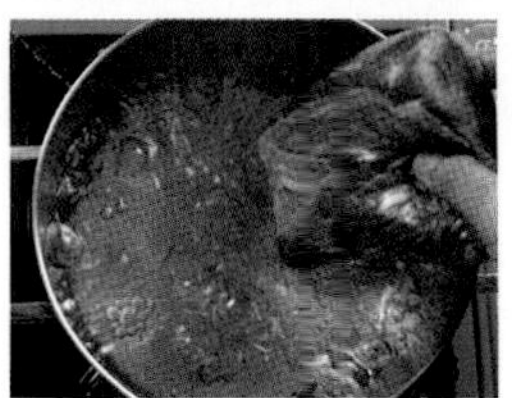

· When cooking a big size meat, bind with thread to help the meat more squared.

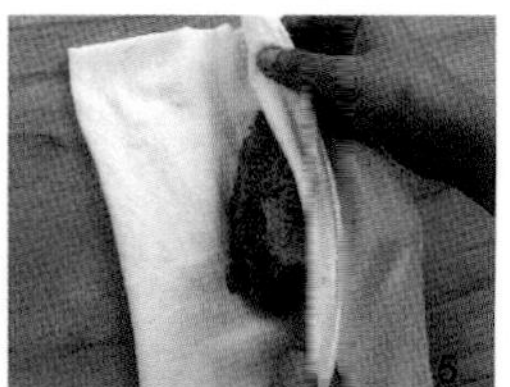

Heating Time	Process	Heat Control
Preparation	Drawing out blood from beef	
0 min	Boiling water	H–heat 9 min.
10 min	Boiling brisket	M–heat 1 hour
70 min	Boiling after adding fragrant seasonings	M–heat 30 min.
100 min	Pressing brisket and cutting	

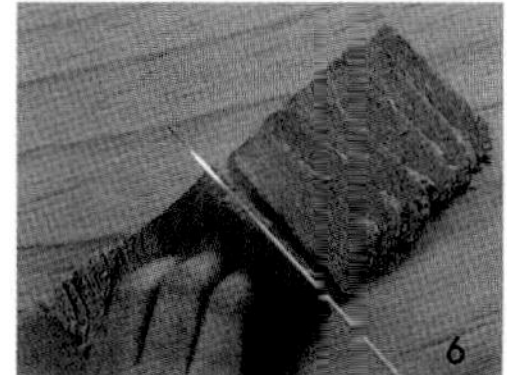

Bugeo-bopuragi 북어보푸라기

Seasoned Dried Pollack Flakes

Bugeo-bopuragi is a dish made of grated dried pollack that is colored and seasoned with soy sauce, ground red pepper and salt. Because *bugeo-bopuragi* is soft, it is often served with porridge, and is good for the elderly and children.

Total weight after cooking	Weight for one serve	Service temperature	Total heating time	Total cooking time	Standard utensil
100 g (4 serves)	25 g	15~25 ℃	0 min.	30 min.	

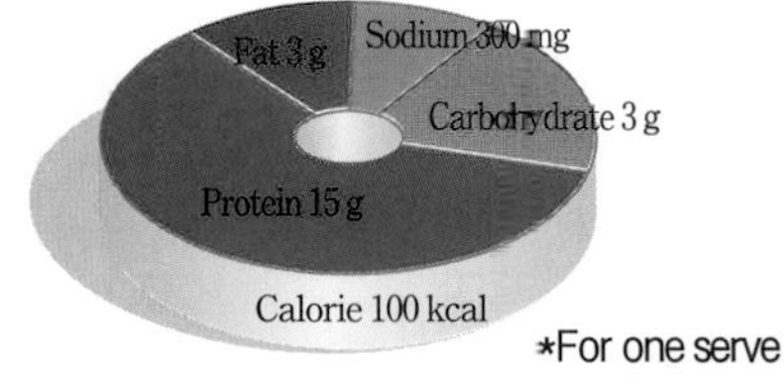

*For one serve

Ingredients & Quantity

70 g (1 body) dried pollack (skinned yellowish dried pollack)

salt seasoning : 1 g (¼ tsp) salt, 4 g (1 tsp) sugar, 1 g (½ tsp) sesame salt, 4 g (1 tsp) sesame oil

red pepper seasoning : 1 g (¼ tsp) salt, 2 g (½ tsp) sugar, 0.5 g (¼ tsp) fine ground red pepper 2 g (1 tsp) sesame salt, 4 g (1 tsp) sesame oil

soy sauce seasoning : 4 g (⅔ tsp) soy sauce, 4 g (1 tsp) sugar, 2 g (1 tsp) sesame salt 2 g (½ tsp) sesame oil

Preparation

1. Remove the head, tail and fins of dried pollack (55 g), wet with water slightly and take out bone and spines. 【Photo 2】

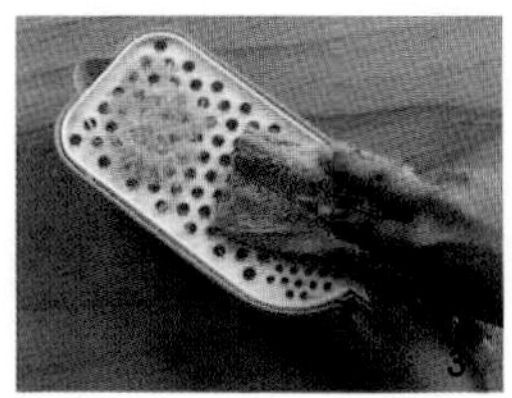

Recipe

1. Grate the dried pollack on a grater (85 g). 【Photo 3】
2. Divide pollack flakes into 3 parts, season each part with each seasonings (salt, red pepper and say sauce) and mix each by hands softly. 【Photos 4 & 5 & 6】

· To make a large volume of pollack flakes, electrical mixer may be used.
· When cooking with an un-spilt pollack, soak it in water. When it is soft enough, pound with wooden mallet and remove bone & spines.
· This is side dish to go with porridge, do not season salty.

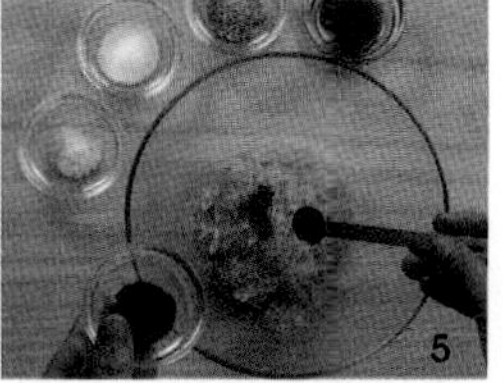

Cooking Time	Process	Heat Control
0 min	Preparing dried pollack	
10 min	Grating dried pollack on grater	
20 min	Seasoning with salt seasoning	
	Seasoning with ground red pepper seasoning	
	Seasoning with soy sauce seasoning	

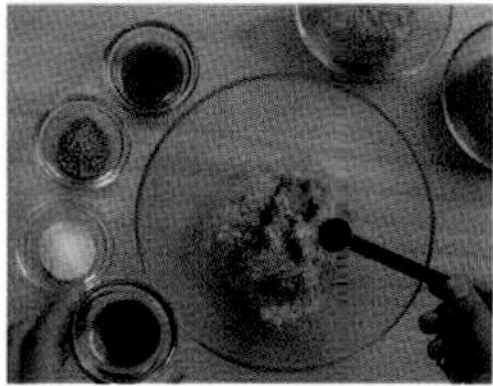

Samhap-janggwa 삼합장과

Three Braised Delicacies

Samhap-janggwa is a dish of three kinds of seafood (mussels, abalone and sea slug) braised with beef and seasonings. Nowadays, the seafood is cooked alive, but in olden days it was dried then cooked after soaking in water because the amino acid and taurine content increases during drying, and it enhances the taste.

Total weight after cooking	Weight for one serve	Service temperature	Total heating time	Total cooking time	Standard utensil
200 g (4 serves)	50 g	15~25 ℃	18 min.	1 hour	18 cm pot

Sodium 410 mg
Fat 3g
Carbohydrate 10 g
Protein 9 g
Calorie 100 kcal
*For one serve

Ingredients & Quantity

160 g abalones, 1 kg (5 cups) water
60 g soaked sea slug
100 g mussel, 600 g (3 cups) water, 8 g (2 tsp) salt, 400 g (2 cups) seafoods scalding water, 2 g (½ tsp) salt
50 g beef (top round)
seasoning sauce : 3 g (½ tsp) soy sauce, 2 g (½ tsp) sugar, 4.5 g (1 tsp) minced green onion
2.8 g (½ tsp) minced garlic, 2 g (1 tsp) sesame salt, 4 g (1 tsp) sesame oil
braising sauce : 27 g (1½ tbsp) soy sauce, 2.8 g (½ tsp) ginger juice, 48 g (2½ tbsp) honey
100 g (½ cup) water
4 g (1 tsp) sesame oil
3.5 g (1 tsp) pine nuts

Preparation

1. Clean the abalones with brush and wash. Take out the flesh and remove entrails. Slice it into 4 cm–wide, 3 cm–long and 0.5 cm–thick, maintaining abalone shape. 【Photo 2 · 3】
2. Wash the soaked sea slug and halve it lengthwise, then cut it into 2.5 cm–square.
3. Cut off the whiskers from the mussel, rinse in salt water softly. 【Photo 4】
4. Clean blood of beef with cotton cloths, cut it into 3 cm–wide/long and 0.3 cm–thick, season with seasoning sauce. 【Photo 5】
5. Prepare pine nuts powder.

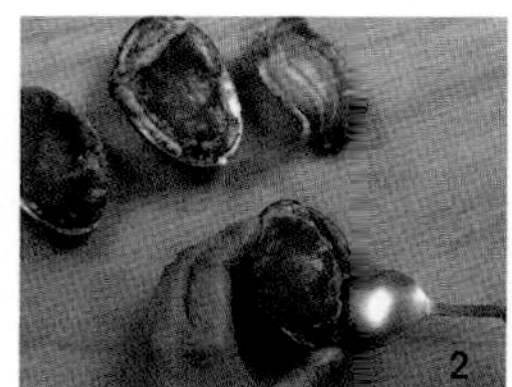

Recipe

1. Pour water into the pot, heat it up for 2 min. on high heat. Scald the abalones, sea slug and mussel for 30 sec. respectively.
2. Put braising sauce into the pot, heat it up for 2 min. on high heat. When it boils, lower the heat to medium, continue to oil it for another 7 min. When the braising sauce is dragged, put the beef and braise for 2 min. Add abalones, sea slug and mussel, braise it for 3 min. with sprinkling broth to set a gloss on. Mix them with sesame oil together. 【Photo 6】
3. Place on a dish and top with pine nuts powder.

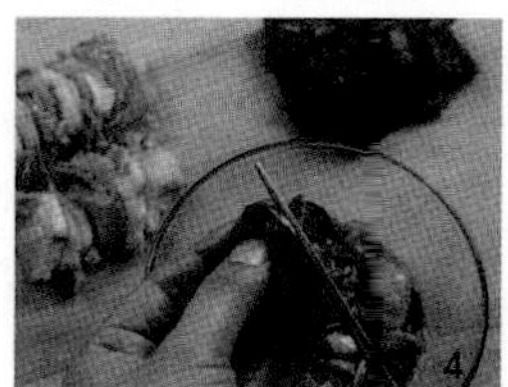

· Braise seafoods on medium heat slowly, or it may become tough.

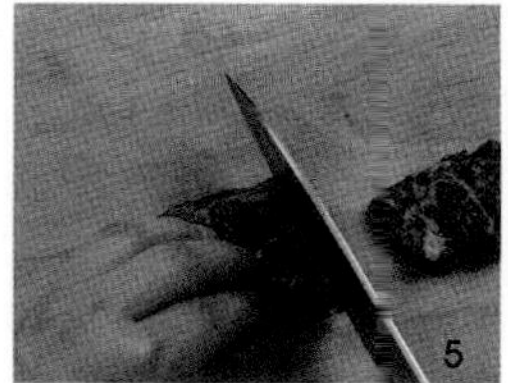

Heating Time	Process	Heat Control
Preparation	Preparing seafoods and beef. Making pine nuts powder	
0 min	Scalding seafoods	H–heat 3 min. and 30 sec.
	Boiling braising sauce	H–heat 2 min. M–heat 7 min.
10 min	Braising after adding beef. Braising after adding seafoods	M–heat 2 min.
	Mixing with sesame oil. Sprinkling pine nuts powder	M–heat 3 min.

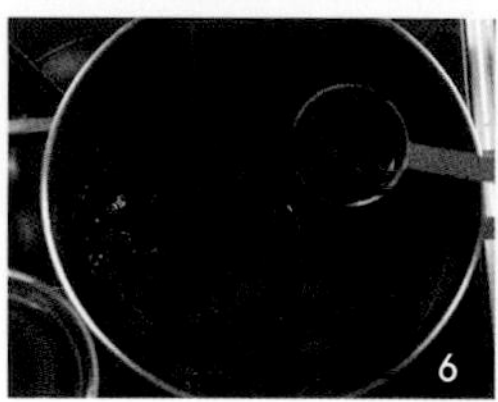

Maneul-jangajji 마늘장아찌

Pickled Garlic

Maneul-jangajji is a pickle of whole garlic heads that are fermented in vinegar or soy sauce. Different kinds of *jangajji* are made by fermenting seasonal ingredients in soy sauce, bean paste, salt-fermented seafood or vinegar. They are served as side dishes. Garlic is a strong, aromatic seasoning. It has been used for medicinal purposes since olden days.

Total weight after cooking	Weight for one serve	Service temperature	Total heating time	Total cooking time	Standard utensil
240 g(12 serves)	20 g	15~25 ℃	4 min.	over 1 month	18 cm pot

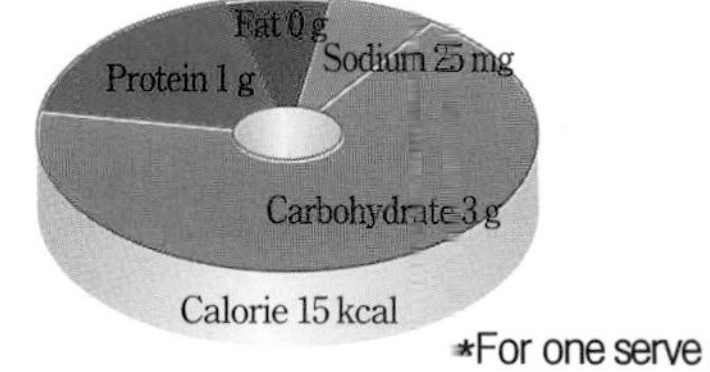

*For one serve

Ingredients & Quantity

300 g (4 heads) whole bulb of garlic, 300 g (1½ cup) water, 150 g (¾ cups) vinegar
seasoning sauce : 36 g (2 tbsp) soy sauce, 36 g (3 tbsp) sugar, 24 g (2 tbsp) salt

Preparation

1. Cut off the roots and stalks of garlic, peel two layer of the skin, wash and drain water on a strainer for 2 hours (275 g). 【Photo 2】

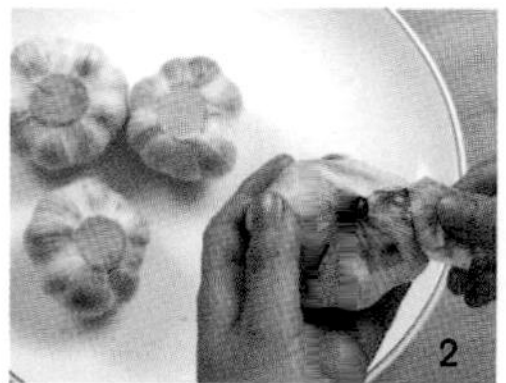

Recipe

1. Put the garlic into a jar, add water and vinegar, ferment it in a cool place for 10 days. 【Photo 3】
2. Filter out the vinegar water into the pot, add seasoning sauce, then heat it up for 3 min. on high heat. When it boils, continue to boil for 1 more minute. 【Photos 4 & 5】
3. Ferment them for 1 month. 【Photo 6】

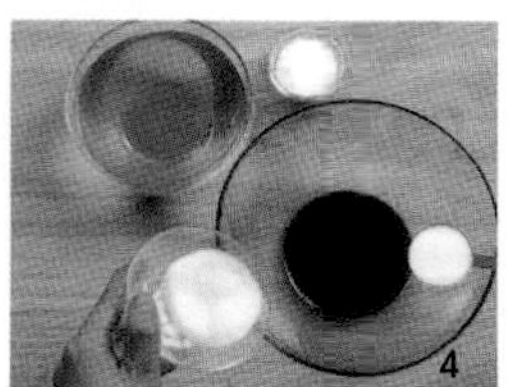

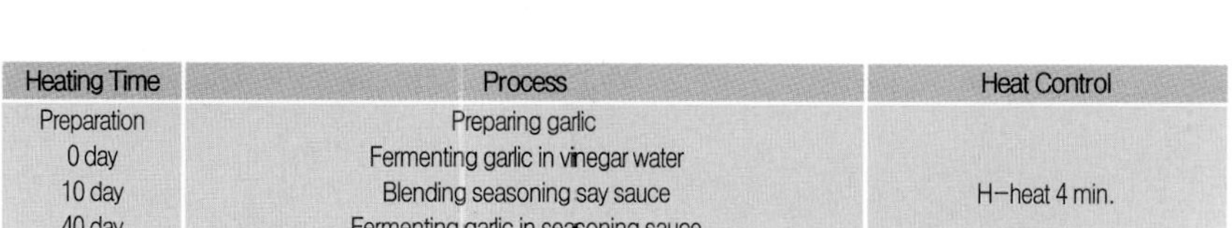

Heating Time	Process	Heat Control
Preparation	Preparing garlic	
0 day	Fermenting garlic in vinegar water	
10 day	Blending seasoning say sauce	H-heat 4 min.
40 day	Fermenting garlic in seasoning sauce	

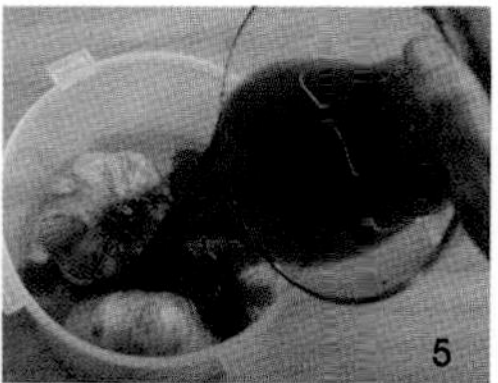

Ojingeojeot 오징어젓

Pickled Squid

Ojingeojeot is a pickle made with thin slivers of squid fermented with salt. Salt–fermented foods have been made since the prehistoric age. There are various kinds of salt–fermented foods with different tastes depending on the ingredients. *Ojingeojeot* is a beloved side dish among Koreans that is high in protein, vitamin and minerals.

Total weight after cooking	Weight for one serve	Service temperature	Total heating time	Total cooking time	Standard utensil
400 g (20 serves)	20 g	4~10 ℃	0 min.	3~4 days	

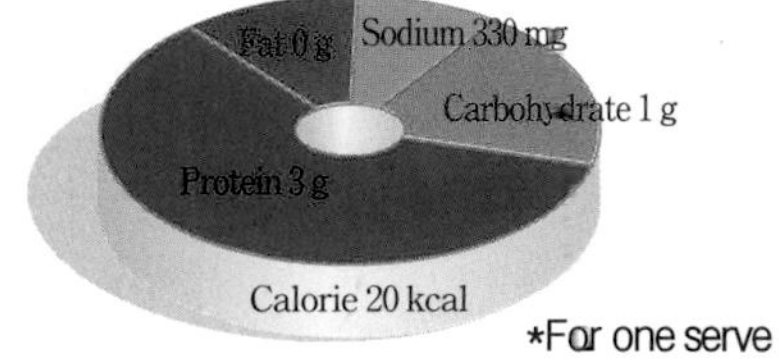

*For one serve

Ingredients & Quantity

500 g (1 body) squid
65 g (¼ cups) salted anchovy juice
21 g (3 tbsp) ground red pepper
30 g (2 ea) green pepper
10 g (½ ea) red pepper
40 g (8 cloves) garlic

Preparation

1. Halve the squid belly lengthwise, remove internal organs and legs (216 g). Skin and wash cleanly. Shred it into 5 cm-long and 0.1 cm-thick. 【Photos 2 & 3】
2. Marinate the squid with salted anchovy juice for 6 hours. 【Photo 4】
3. Cut the green/red pepper into 2 cm-long and 0.3 cm-thick diagonally, seed by shaking.
4. Slice the garlic at intervals of 0.3 cm-thick.

Recipe

1. Mix the marinated squid with ground red pepper thoroughly. 【Photo 5】
2. Add the green/red pepper and garlic to the squid, mix them together evenly. 【Photo 6】
3. Put them into a jar and ferment for 3~4 days.

· Salted anchovy juice may be replaced by salt.
· Shred and salt marinated radish may be added.
· Put sesame oil and sesame seeds just before serving.

Cooking Time	Process	Heat Control
0 min	Preparing squid. Marinating with salted anchovies juice	
360 min	Mix with ground red pepper	
370 min	Adding green/red pepper and garlic	
380 min	Putting into a jar and fermenting	

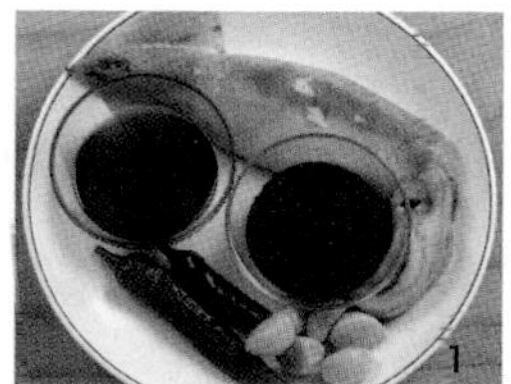

Baechu-kimchi 배추김치

Cabbage Kimchi

Baechu-kimchi is made by fermenting brined Korean cabbage with Korean radish, vegetables, salt-fermented seafood, ground red pepper and various seasonings. Kimchi is a quintessential side dish that is served without fail on dining tables in Korea. Kimchi was approved as an International Standard Food by Codex in 2001. Certain studies have shown a link between Kimchi and cancer prevention.

Total weight after cooking	Weight for one serve	Service temperature	Total heating time	Total cooking time	Standard utensil
4.8 kg (60 serves)	80 g	4~10 ℃	0 min.	over 5 hours	

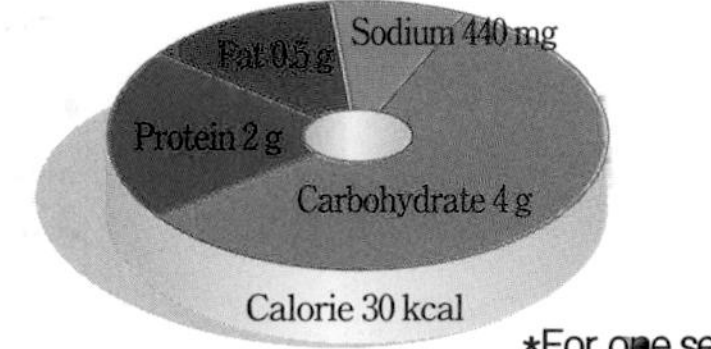

*For one serve

Ingredients & Quantity

4.8 kg (2 heads) Korean cabbage, 700 g (4⅓ cups) coarse salt, 4 kg (20 cups) water
1 kg (1 ea) radish, 100 g watercress, 200 g small green onion, 200 g mustard leaf
200 g (1 cup) oyster : 6 g (½ tbsp) salt, 400 g (2 cups) water
seasonings : 130 g (1⅓ cups) ground red pepper, 100 g (½ cup) salted anchovy juice
100 g salted shrimps, 12 g (1 tbsp) sugar, 200 g green onion, 80 g (5 tbsp) minced garlic
36 g (3 tbsp) minced ginger,
Kimchi liquid : 100 g (½ cup) water, 2 g (½ tsp) salt

Preparation

1. Trim the bottom and outer leaves of the cabbage (4.5 kg), put a deep knife slit lengthwise and split it into two parts by hands, marinate them in salt water in which half (350 g) of the coarse salt dissolved, and spread remained half of the salt in between the petioles. Let it sit cutting side up for 3 hours, and then another 3 hours after turn over. 【Photo 2】
2. Rinse the cabbage under running water for 3~4 times, drain water on a tray for about 1 hour (3.2 kg).
3. Trim and wash the radish, shred into 5 cm−long, 0.3 cm−wide/thick. Trim and wash watercress stalks, small green onion and mustard leaf, cut them into 4 cm−long. (watercress 60g, small green onion 150 g, mustard leaf 150 g). 【Photo 3】
4. Wash the fresh oyster softly in mild salt water and drain.
5. Mince the solid ingredients of salted shrimps finely. Soak ground red pepper in the salted shrimps juice and salted anchovy juice.

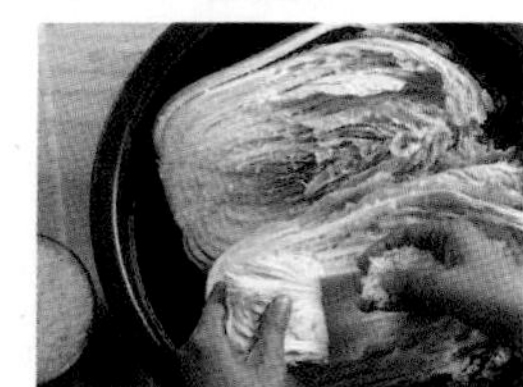

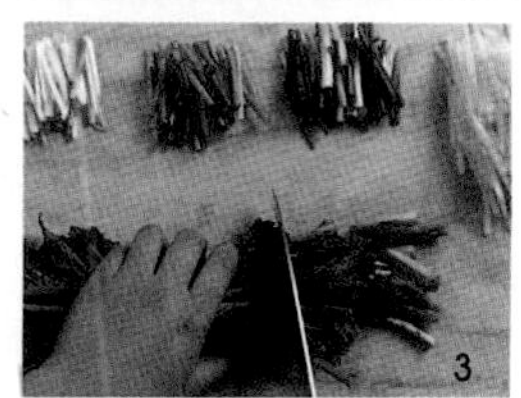

Recipe

1. Add soaked red pepper to the shred radish, mix well, add remained seasonings, and mix well again. Add vegetables and oyster, mix softly and season with salt (1.5 kg). 【Photo 4】
2. Pack the seasonings in between each leaf of the cabbage, fold over the outer leaves to hold the seasonings. 【Photos 5 & 6】
3. Place it in a jar one by one until 70~80 % of the jar filled, cover the top with marinated outer leaves.
4. Make Kimchi liquid by adding some water and salt into the Kimchi mixing container. Then finish by pouring Kimchi liquid into the jar and pressing down.

· For the good taste and better nutrition of the winter cabbage Kimchi, it may be fermented under the ground at 10 ℃ for around 3 weeks.
· Fresh shrimps and/or glue plants may be added into the Kimchi.

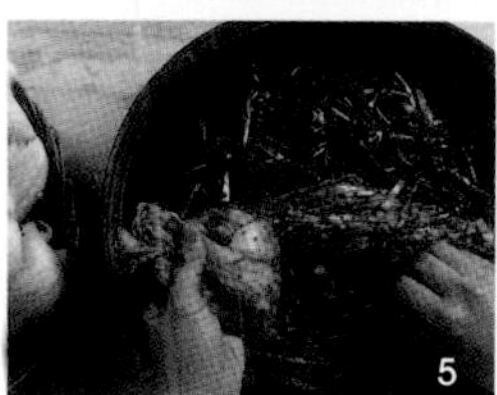

Cooking Time	Process	Heat Control
0 min	Preparing cabbage, vegetables, salted shrimps and fresh oyster	
30 min	Marinating cabbage	
390 min	Washing cabbage and draining water	
460 min	Mixing cabbage Kimchi and placing in a jar	

Baek-kimchi 백김치

White Cabbage Kimchi

Baek-kimchi is a type of Kimchi made of brined Korean cabbage that is fermented with various seasonings and garnishes. It does not contain ground red pepper so it is white in color and not spicy. *Baek-kimchi* cannot be stored for a long period of time due to the absence of ground red pepper as a preservative, but it is preferred by the elderly and others who cannot eat spicy food.

Total weight after cooking	Weight for one serve	Service temperature	Total heating time	Total cooking time	Standard utensil
3.6 kg(45 serves)	80 g	4~10 ℃	17 min.	over 5 hours	16 cm pot

Sodium 800 mg
Fat 1 g
Protein 1 g
Carbohydrate 3 g
Calorie 20 kcal
*For one serve

Ingredients & Quantity

2.4 kg (1 head) Korean cabbage, 2 kg (10 cups) water, 350 g coarse salt
200 g radish, 25 g green mustard leaf, 25 g watercress, 30 g small green onion
250 g (½ ea) pear, 100 g (5 ea) chestnut, 12 g (3 ea) jujube
10 g (2 sheets) brown oak mushrooms, 2 g stone mushrooms, 10 g (1tbsp) pine nuts
15 g (3 cloves) garlic, 5 g ginger, 2 g shred red pepper
50 g salted yellow croaker (young croaker)
10 g (2½ tsp) salt
boiled salted yellow croaker liquid : 20 g salted croaker bone, 100 g (½ cup) water
white Kimchi liquid : 900 g (4½ cups) water, 30 g boiled salted croaker liquid, 12 g (1 tbsp) salt

Preparation

1. Trim the bottom and outer leaves of the cabbage (2.2 kg), cut in half lengthwise and split it into two parts by hands. Marinate it in salt water in which half (175 g) of the coarse salt dissolved, and spread remained half of the salt in between the petioles. Let them sit cutting side up for 3 hours, and then another 3 hours after turn over. Rinse the cabbage under running water for 3~4 times and drain water on a strainer for 1 hour (1.6 kg). 【Photo 2】
2. Trim and wash the radish and shred into 4 cm−long, 0.2 cm−wide (170 g). Trim and wash green mustard leaf, watercress and small green onion, Cut them into same length of the radish (mustard leaf 25 g, watercress 16 g, small green onion 24 g). 【Photo 3】
3. Skin pear and chestnut, shred them into 3 cm−long, 0.2 cm−wide. Wipe jujube with damp cotton cloths, cut the flesh round and shred into 0.2 cm of width (pear 146 g, chestnut 54 g, jujube 9 g).
4. Soak mushrooms in water for 1 hour, remove stems of brown oak mushrooms, wipe with cotton cloths, then shred into 0.2 cm−wide (20 g). Wash the stone mushrooms by rubbing, remove belly buttons, and shred into 0.1 cm−wide (3 g). 【Photo 4】
5. Remove tops of the pine nuts and wipe them with dry cloths.
6. Shred the garlic and ginger into 0.1 cm of width. Cut the shred red pepper into 2~3 cm−long. (garlic 12 g, ginger 4 g).
7. Slice the flesh of salted yellow croaker and leave the head and bone aside (flesh 18 g, bone 32 g).

1

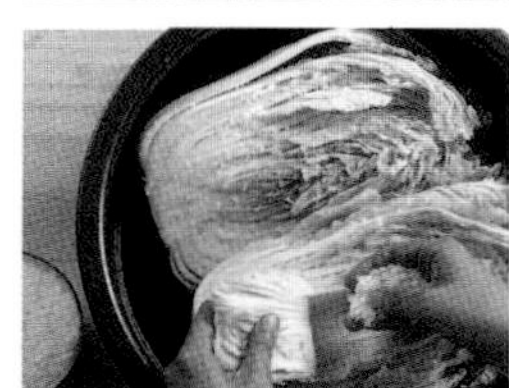
2

3

4

Recipe

1. Put water and the head and bone in the pot, heat it up for 2 min. on high heat. When it boils, reduce the heat to low, boil it for 15 min. then strain and cool down for white Kimchi liquid.
2. Put the sliced croaker flesh into the prepared stuffs and season with salt to make Kimchi filling stuffs. 【Photo 5】
3. Pack the filling stuffs between each leaf of the cabbage, fold over the outer leaves to hold the filling stuffs. Place it in a jar one by one, cover the top with marinated outer leaves and press down. Then add Kimchi liquid just up to the top of the Kimchi. 【Photo 6】

5

6

· Less salty, less spicy Kimchi may spoil easily. The Kimchi should be covered with outer leaves and pressed down everytime when you take some Kimchi out.
· When marinating cabbage, turn over upside down 2~3 times.

Heating Time	Process	Heat Control
Preparation	Marinating cabbage and washing. Soaking mushrooms.	
	Preparing sub stuffs and nuts	
0 min	Boiling salted yellow croaker head and bone	H−heat 2 min. L−heat 15 min.
20 min	Preparing Kimchi filling stuffs.	
	Making white cabbage Kimchi and placing in a jar	

Bossam-kimchi 보쌈김치

Wrapped Kimchi

Bossam-kimchi is brined Korean cabbage stuffed with fruit, seafood, mushrooms, vegetables and various garnishes. *Bossam-kimchi* is made by wrapping the stuffed cabbage with cabbage leaves, and it is also called '*bokimchi.*' It has been popular in the *Gaeseong* area where good quality cabbage was grown in olden days.

Total weight after cooking	Weight for one serve	Service temperature	Total heating time	Total cooking time	Standard utensil
1.68 kg(24 serves)	70 g	4~10 ℃	5 min.	over 5 hours	16cm pot

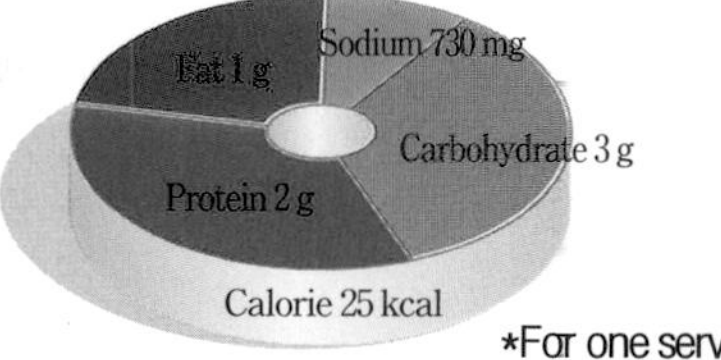

*For one serve

Ingredients & Quantity

2.4 kg (1 head) Korean cabbage, 2 kg (10 cups) water, 350 g coarse salt,
250 g (¼ ea) radish, 125 g (¼ ea) pear, 30 g mustard leaf, 25 g small green onion,
30 g watercress, 25 g green onion
garnish : 10 g (2 sheets) brown oak mushrooms, 3 g stone mushrooms, 30 g (2 ea) chestnut
12 g (3 ea) jujube, 2 g shred red pepper, 10 g (1 tbsp) pine nuts
25 g salted shrimps, 25 g salted yellow corvena (salted young corvena), 200 g(1 cup) water
50 g oyster, 400 g (2 cups) water, 6 g (½ tbsp) salt ,
80 g young octopus, 12 g (1 tbsp) salt
28 g (4 tbsp) ground red pepper
seasoning : 32 g (2 tbsp) minced garlic, 12 g (1 tbsp) minced ginger, 2 g (½ tsp)sugar
12 g (1 tbsp) salt

Preparation

1. Trim the bottom and outer leaves of the cabbage, put a deep knife slit lengthwise and split it into two parts by hands. Marinate it in salt water in which half of the coarse salt dissolved, and spread remained half of the salt in between the petioles. Let it sit cutting side up for 3 hours, and then another 3 hours after turn over.
2. Rinse the marinated cabbage under running water for 3~4 times, drain water on a tray as facing down for 1 hour (2 kg).
3. Cut the cabbage, radish and pear into 2.5 cm-wide, 2.5 cm-long and 0.3 cm-thick. Save outer leaves. (radish 180 g, pear 100 g). Cut the mustard leaf, small green onion, watercress and green onion into 3 cm-long. 【Photos 2 & 3】
4. Soak the mushrooms in water for 1 hour, remove stems of brown oak mushrooms, wipe water with cotton cloths, shred it at intervals of 0.3 cm of width. Remove belly button of stone mushrooms, wash by rubbing, shred it into 3 cm-long and 0.2 cm-wide.
5. Skin the chestnuts and slice it into 0.3 cm-thick. Cut the jujube flesh round, and shred them into the same size of brown oak mushrooms. 【Photo 4】
6. Cut the shred red pepper into 2 cm-long. Remove tops of pine nuts and wipe the nuts with dry cotton cloths.
7. Mince the solid ingredients of the salted shrimps finely.
8. Cut the flesh of the salted yellow corvena, save the heads and bones.
9. Rinse the oyster in salt water, drain water. Wash the young octopus by fumbling with salt, cut into 3cm-long.

1

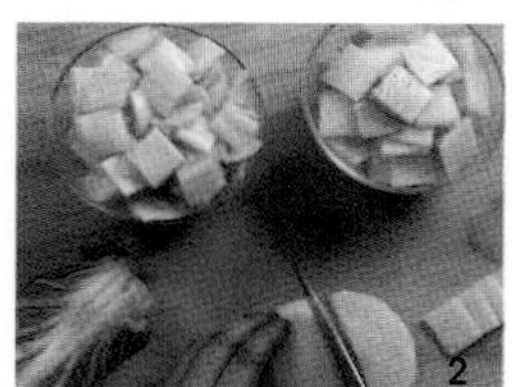
2

3

Recipe

1. Put water and the heads and bones of salted corvena in the pot, boil for 5 min. on medium heat, drain it on a strainer to make corvena liquid (50 g).
2. Mix the shred cabbage and radish with ground red pepper together, add salted shrimps and corvena flesh and seasoning, mix them together thoroughly. Add all the prepared stuffs and mix evenly. Add ⅔ of seafoods into it, mix them softly, then season with salt. 【Photo 5】
3. Put 3~4 sheets of cabbage outer leaves on the bowl. Heap up with the mixed stuffs, place remained ⅓ of seafoods and garnish on it. Roll the outer leaves up and wrap them tightly. 【Photo 6】
4. Put the wrapped kimchi into a jar one by one and press down. Add the boiled corvena liquid into the jar.

4

5

· Discard a few tough outer leaves from cabbage, and use remained leaves as much as possible.
· This wrapped Kimchi has been called as 'Bokimchi' (restorative Kimchi), because wrapped all sorts of delicacies with marinated cabbage and fermented.

6

Heating Time	Process	Heat Control
Preparation	Marinating cabbage. Draining water from cabbage. Cutting stuffs. Cutting garnish. Mincing salted shrimps. Preparing seafoods	
0 min	Boiling salted yellow corvena Mixing Kimchi filling stuffs Making wrapped Kimchi Putting into a jar and pouring Kimchi liquid	M-heat 5 min.

Chonggak-kimchi 총각김치

Whole Radish Kimchi

Chonggak-kimchi is a type of Kimchi made of brined young radishes and their leaves. The word *chonggak-kimchi* came from the name of the young radish, *chonggak-mu*, which looked like the hairstyle of a young boy (*chonggak*) in olden days.

Total weight after cooking	Weight for one serve	Service temperature	Total heating time	Total cooking time	Standard utensil
2.8 kg(40 serves)	70 g	4~10 ℃	5 min.	4 hours	

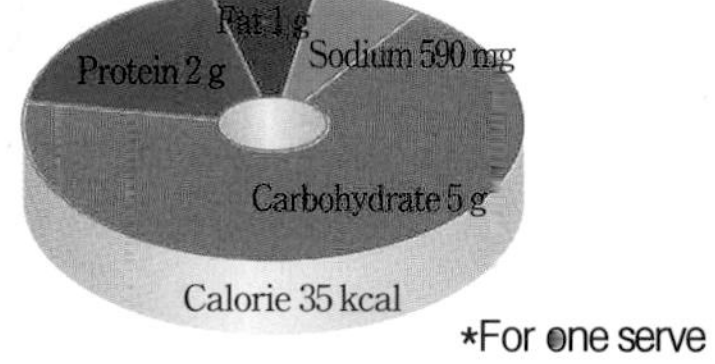

*For one serve

Ingredients & Quantity

2.6 kg young radish, 400 g (2 cups) water, 160 g (1 cup) coarse salt
50 g (1/4 cup) salted anchovies, 40 g salted shrimps
70 g (3/4 cups) ground red pepper
glutinous rice soup : 200 g (1cup) water, 12 g (2 tbsp) glutinous rice powder
200 g small green onion, 48 g (3 tbsp) minced garlic, 6 g (1/2 tbsp) minced ginger
30 g (2 1/2 tbsp) sugar, 6 g (1/2 tbsp) salt

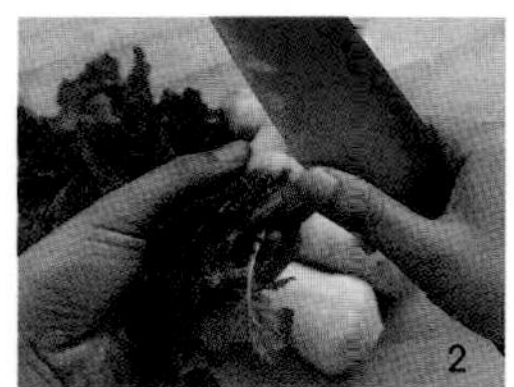

Preparation

1. Remove fine roots from the radish body, trim and wash cleanly. 【Photo 2】
2. Marinate the radish in coarse salt water for 3 hours (2.2 kg). Wash them in water and drain water on a strainer for 30 min. 【Photo 3】
3. Trim and wash small green onion and cut it into 4 cm−long (150 g).
4. Mince the solid ingredients of salted shrimps finely.

Recipe

1. Put water and glutinous rice powder in the pot, mix, then boil it for 5 min. on high heat, and cool it down (130 g).
2. Mix the salted anchovies, salted shrimps, ground red pepper and glutinous rice soup together to make Kimchi seasoning. 【Photo 4】
3. Mix the marinated radish with prepared seasonings and other stuffs together, and season with sugar and salt. 【Photo 5】
4. Place them into a jar and press down. 【Photo 6】

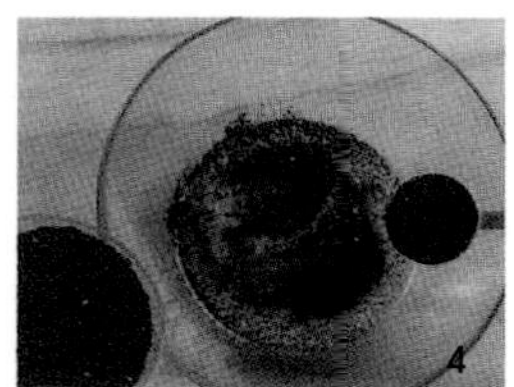

· Small bundles of marinated mustard leaf and small green onion may be add to the whole radish Kimchi.
· Dried red pepper after being soaked and ground may be substituted for the ground red pepper.

Heating Time	Process	Heat Control
Preparation	Marinating young radish. Preparing stuffs	
0 min	Boiling glutinous rice soup	H−heat 5 min.
5 min	Making Kimchi seasoning	
	Mixing Kimchi with stuffs together	
	Pacing into a jar	

Kkakdugi 깍두기

Diced Radish Kimchi

Kkakdugi is a type of Kimchi made with cubed Korean radish, ground red pepper, salted anchovy, green onions, garlic and minced ginger. Pregnant women would eat *jeong-kkakdugi*, made of regular cubed radish, in hopes their child would grow to be honest and upright like a cubed radish. *Suk-kkakdugi*, made with steamed cubed radish, is good for the elderly and others with weak teeth.

Total weight after cooking	Weight for one serve	Service temperature	Total heating time	Total cooking time	Standard utensil
1.6 kg (20 serves)	80 g	4~10 ℃	0	2 hours	

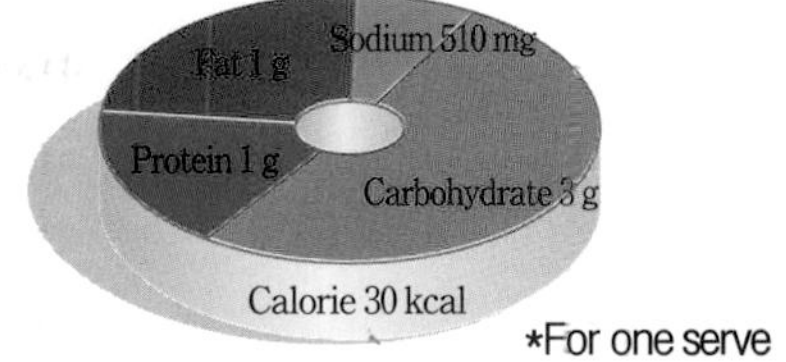

*For one serve

Ingredients & Quantity

1.5 kg (1½ ea) radish, 18 g(1½ tbsp) salt, 6 g (½ tbsp) sugar

seasonings : 42 g (6 tbsp) ground red pepper, 60 g salted shrimps, 24 g (1½ tbsp) minced garlic
8 g (¾ tbsp) minced ginger, 100 g small green onion, 100 g watercress, 6 g (½ tbsp) salt

Preparation

1. Trim and wash the radish, peel the skin and cut it into 2.5 cm–wide/long/thick dice. 【Photo 2】
2. Add salt and sugar to the diced radish, marinate it for 1 hour and drain water for 10 min. (1.3 kg). 【Photo 3】
3. Trim and wash small green onion and watercress, cut them into 3 cm–long (small green onion 80 g, watercress 70 g). 【Photo 4】
4. Mince salted shrimps finely.

Recipe

1. Add ground red pepper to the marinated radish, mix it evenly until colored in red, add salted shrimps, garlic and ginger, mix them together thoroughly. Add small green onion and watercress, mix them softly, season with salt. 【Photos 5 & 6】
2. Put them into a jar and press down.

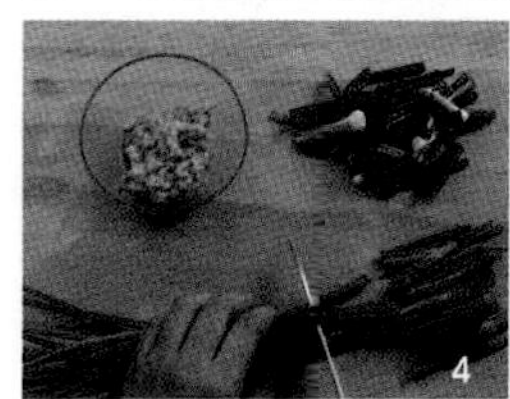

· Add sugar to the spring radish, not to the autumn radish, because autumn radish tastes sweet already.
· Fresh oyster may be add to the radish Kimchi for immediately serving. Kimchi juice will be clean and cool in taste.

Cooking Time	Process	Heat Control
0 min	Trimming and washing vegetables	
20 min	Marinating radish. Mincing salted shrimps	
90 min	Mixing diced radish Kimchi and putting into a jar	

Nabak-kimchi 나박김치

Radish Water Kimchi

Nabak-kimchi is a radish water Kimchi made of brined and seasoned Korean radish and cabbage in Kimchi liquid that is colored with ground red pepper. The word "*nabak*" refers to the shape of the radish which is square and thin. With its refreshing and milder taste, *nabak-kimchi* is enjoyed by men and women of all ages.

Total weight after cooking	Weight for one serve	Service temperature	Total heating time	Total cooking time	Standard utensil
1.76 kg(16 serves)	110 g	4~10 ℃	0 min.	30 min.	

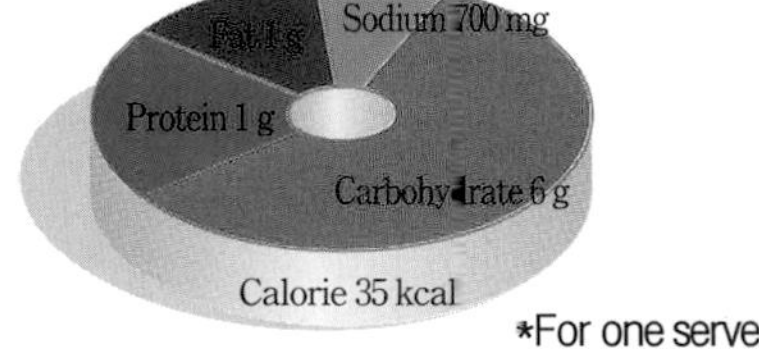

*For one serve

Ingredients & Quantity

200 g Korean cabbage, 200 g radish, 10 g (2½ tsp) salt

20 g small green onion, 30 g (1½ ea) red pepper, 50 g watercress, 3 g (1 tsp) pine nuts

Kimchi liquid : 1.2 kg (6 cups) water, 18 g (1½ tbsp) salt, 4 g (1 tsp) sugar, 14 g (2 tbsp) ground red pepper

24 g (1½ tbsp) minced garlic, 15 g (1¼ tbsp) minced ginger

Preparation

1. Trim the cabbage and radish, wash, cut them into 2.5 cm-wide, 3 cm-long and 0.3 cm-thick, marinate the cabbage with salt for 5 min. and then add radish. After another 5 min. marinating, drain. (save the drained salt water) (cabbage 140 g, radish 180 g). 【Photos 2 & 3】
2. Trim and wash small green onion and watercress, cut them into 3 cm-long. Cut the red pepper lengthwise, seed, and shred into 3 cm-long and 0.3 cm-thick (small green onion 15 g, watercress 40 g, red pepper 23 g). 【Photo 4】
3. Add water, salt and sugar into the saved salt water. Put the ground red pepper into the cotton cloths bag, fumble with hands in the salt water around 10 times to make color Kimchi liquid. 【Photo 5】
4. Remove tops of the pine nuts and wipe them with dry cotton cloths.
5. Put the ginger and garlic into the cotton cloths bag.

Recipe

1. Mix the marinated cabbage and radish, green onion, red pepper thoroughly. Put them into a jar and pour the Kimchi liquid. 【Photo 6】
2. Put the ginger and garlic bag into the jar.
3. When the Kimchi is well-done, serve with watercress and pine nuts topping.

· To keep the Kimchi not to be soften, add the Kimchi liquid later, after mixing with seasonings.

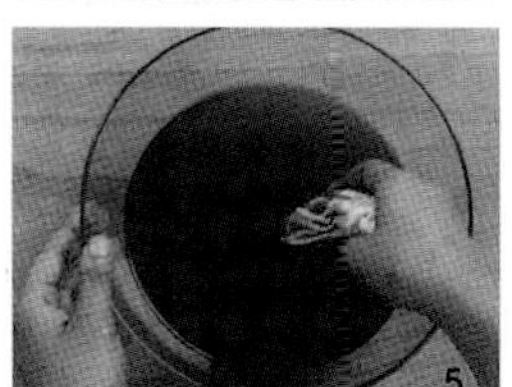

Cooking Time	Process	Heat Control
0 min	Marinating cabbage and radish. Making Kimchi liquid	
10 min	Trimming small green onion, watercress and red pepper, Making Kimchi	
20 min	Putting in a jar. Topping with watercress and pine nuts	

Jangkimchi 장김치

Soy Sauce Kimchi

Jangkimchi is a watery Kimchi made with cabbage and Korean radish brined in soy sauce with various ingredients. *Jangkimchi* is a delicacy with its deep soy sauce fragrance and sweet taste. It was enjoyed in the royal court in olden days.

Total weight after cooking	Weight for one serve	Service temperature	Total heating time	Total cooking time	Standard utensil
1.44 kg (12 serves)	120 g	4~10 ℃	0 min.	2 hours	

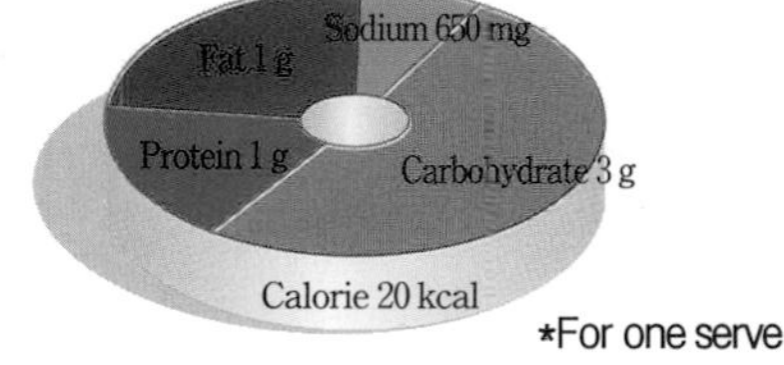

*For one serve

Ingredients & Quantity

200 g Korean cabbage leafstalk, 180 g radish, 90 g (5 tbsp) soy sauce
60 g (3 ea) chestnut, 60 g pear, 30 g watercress, 30 g green onion (white part)
10 g (2 sheets) brown oak mushrooms, 3 g stone mushrooms
11 g (2 tsp) minced garlic, 4 g (1 tsp) minced ginger
5 g (½ tbsp) pine nuts, 1 g shred red pepper
1 kg (5 cups) water, 6 g (½ tbsp) sugar, 16 g (1⅓ tbsp) salt

1

Preparation

1. Trim and wash the cabbage leafstalk and radish, cut them into 2.5 cm-wide, 3 cm-long and 0.5 cm-thick (cabbage 150 g, radish 160 g). 【Photo 2】
2. Add the soy sauce to the cabbage, marinate for 30 min. Add radish and marinate together for another 30 min. drain soy sauce water (120 g). 【Photos 3 & 4】
3. Trim the chestnut and slice it into 0.2 cm-thick (18 g). Trim the watercress and cut them into 3 cm-long (15 g). Trim the green onion and shred into 3 cm-long and 0.1 cm-wide (16 g). Soak mushrooms in water for 1 hour, remove stems of brown oak mushrooms, wipe with cotton cloths, then shred into 0.2 cm-wide (20 g). Cut the shred red pepper into 2 cm-long. Wash the stone mushrooms by rubbing, remove the belly buttons, roll up, and shred into 0.2 cm-wide (3 g). Peel the pear and cut into 2.5 cm-wide, 3 cm-long and 0.3 cm-thick (46 g). 【Photo 5】
4. Put the ginger and garlic into the cotton cloths bag.
5. Remove tops of the pine nuts and wipe the nuts with dry cotton cloths.

2

3

Recipe

1. Mix marinated cabbage and radish with chestnut, pear, watercress, green onion, mushrooms, pine nuts and shred red pepper together thoroughly, then place them into a jar. 【Photo 6】
2. Add water, sugar and salt to the half of the soy sauce water (60 g) and season. Then pour it into the jar and put the garlic and ginger bag in it.

4

· Do not blend soy sauce too dark for this Kimchi.
· Top the watercress and pine nuts just before serving.

5

Cooking Time	Process	Heat Control
0 min	Trimming and washing cabbage and radish. Soaking mushrooms.	
10 min	Marinating cabbage in soy sauce	
40 min	Marinating after adding radish	
70 min	Preparing filling stuffs	
90 min	Mixing Kimchi. Placing into a jar	

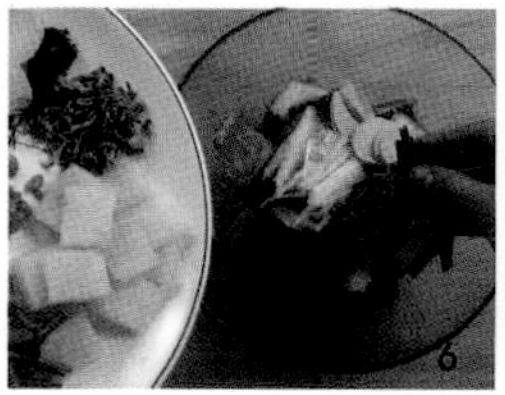
6

Oi-sobagi 오이소박이

Stuffed Cucumber Kimchi

Oi-sobagi is a type of Kimchi made with slightly fermented cucumbers that have been slit and stuffed with seasoned Korean leeks. *Oi-sobagi* may also be served without fermenting.

Total weight after cooking	Weight for one serve	Service temperature	Total heating time	Total cooking time	Standard utensil
600 g(8 serves)	75 g	4~10 ℃	0 min.	3 hours	

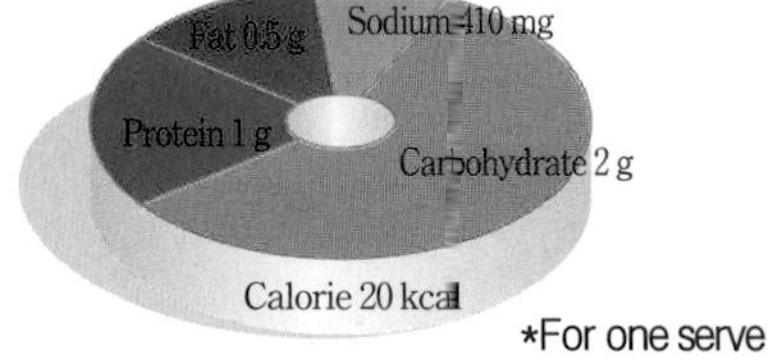

*For one serve

Ingredients & Quantity

600 g (3 ea) cucumber(white), 30 g coarse salt
saltwater : 380 g water, 20 g coarse salt
50 g small wild leaks
15 g (1 tbsp) salted shrimps
seasoning : 28 g (2 tbsp) minced green onion, 16 g (1 tbsp) minced garlic, 4 g (1 tsp) minced ginger
14 g (2 tbsp) ground red pepper, 4 g (1 tsp) salt
stuffed cucumber liquid : 45 g (3 tbsp) water, 1 g (¼ tsp) salt

Preparation

1. Clean the cucumber by rubbing with salt and wash, cut them into 6 cm−long (515 g), put 3~4 knife slits on it, inside of 1cm on both sides. 【Photo 2】
2. Marinate cucumber in salt water for 2 hours, drain water on a strainer for 30 min. 【Photo 3】
3. Trim and wash small wild leaks, cut them into 0.5 cm−long finely. 【Photo 4】
4. Mince the solid ingredients of salted shrimps.

Recipe

1. Prepare filling stuffs with small wild leaks, salted shrimps and seasoning sauce by fumbling with hands. 【Photo 5】
2. Fill up the slits on the cucumber with seasoned filling stuffs. 【Photo 6】
3. Put the stuffed cucumber into a jar. Add water and salt in the mixing container to make stuffed cucumber Kimchi liquid, pour it into the jar and press the cucumber down.

· Young and straight cucumber is good for this Kimchi.

Cooking Time	Process	Heat Control
0 min	Trimming cucumber. Marinating cucumber	
120 min	Draining water on a strainer	
150 min	Preparing filling stuffs	
160 min	Filling up with stuffs	
170 min	Placing in a jar	

Hobaktteok 호박떡

Pumpkin Rice Cake

Hobaktteok is a type of rice cake made with non-glutinous rice powder and steamed pumpkin flesh. *Tteok* is a grain cuisine and has a long history in Korea. It can be served as a main dish to substitute for rice, or as a special food for a festive day or birthday. There are various kinds of *tteok* with different main ingredients.

Total weight after cooking	Weight for one serve	Service temperature	Total heating time	Total cooking time	Standard utensil
720 g (8 serves)	90 g	15~25 ℃	50 min	1 hour	26 cm steamer, 18 cm stainless steel cake mold

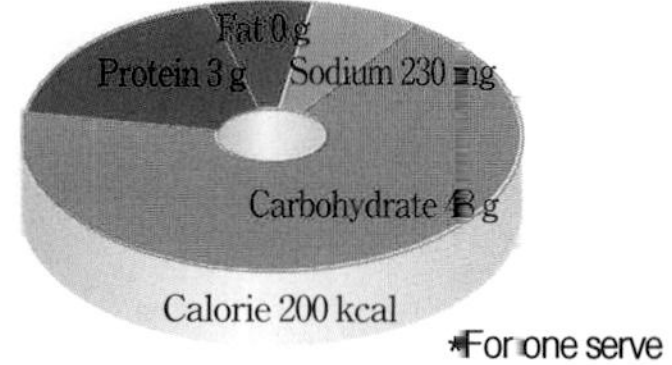

Ingredients & Quantity

500 g (5 cups) non-glutinous rice powder, 6 g (½ tbsp) salt, 100 g (⅔ cups) sugar
250 g (2 ea) sweet pumpkin
2kg (10 cups) pumpkin-rice cake steaming water
garnish : 8 g (2 ea) jujube, 8 g (16 ea) pumpkin seeds

Preparation

1. Scrape out the inside stuffs from the sweet pumpkin.
2. Sprinkle salt on the rice powder and sieve.
3. Wipe the jujube with damp cotton cloths, cut the flesh round, make it into flower shape. Wipe the pumpkin seeds with dry cotton cloths.

Recipe

1. Pour water into the steaming pot, heat it up for 9 min. on high heat. When it gives off steam, put the sweet pumpkin, steam it for 15 min. Scrape the flesh from the pumpkin (170 g). 【Photo 2】
2. Add pumpkin flesh and sugar into the rice powder, mix thoroughly by rubbing, then sieve. 【Photos 3 & 4】
3. Pour water into the steaming pot, heat it up for 9 min. on high heat. When it boils, layer damp cotton cloths on the bottom of the pot, put the cake mold on, put the mixture of rice and pumpkin into the mold, Plane the surface. Put crisscross knife slits on the mixture at intervals of 5 cm, top with jujube and pumpkin seeds. 【Photos 5 & 6】
4. Steam it for another 15 min. after steam bursting up.

· To steam the sweet pumpkin not to be watery, pumpkin should be kept upright.
· Pumpkin skin may be used for garnish after cutting into sheets and boiling down with sugar.

Heating Time	Process	Heat Control
Preparation	Sieving non-glutinous rice powder	
0 min	Steaming sweet pumpkin	H-heat 24 min.
20 min	Mixing rice powder with sweet pumpkin	
30 min	Steaming rice cake	H-heat 24 min.
50 min	Completion	

Songpyeon 송편

Half-moon shape Rice Cake

Songpyeon is a type of rice cake made by kneading rice powder with hot water and stuffing the dough with beans, sesame, chestnuts and other fillings. The rice cake is shaped into a half-moon and steamed. *Songpyeon* is served without fail on *Chuseok* (Korean Thanksgiving) the biggest holiday in Korea. On the eve of *Chuseok*, all the family members gather around the table and make *songpyeon*. They try to make pretty shapes because there is a belief that if you make pretty *songpyeon*, you will have a beautiful daughter.

Total weight after cooking	Weight for one serve	Service temperature	Total heating time	Total cooking time	Standard utensil
880 g(8 serves)	110 g(5 ea)	15~25 ℃	1 hour 3 min	over 5 hours	26 ㎝ steamer

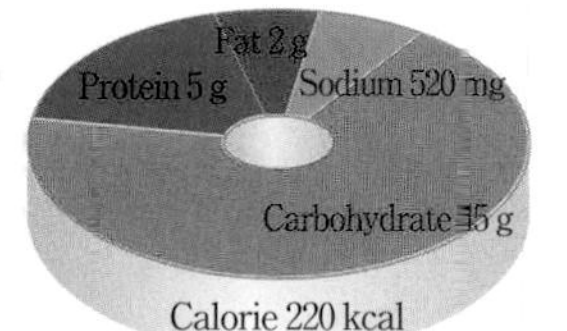

*For one serve

Ingredients & Quantity

500 g (5 cups) non-glutinous rice powder, 5 g salt, 200~210 g water
coloring stuffs : 2.5 g mugwort powder, 7 g (gardenia 2 g + water 25 g) gardenia soaked water , 9 g (strawberry powder 1 g + water 8 g) strawberry powder liquid, 1 g cinnamon powder
filling stuffs : 50 g fresh green bean, 1 g (¼ tsp) salt, 30 g sesame seeds, 9.5 g (½ tbsp) honey 12 g (1 tbsp) sugar, 0.5 g (⅛ tsp) salt, 30 g geopi-pat (dark blue, thin skin sweet bean) 14 g (⅔ tbsp) honey, 1 g (¼ tsp) salt, 0.6 g cinnamon powder
300 g pine needles, 2 kg (10 cups) steaming water
13 g (1 tbsp) sesame oil

Preparation

1. Halve the gardenia, soak in water for 30 min. to make gardenia soaked water. Mix strawberry powder with water to make strawberry powder liquid.
2. Sprinkle salt on the rice powder and sieve. Divide it into 5 parts. Mix each part of rice powder with each coloring stuff well and sieve. 【Photo 2】
3. Sprinkle salt on the fresh green bean. Grind half of the fried sesame seeds, mix with honey, sugar and salt together. 【Photo 3】
4. Wash the geopi-pat and soak them in 7 times volume of water for 8 hours, skin by rubbing, rinse in water, drain water on a strainer for 10 min. (60 g).
5. Rinse pine needles in water and drain water on a strainer.

1

2

Recipe

1. Strongly knead each colored rice powder with hot water quite for a long time.
2. Pour water into the steaming pot and heat it up for 9 min. on high heat. When it gives off steam, layer damp cotton cloths on the bottom of the pot. Put the geopi-pat in the pot, steam it for 25 min. Pound the geopi-pat with salt and sieve (55 g), then mix with honey, salt and cinnamon powder thoroughly. 【Photo 3】
3. Pull off around 15~16 g of rice powder dough, roll it into a small ball and make a dent in the center. Put the filling stuffs in it, close up the balls edges and make it into a half-moon shape (20 g after stuffing).【Photo 4】
4. Pour water into the steaming pot, heat it up for 9 min. on high heat. When it boils, layer pine needles on the bottom. Place the shaped dough and steam for 20 min. on high heat. 【Photo 5】
5. Take out the steamed rice cake, quickly rinse in cold water, remove the pine needles, drain water and coat with sesame oil. 【Photo 6】

3

4

- Shaping dough should be covered with damp cotton cloths not to be dried.
- Dough should be kneaded with hot water strongly, then the dough will be pretty.
- Thick Omija(Chinese magnolia vine) tea (Omija 1 : water 2) may be replaced to strawberry juice for pink color.
- Potato, sweet potato, sweet pumpkin, acorn, arrowroots starch and ramie leaves may be added to the dough.
- Black bean, mung bean, chestnut, jujube, and/or sweet potatoes may be used for filling stuffs.

5

Heating Time	Process	Heat Control
Preparation	Soaking geopipat, Kneading rice powder Preparing filling stuffs, Trimming and cleaning pine needles	
0 min	Steaming geopi-pat	H-heat 34 min.
30 min	Shaping dough and steaming	H-heat 29 min.
60 min	Coating with sesame oil	

6

Yaksik 약식

Sweet Rice with Nuts and Jujubes

Yaksik is a sweet dish made with steamed glutinous rice, honey, soy sauce, jujubes, chestnuts and pine nuts. It may also be called *yakbap* (medicinal *bap*). It is said that *yaksik* was prepared and served to the crows as a reward for saving the king's life in the *Silla* Dynasty.

Total weight after cooking	Weight for one serve	Service temperature	Total heating time	Total cooking time	Standard utensil
600 g (8 serves)	75 g	15~25 ℃	2 hours 17 min	5 hours	20 cm pot, 26 cm steamer

Fat 1 g
Protein 3 g
Sodium 125 mg
Carbohydrate 4[illegible] g
Calorie 180 kcal
*For one serve

Ingredients & Quantity

270 g (1½ cups) glutinous rice, 1.6 kg (8 cups) rice steaming water
salt water : 45 g (3 tbsp) water, 2 g (½ tsp) salt
20 g (5 ea) jujube, 45 g (3 ea) chestnut, 3.5 g (1 tsp) pine nuts
jujube stone tea : 5 ea jujube stone, 200 g (1 cup) water
sweet steamed rice seasoning : 15 g (2½ tsp) soy sauce, 32 g (2 tbsp) sweet steamed rice sauce
36 g (3 tbsp) yellow sugar, 0.5 g (¼ tsp) cinnamon powder
6.5 g (½ tsp) jujube stone tea, 38 g (2 tbsp) honey, 24 g (2 tbsp) sugar
6.5 g (½ tbsp) sesame oil
sweet steamed rice sauce : 24 g (2 tbsp) sugar, 4 g (1 tsp) edible oil, 2 g (½ tbsp) starch powder
45 g (3 tbsp) warm water

1

Preparation

1. Wash the glutinous rice and soak in water for about 3 hours, drain water through a strainer for 10 min (330 g).
2. Wipe the jujube with damp cotton cloths, cut the flesh round and cut it into 6 pieces (16 g). Skin the chestnut and cut it into 6 pieces (30 g). 【Photo 2】
3. Remove tops of the pine nuts and wipe the nuts with dry cotton cloths.

2

Recipe

1. Pour water into the steaming pot, heat it up for 8 min. on high heat. When it gives off steam, layer a damp cotton cloths on the bottom, put the glutinous rice and steam it for 20 min. Sprinkle salt water, mix well with wooden scoop, steam it for another 30 min. 【Photo 3】
2. Put the jujube stones and water in the pot, cover the lid and simmer it for 15 min. on medium heat, strain it (19 g).
3. Put the sugar in the pot, heat it up for 3 min. on medium heat. When the sugar melted, coat the pan with edible oil. When the sugar turns to brownish liquid, add the starch powder and boil it with stirring for 1 min. to make sweet steamed rice sauce.
4. While the steamed rice is still warm, add soy sauce, sweet steamed rice sauce, yellow sugar, cinnamon powder, jujube stone tea, honey, regular sugar and sesame oil into the steamed rice and mix them well. Mix them well again after adding chestnuts, jujube and pine nuts. 【Photo 4 · 5】
5. Put the mixture of above steamed glutinous rice into the steaming pot for steaming in boiling water, steam it for 10 min. on high heat. Then lower the heat to medium, steam for 20 min. mix it well. Reduce the heat to low, steam it for 20 min. mix it again to be admixed with seasonings evenly and steam it for another 10 min. 【Photo 6】

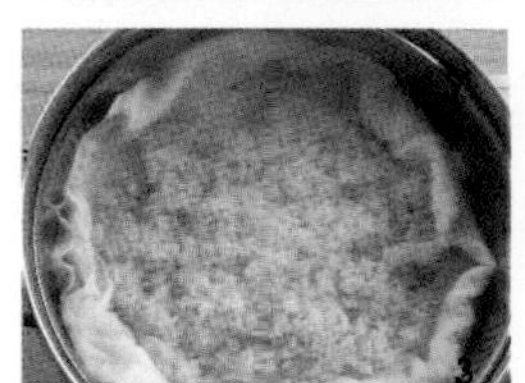
3

4

- To cook good taste steamed rice, rice should be steamed to be pretty tender, neither too hard nor too soft or watery.
- Steaming in boiling water would produce deeper brown color, better taste and sweet smell.
- Two hours may be proper for steaming in boiling water.
- For the sweet steamed rice sauce, caramel sauce may produces good color and sweet smell.

5

Heating Time	Process	Heat Control
Preparation	Soaking glutinous rice and draining. Trimming nuts	
0 min	Steaming glutinous rice	H-heat 8 min. H-heat 50 min.
60 min	Simmering jujube stones	M-heat 15 min.
70 min	Blending sweet steamed rice sauce. Seasoning glutinous rice	M-heat 4 min.
80 min	Steaming in boiling water	H-heat 10 min. M-heat 20 min. L-heat 30 min.

6

Jeungpyeon 증편

Rice Wine Cake

Jeungpyeon is a type of rice cake made by kneading rice powder with milky rice wine, garnishing it with jujubes, chestnuts, pine nuts and stone mushrooms, and then steaming it in a cake mold. *Jeungpyeon* is a good rice cake for the summer because it is fermented with wine, and does not spoil easily. It has a unique wine aroma, slightly sour taste and soft texture.

Total weight after cooking	Weight for one serve	Service temperature	Total heating time	Total cooking time	Standard utensil
400 g(4 serves)	100 g	15~25 ℃	39 min	1 hour	26 cm steamer cake mold (dia.– 4 cm)

Fat 0 g
Protein 3 g
Sodium 240 mg
Carbohydrate 47 g
Calorie 200 kcal
*For one serve

Ingredients & Quantity

250 g non-glutinous rice powder, 3 g (¼ tbsp) salt
50 g (¼ cups) milky rice wine
100 g (½ cups) tepid water (40 ℃), 5 g fresh yeast, 40 g (¼ cups) sugar
garnish : 8 g (2 ea) jujube, 1g stone mushrooms, 1.7 g (½ tsp) pine nuts, 1 g pumpkin seed
coloring : yellow : 7.5 g (½ tbsp) water, 2 g (1 ea) gardenia
pink color : 7.5 g (½ tbsp) water, 3 g strawberry powder
2 kg (10 cups) rice wine cake steaming water
13 g (1 tbsp) edible oil

Preparation

1. Sprinkle salt over the rice powder and sieve through fine mesh two times. Add milky rice wine, tepid water, fresh yeast and sugar to the rice powder. Mix them with wooden scoop thoroughly. Place it in a container, cover with poly–vinyl film, electrical thermo–floor and thick blanket. Maintain the temperature within 40~45 ℃. 【Photo 2】
2. Ferment it for 2 hours. When the dough swells up, stir it strongly and draw the air out. Ferment it again for another 1 hour (470 g). 【Photo 3】
3. Wipe the jujube with damp cotton cloths, cut the flesh round, make it into flower shape. Soak stone mushrooms in water for 1 hour, wash it by rubbing, wipe water with cotton cloths, roll it up, and shred it into 0.1 cm–thick.
4. Remove tops of the pine nuts, wipe the nuts with dry cotton cloths. Halve it lengthwise to make scale–like pine nuts. Wipe the pumpkin seeds with dry cotton cloths.
5. Halve the gardenia, soak it in water for 1 hour for yellow color. Dissolve the strawberry powder in water for pink color.

Recipe

1. When the 2nd fermentation completed, divide the dough into 3 parts. Leave one part for white, and color one part of the dough with 1.5 g of gardenia water in yellow, the other part with 2 g of strawberry water in pink. 【Photo 4】
2. Put the dough in the cake mold. Garnish with jujube, mushrooms, pine nut and pumpkin seeds (18 ea). 【Photo 5】
3. Pour water into the steaming pot, heat it up for 9 min. on high heat. When it is steaming, turn off the heat, put the cake mold in the pot. Let it sit there for 10 min. for third fermentation(water temperature 83 ℃). 【Photo 6】
4. When the dough swells up again, steam it for 20 min. on high heat, another 10 min. on low heat.
5. When it gives off steam, take out the cakes and coat with edible oil.

- The finer rice power is better for rice wine cake. Thicker dough is better than thinner.
- Mugwort powder brings out green color rice wine cakes.
- Traditionally, Omija water(Omija : water = 1 : 2) may be used for pink color.
- This cake is made with milky rice wine, has sweet smelling. This cake is good for summer season, because it is not easily spoiled even in summer.

Heating Time	Process	Heat Control
Preparation	Kneading dough. 1st fermentation. 2nd fermentation	
	Preparing garnish	
0 min	Coloring dough	
	Boiling rice cake steaming water. 3rd fermentation	H–heat 9 min.
10 min	Steaming rice wine cake	H–heat 20 min. L–heat 10 min.
40 min	Coating the cake with edible oil	

Gyeongdan 경단

Sweet Rice Balls

Gyeongdan is a type of rice cake made by kneading glutinous rice powder with hot water, shaping the dough into balls, boiling them in hot water and coating them with various sweet powders. It gets its name because the shape is similar to round jade (*gyeongdan*). The color or taste varies depending on the coating powder.

Total weight after cooking	Weight for one serve	Service temperature	Total heating time	Total cooking time	Standard utensil
680 g(8 serves)	85g(6 ea)	15~25 ℃	1 hour 36 min	over 5 hours	24 ㎝ pot, 26 cm steamer

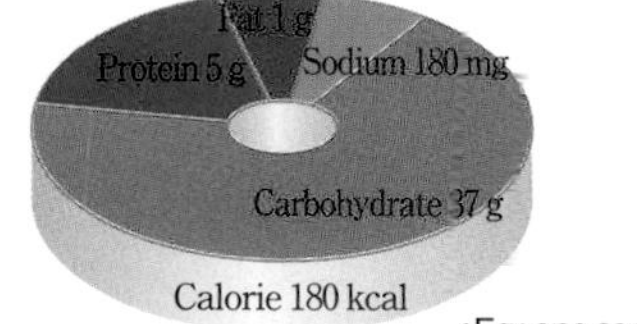

*For one serve

Ingredients & Quantity

500 g (5 cups) glutinous rice powder, 4 g (1 tsp) salt, 120 g water
20 g (¼ cups) yellow bean powder, 20 g (¼ cups) green bean powder, 20 g (¼ cups) black sesame powder
28 g geopi-pat (dark blue, thin skin sweet bean), 0.5 g (⅛ tsp) salt, 4 g (1 tsp) sugar
27 g red bean, 200 g (1 cup) scalding water, 400 g (2 cups) boiling water, 0.5 g (⅛ tsp) salt, 4 g (1 tsp) sugar
2 kg sweet rice ball steaming water

Preparation

1. Wash the geopi-pat and soak in 7 times volume of water for 8 hours, skin by rubbing, rinse in water, drain water on a strainer for 10 min. (55 g).
2. Wash the red bean and drain water on a strainer for 10 min.

Recipe

1. Pour water into the steaming pot and heat it up for 9 min. on high heat. When it gives off steam, layer damp cotton cloths on the bottom of the pot, put the geopi-pat in the pot and steam it for 25 min. pound with salt, sieve (53 g), then mix with sugar thoroughly. 【Photo 2】
2. Put water and red bean in the pot, heat it up for 5 min. on high heat. When it boils, discard the boiling water and pour new water, boil it for 20 min. on medium heat. Reduce the heat to low, steam it for 25 min. until the red bean very tender, pound with salt, sieve, and mix it with sugar thoroughly (52 g). 【Photo 3】
3. Add salt in the glutinous rice powder and knead with hot water. Pull off around 12~13 g of dough and roll it into 2 cm-diameter balls (total 48 ea). 【Photo 4】
4. Pour water in the pot and heat it up for 9 min. on high heat. When it boils, put the rolled dough into the boiling water, boil it for about 2 min. and 30 sec. When balls float up on the surface, let them float there for 20~30 sec. more. Take them out with strainer, quickly rinse in cold water and drain. 【Photo 5】
5. Divide rice-cake balls into 5 parts and coat the balls with each sweet powder. 【Photo 4】

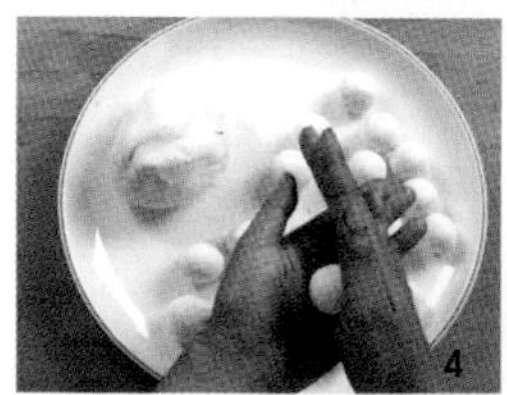

· Red bean stuffs or sponge cake powder may be available in the market.
· The dough, mixed with 4 parts of glutinous and 1 part of non-glutinous rice powder would not hang down.

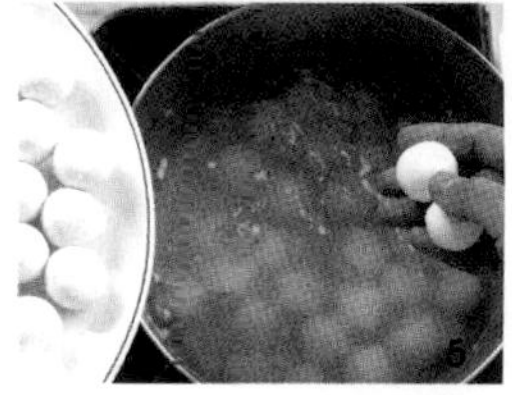

Heating Time	Process	Heat Control
Preparation	Soaking geopi-pat. Kneading glutinous rice powder with hot water	
0 min	Steaming geopi-pat	H-heat 34 min.
30 min	Boiling red bean and preparing red bean powder stuffs	H-heat 5 min. M-heat 20 min. L-heat 25 min.
80 min	Boiling rolled dough	H-heat 9 min. H-heat 3 min.
90 min	Coating with sweet powder	

Yakgwa 약과

Deep-fried Honey Cookies

Yakgwa is a type of cookie made by kneading wheat flour with sesame oil, honey and refined rice wine. It is pressed into a square mold, or flattened with a mallet and cut into a square. It is then fried in oil and dipped in honey. This is the most luxurious and tasteful traditional Korean cookie. It is served without fail on festive days, at ceremonial feasts and memorial services.

Total weight after cooking	Weight for one serve	Service temperature	Total heating time	Total cooking time	Standard utensil
240 g(4 serves)	60 g(3 ea)	15~25 ℃	30 min	over 5 hours	28㎝ round pan

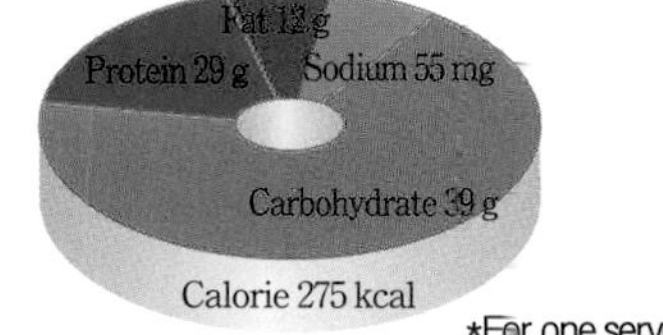

*For one serve

Ingredients & Quantity

151 g (1 cup, 8 tbsp) wheat flour (medium viscidness), 26 g (2 tbsp) sesame oil

honey cookie seasoning : 38 g (2 tbsp) honey, 30 g (2 tbsp) refined rice wine, 1 g (¼ tsp) salt
8 g (½ tbsp) ginger juice, 0.1 g ground white pepper, 0.5 g (¼ tsp) cinnamon powder

honey syrup : 300 g (1 cup) honey, 0.5 g (¼ tsp) cinnamon powder

10 g (1 tbsp) pine nuts, 8 g (2 ea) jujube, 2 g pumpkin seeds

680 g (4 cups) edible oil

1

Preparation

1. Sieve wheat flour, mix with the sesame oil thoroughly and sieve again. 【Photo 2】
2. Add seasonings to the wheat flour, mix thoroughly and knead it softly like as making a snowball.
3. Roll the dough flat with roller, fold over three times, roll and fold again. Finally roll it down to 0.5 cm–thick, cut it into 3.5 cm–square and make 5~6 holes with a chopstick. 【Photo 3】
4. Blend honey syrup.
5. Remove tops of the pine nuts, wipe pine nuts and pumpkin seeds with dry cotton cloths. Wipe jujube with damp cloths, cut the flesh round and make it flower shape.

2

3

Recipe

1. Pour edible oil into the pan and heat it up for 5 min. on medium heat. When oil temperature comes up to 85~90 ℃, put the cookie dough, oil–fry for 15 min. When the dough float on the surface, raise the heat to high heat. When oil temperature comes up to 140~145 ℃, fry it for another 10 min. until the both sides color turns to brown. 【Photo 4】
2. Drain oil on a strainer for 5~10 min, dip in honey syrup for 5~6 hours, put them on a strainer again for 2 hours. 【Photo 5】
3. Garnish with pine nuts, jujube and pumpkin seeds. 【Photo 6】

4

5

· Do not knead too strong. Soft kneading like as folding will make the cookies non–sticky and crispy.
· Citron syrup may be added into the honey syrup upon taste.

Heating Time	Process	Heat Control
Preparation	Kneading cookie dough. Preparing honey syrup. Preparing garnish	
0 min	Oil–frying honey cookies	M–heat 20 min. H–heat 10 min.
30 min	Draining oil	
	Dipping in honey syrup	
	Draining honey syrup. Garnishing	

6

Maejakgwa 매작과

Fried Ribbon Cookies

Maejakgwa is a type of cookie made by kneading wheat flour with salt and ginger juice. It is sliced thinly and slit, then flipped over after squeezing one end into the slit. The cookies are fried in oil, coated with sugar syrup, and sprinkled with pine nut and cinnamon powder. *Maejakgwa* gets its name from its shape which is similar to a sparrow (*jak*) in an apricot (*maehwa*) tree.

Total weight after cooking	Weight for one serve	Service temperature	Total heating time	Total cooking time	Standard utensil
160 g (4 serves)	40 g	15~25 ℃	24 min	1 hour	16 cm pot, 28 cm round pan

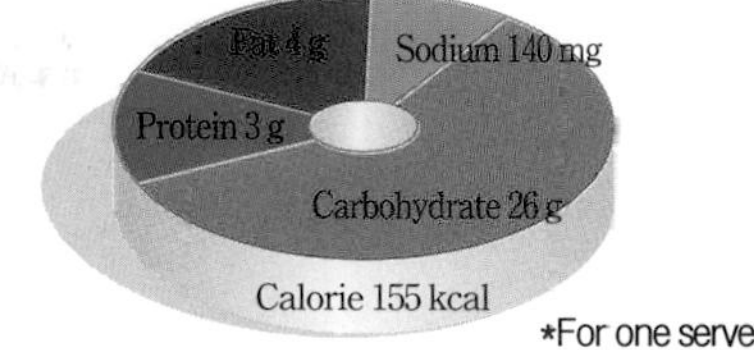

*For one serve

Ingredients & Quantity

white dough : 70 g wheat flour, 0.5 g salt, 30 g ginger juice
pink color dough : 25 g wheat flour, 0.2 g salt, 1 g (¼ tsp) strawberry powder, 15 g ginger juice
mugwort color dough : 25 g wheat flour, 0.2 g salt, 1 g (½ tsp) mugwort powder, 15g ginger juice
yellow dough : 25 g wheat flour, 0.2g salt, 2 g (gardenia 2 g, water 30 g) gardenia water, 10 g ginger juice
syrup : 80 g (½ cup) sugar, 100 g (½ cup) water
6 g (1 tbsp) pine nuts powder

Preparation

1. Sprinkle salt to the each wheat flour and sieve.
2. Knead white wheat flour with ginger juice and add strawberry powder, mugwort powder, and gardenia water to the remained each wheat flour respectively, mix them thoroughly individually, and knead with ginger juice. 【Photo 2】
3. Wrap the each dough with cotton cloths individually and let them sit for 20 min. (white 160 g, yellow/pink/mugwort 40 g each).
4. Roll the white dough down into 0.2 cm−thick, and divide it into 3 parts. Roll the remained 3 color doughs down into 0.2 cm−thick respectively. Stick each colored dough to the white dough together face to face, and roll it down into 0.2 cm−thick again.
5. Cut the rolled dough into 2 cm−wide and 4 cm−long, then put 3 stream line slits, insert one end into the center slit, then flip over. 【Photo 4】

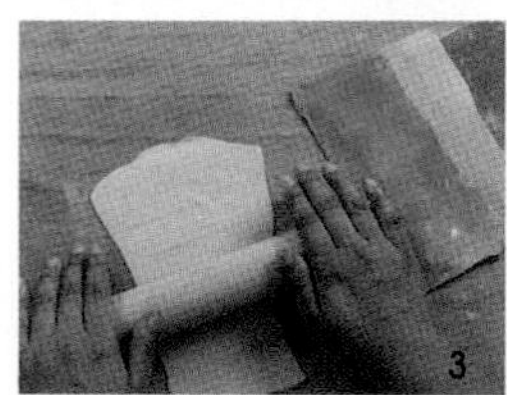

Recipe

1. Put sugar and water in the pot, boil it on low heat for 15 min to make syrup.
2. Pour edible oil into the pan and heat it up for 5 min. on medium heat. When oil temperature comes up to 130 ℃, put the doughs in the pan and let it sit for 2 min. Fry for another 2 min. after turn over, drain oil on a strainer. 【Photo 5】
3. Then put the fried doughs into the syrup to coat with. Place cookies on a dish and sprinkle pine nuts powder. 【Photo 6】

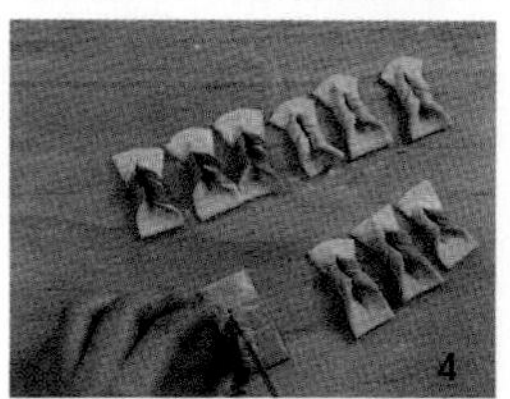

· Traditional twisted cookie is white and much bigger.
· It may be called as 'Taraegwa'.
· Saturated Omija water (Omija : water = 1 : 2) may be used for pink dough.

Heating Time	Process	Heat Control
Preparation	Kneading. Shaping ribbon cookies	
0 min	Oil frying cookies	M−heat 9 min.
10 min	Blending syrup and coating syrup.	L−heat 15 min.
	Sprinkling pine nuts powder	

Jatbaksan 잣박산

Pine Nut Cookies

Jatbaksan is a mixture of toasted pine nuts, wheat gluten and honey. Pine nuts are a special ingredient from olden days. Like ginseng, they have been used in many ways, for example, in cookies, *tteok* and as a garnish for noodle dishes. According to Oriental medicine, pine nuts promote physical strength.

Total weight after cooking	Weight for one serve	Service temperature	Total heating time	Total cooking time	Standard utensil
140 g (4 serves)	35 g	15~25 ℃	2 min	30 min	28 ㎝ round pan

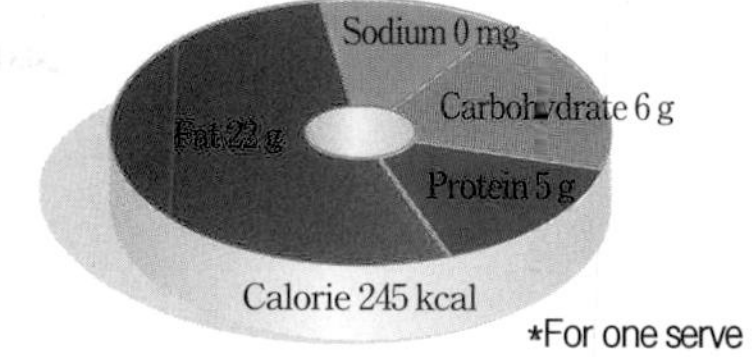

*For one serve

Ingredients & Quantity

120 g (1 cup) pine nuts

syrup : 28.5 g (1½ tbsp) glutinous starch syrup, 12 g (1 tbsp) sugar, 5 g (1 tsp) water

2 g (½ tsp) edible oil

Preparation

1. Remove tops of the pine nuts and wipe the nuts with dry cotton cloths. 【Photo 2】

Recipe

1. Put the glutinous starch syrup, sugar and water in the pan, heat it up for 1 min. on medium heat to make syrup. 【Photo 3】
2. Add pine nuts in the syrup, boil it down for 1 min. with stirring. 【Photo 4】
3. Coat the surface of vynil sheet with edible oil. Spread the boiled syrup on the vynil, press and roll it down with roller into 0.5 ㎝-thick. 【Photo 5】
4. Cut it into 2 ㎝-wide and 3 ㎝-long. 【Photo 6】

· Add pine nuts when the syrup boiled down slightly hard, then it will be crispy.

· In winter season, the amount of sugar may be reduced.

Heating Time	Process	Heat Control
Preparation 0 min	Preparing pine nuts Making syrup Boiling down after adding pine nuts Oiling on the surface of vynil sheet Press-rolling boiled pine nuts and cutting	 M-heat 1 min. M-heat 1 min.

Dasik 다식

Traditional Pressed Sweet

Dasik is a traditional pressed cookie, made by kneading fried grain powder, Oriental medicinal herbs or flower pollen with honey. The dough is pressed with *dasik* molds that have carvings of birds, flowers or Chinese characters. *Dasik* has a unique taste that harmonizes well with the sweet honey and other ingredients. It was named '*dasik*,' which means tea and food, because it is usually served with tea.

Total weight after cooking	Weight for one serve	Service temperature	Total heating time	Total cooking time	Standard utensil
200g (8 serves)	25g (6 ea)	15~25℃	0 min	1 hour	cookie mold (dia.– 2.3 cm)

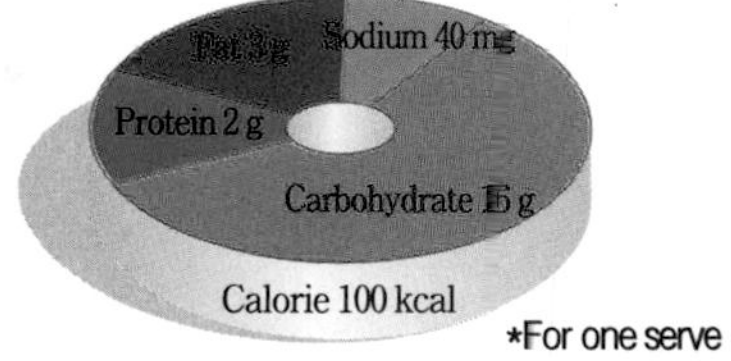

*For one serve

Ingredients & Quantity

20 g green bean flour, 13 g honey
20 g yellow bean flour, 13 g honey
25 g black sesame powder, 9 g honey
10 g pine pollen, 13 g honey
25 g mung bean starch, 13 g honey
25 g mung bean starch, 11 g honey
strawberry liquid : 7.5 g (½ tbsp) water, 3 g strawberry powder
13 g (1 tbsp) edible oil

1

2

Preparation

1. Dissolve strawberry powder in water to make strawberry liquid.

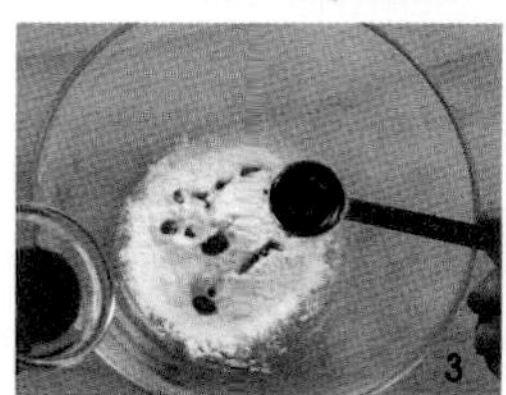
3

Recipe

1. Add honey to the green bean flour, yellow bean flour, black sesame powder, pine pollen, mung bean starch respectively. 【Photo 2】
2. Add 1.7 g of strawberry liquid to the mung bean starch, rubbing by hand and sieve finely, then add honey. 【Photo 3】
3. Knead each stuff strongly. 【Photo 4】
4. Oil over the press mold, put small amount of the dough into the mold and press down (48 ea). 【Photos 5 & 6】

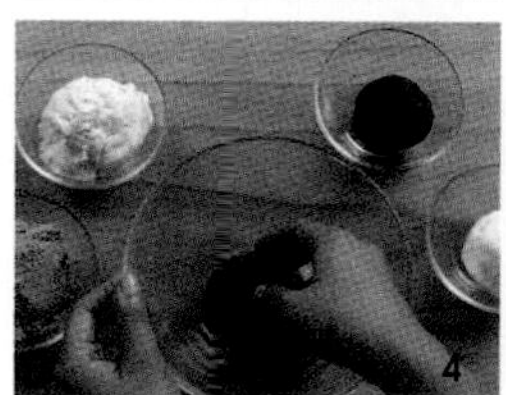
4

· The amount of the honey for the dough will be varied upon the moisture level of the ingredients. Knead the dough neither too hard nor too watery.
· Traditionally, Omija water(Omija : water = 1:2) has been used for pink color.

Cooking Time	Process	Heat Control
0 min	Making strawberry liquid	
10 min	Kneading sweet cookies	
30 min	Pressing on a mold	

6

Omijapyeon 오미자편

Omija-flavored Jelly

Omijapyeon is a Korean cookie made of a mixture of *omija* liquid, mung bean starch and sugar, that is boiled down into a jelly. It has a pretty color and shape, soft texture, and sweet and sour taste. *Omija* is a fruit that has five tastes. The skin is sour and sweet, the stone is spicy and bitter, and the whole body is salty.

Total weight after cooking	Weight for one serve	Service temperature	Total heating time	Total cooking time	Standard utensil
240 g(4 serves)	60 g	4~10 ℃	12 min	over 5 hours	18cm pot

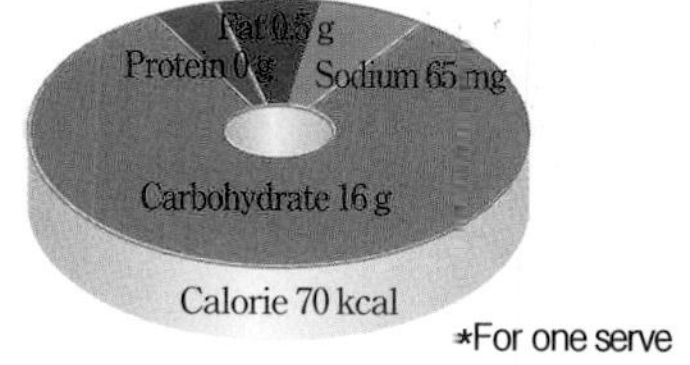

*For one serve

Ingredients & Quantity

33 g (⅓ cup) Omija, 400 g (2 cups) water
32 g (4 tbsp) mung bean starch
53 g (⅓ cups sugar
1 g (¼ tsp) salt

Preparation

1. Wash Omija cleanly, soak in water for 12 hours. Sieve the water through cotton cloths (300 g (1½ cup)). 【Photos 2 & 3】
2. Mix mung bean starch with 100 g of Omija water thoroughly.

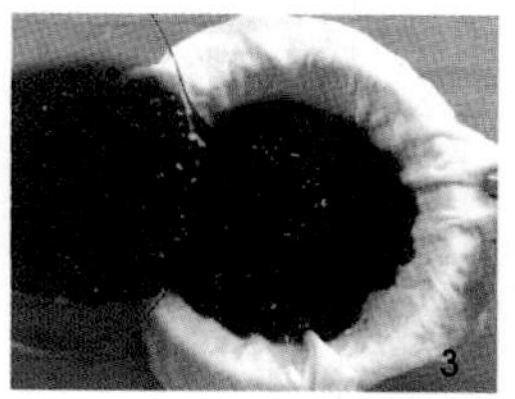

Recipe

1. Put sugar and salt into the 200g (1 cup) of Omija water, boil it for 5 min. on medium heat, then add mung bean starch dissolved in Omija water, boil it with stirring for 5 min. on low heat. 【Photo 4】
2. When the liquid concentrated into droplet viscosity, steam for 2 min. Pour into a square container and let it be solidified. 【Photo 5】
3. When it solidified as jelly, cut into 3 cm−wide by 4 cm−long. 【Photo 6】

· Omija cookies may be served with plentiful shred chestnut and/or fruits on the bottom.

Heating Time	Process	Heat Control
Preparation	Trimming Omija, Mixing mung bean starch with Omija water	
0 min	Boiling Omija water	M−heat 5 min.
5 min	Boiling after adding mung bean starch liquid	L−heat 5 min.
10 min	Steaming. Solidifing	L−heat 2min.
	Cutting Omija jelly	

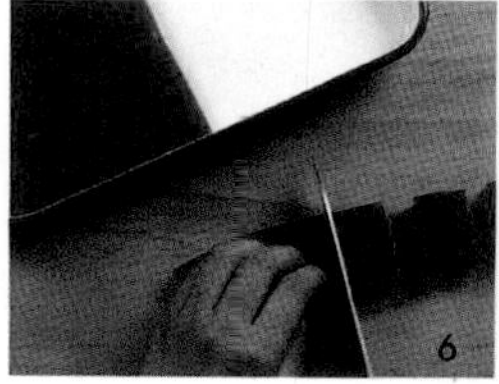

Sikhye 식혜

Rice Punch

Sikhye is a punch made by fermenting steamed rice in malt water. Chilled *sikhye* has a unique sweet taste and is beloved by Koreans. *Sikhye* is usually served on national holidays because it is believed to help digestion and stimulate blood circulation.

Total weight after cooking	Weight for one serve	Service temperature	Total heating time	Total cooking time	Standard utensil
2.21 kg(16 serves)	120 g	4~10 ℃	26 min	over 5 hours	thermo-pot, 18 cm, 24 cm pot

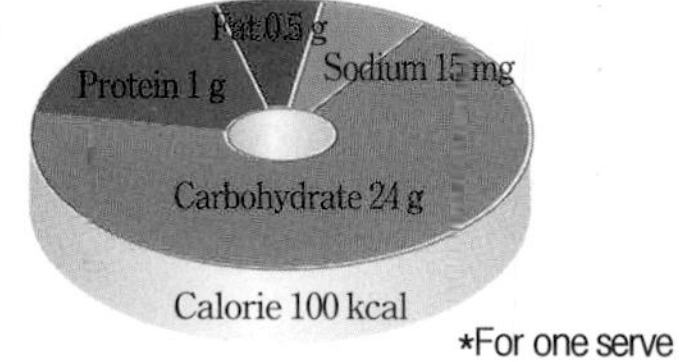

*For one serve

Ingredients & Quantity

115 g (1 cup) malt powder, 2.4 kg (12 cups) water
360 g (2 cups) non-glutinous rice, 480 g (2⅓ cups) water
160 g (1 cup) sugar
10 g (1 tbsp) pine nuts

Preparation

1. Put the malt powder in warm water which is around 40 ℃, and let it sit for 30 min. 【Photo 2】
2. Fumble the soaked malt powder with hands, sieve through a strainer. Discard the solids after squeezing, sink the malt water. When the sediments settle down, pour the top clean water out gently for malt liquid. (1.8 kg) 【Photo 3】
3. Wash the non-glutinous rice, soak in water for 30 min. Then drain water through a strainer for 10 min.
4. Remove tops of the pine nuts and wipe the nuts with dry cotton cloths.

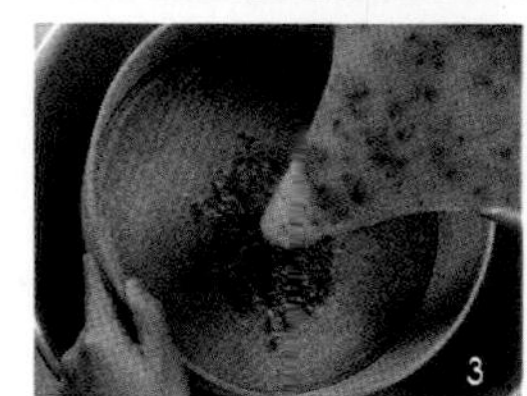

Recipe

1. Put the rice and water in the pot, heat it up for 4 min. on high heat. When it boils, continue to boil for 4 min. Lower the heat to medium, boil for 3 min. When the rice become sodden, lower the heat to low, steam it for 10 min. (880 g).
2. Put the steamed rice, malt water and sugar into the thermo-pot (60~65 ℃), keep in there for 3~4 hours. 【Photo 4】
3. When 7~8 of rice grains floated up, take out the all rice grains from the pot. 【Photos 5 & 6】
4. Rinse the rice grains in cold water until sweet taste is soaked out. Pour the fermented water into the pot, heat it up for 5 min. on high heat. When it boils, skim the foam out cleanly.
5. Cool down the rice punch, fill in a bowl, top with rice grains and pine nuts.

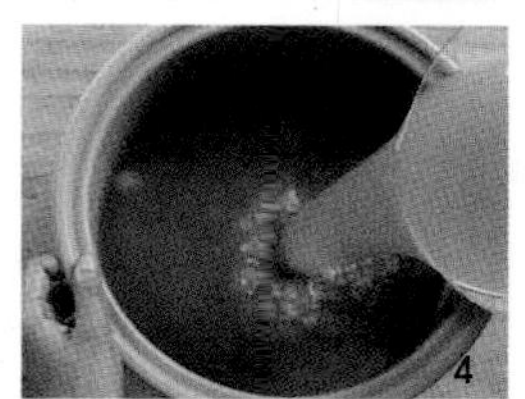

- **If the rice grains taken out from the pot after lots of grains are floated, rice punch may be soured.**
- **When the rice punch volume is so much, boil it for 20 min. more.**

Heating Time	Process	Heat Control
Preparation	Preparing malt water. Soaking non-glutinous rice.	
	Preparing pine nuts	
0min	Cooking steamed rice	H-heat 8 min. M-heat 3 min. L-heat 10 min.
	Fermenting steamed rice	
	Boiling rice punch	
20min	Topping with rice grains and pine nuts	H-heat 5 min.

Sujeonggwa 수정과

Cinnamon Punch with Dried Persimmons

Sujeonggwa is a cinnamon punch made by soaking cinnamon and ginger in water. The soaking liquid is mixed with sugar and boiled, then garnished with dried persimmons and pine nuts. *Sujeonggwa* means 'cookies in water.' To enjoy the real *sujeonggwa* taste, drink it like as to drink sweet honey and cold ice.

Total weight after cooking	Weight for one serve	Service temperature	Total heating time	Total cooking time	Standard utensil
2.6 kg (20 serves)	130 g	4~10 ℃	2 hours 40 min	3 hours	20 cm pot, 24 cm pot

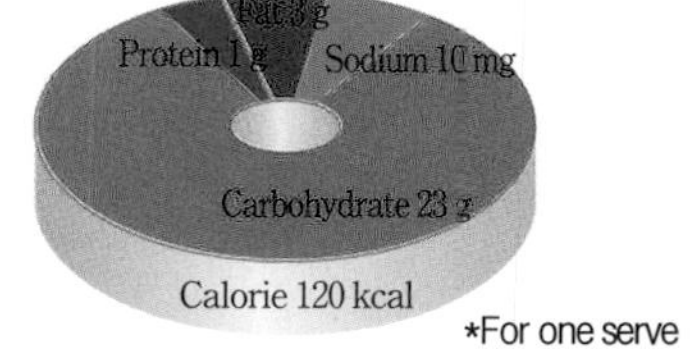

*For one serve

 Ingredients & Quantity

200 g ginger, 2 kg (10 cups) water
120 g un-spilt cinnamon, 2 kg (10 cups) water
150 g (1 cup) yellow sugar, 213 g (1⅓ cups) sugar
200 g (5 ea) dried persimmons, 50 g (10 ea) walnut
5 g pine nuts

Preparation

1. Skin the ginger (160 g) and cut it into 0.3 cm-thick. Wash un-spilt cinnamon, cut it into half if it is too long. 【Photo 2】
2. Remove stalks of dried persimmons, slit one side with knife and make it flat strip (185 g).
3. Soak the walnut in warm water for 5 min, skin (45 g). Put the walnut on the flat dried persimmons and roll it up, cut it into 1 cm-thick. (200 g, 20 pieces). 【Photo 3】
4. Remove tops of the pine nuts and wipe the nuts with dry cotton cloths.

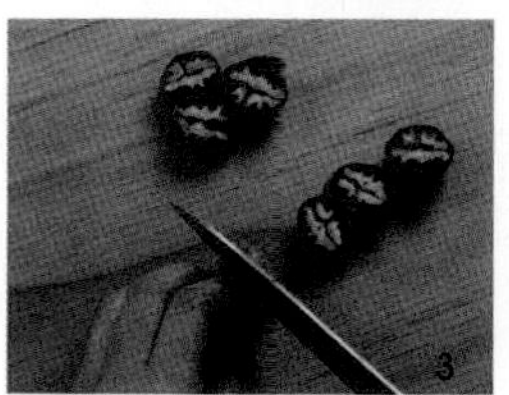

Recipe

1. Put water and ginger in the pot, heat it up for 9 min. on high heat. When it boils, reduce the heat to medium, boil it for 1 hour, sieve through cotton cloths (1.3 kg). 【Photo 4】
2. Put water and cinnamon in the pot, heat it up for 9 min. on high heat. When it boils, reduce the heat to medium, boil it for 1 hour, sieve through cotton cloths (1.2 kg). 【Photo 5】
3. Pour ginger liquid and cinnamon liquid in the pot, add yellow sugar and regular sugar, heat it up for 12 min. on high heat. When it boils, reduce the heat to medium, boil it for another 10 min. Cool it down, and top with persimmons and pine nuts. 【Photo 6】

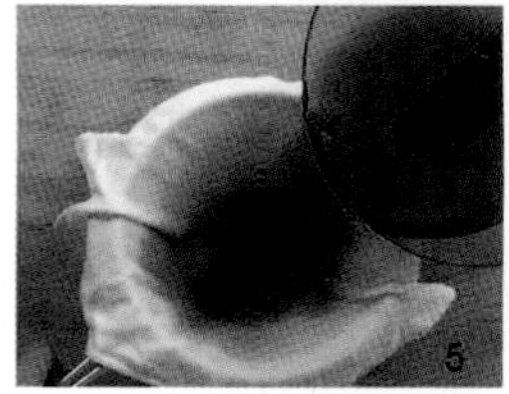

- Ginger and cinnamon may be boiled together, but separate boiling will save each taste and smell.
- Un-spilt dried persimmons may be topped, instead of chestnut wrapped in persimmons.

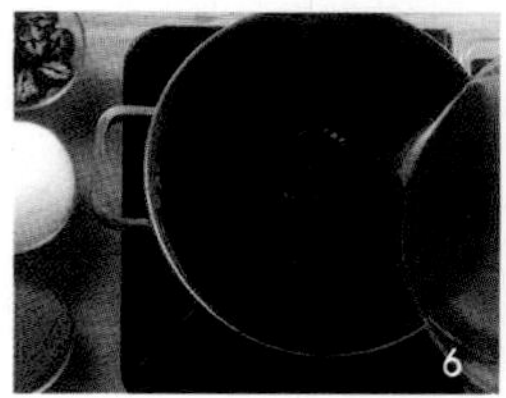

Heating Time	Process	Heat Control
Preparation	Preparing ginger, cinnamon, dried persimmons, walnuts and pine nuts	
0 min	Boiling ginger	H-heat 9 min. M-heat 1hour
70 min	Boiling cinnamon	H-heat 9 min. M-heat 1hour
140 min	Boiling cinnamon punch	H-heat 12 min. M-heat 10 min.
160 min	Topping with persimmons and pine nuts	

Maesilcha 매실차

Plum Tea

Maesilcha is Asian plum tea made by marinating *maesil* (Asian plum) with sugar or honey, and then diluting that liquid with cold or boiling water. *Maesilcha* is served chilled in the summer. It is high in organic acids which are good for relieving physical fatigue, quenching thirst and stimulating appetite.

Total weight after cooking	Weight for one serve	Service temperature	Total heating time	Total cooking time	Standard utensil
2.88 kg(24 serves)	120 g	4~10 ℃	0 min	over 2 months	

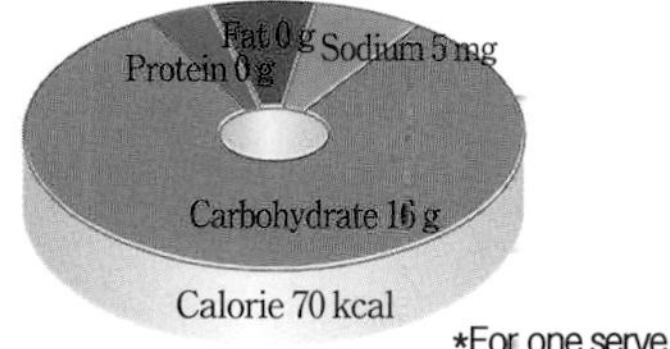

*For one serve

Ingredients & Quantity

500 g plum, 500 g sugar, 7 g (2 tsp) pine nuts, 2.16 kg water

1

Preparation

1. Wash the plums in water, remove stems, wash again in water, then drain water on a strainer for 2 hours (499 g).

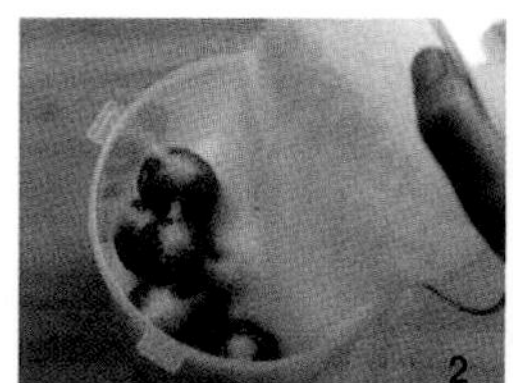
2

Recipe

1. Put the plum and sugar in a jar layer by layer.
2. Cover the top with plentiful sugar to cover all the plums. 【Photo 2】
3. Seal the jar tightly and let it sit for over 2 months until the plums withered. 【Photo 3】
4. Filter the plums out through strainer, and collect only plum liquid (720 g). 【Photos 4 & 5】
5. Dilute 30 g of plum liquid with 90 g of water, top with pine nuts. 【Photo 6】

3

- Plum liquid may be diluted in hot water for drinking.
- Plum liquid can be kept in cold storage for a long time.
- The jar for fermenting plum liquid should be kept in a cool place.

Cooking Time	Process	Heat Control
0min	Preparing plums	
120min	Adding sugar to the plum	
60day	Filtering plum liquid. Blending plum tea. Topping with pine nuts	

5

6

Insamcha 인삼차

Ginseng Tea

Insamcha is a tea made with tiny ginseng. It has a strong fragrance and taste. Ginseng is a special product of Korea, and is good for physical strength. Certain studies have found saponin in ginseng to have anti-cancer properties. Korean ginseng has been identified with the highest saponin content and the best effects.

Total weight after cooking	Weight for one serve	Service temperature	Total heating time	Total cooking time	Standard utensil
480 g(4 serves)	120 g	65~70 ℃	1 hour 7 min	1 hour	20 ㎝ pot

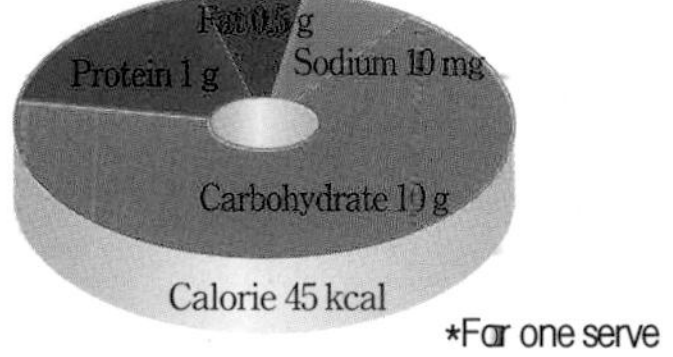

*For one serve

Ingredients & Quantity

100 g ginseng (fresh wet ginseng)
40 g (10 ea) jujube
1.4 kg (7 cups) water
3.5 g (1 tsp) pine nuts
38 g (2 tbsp) honey

Preparation

1. Trim and wash ginseng cleanly, remove the head part. 【Photo 2】
2. Wipe the jujube with damp cotton cloths.
3. Remove tops of the pine nuts and wipe the nuts with dry cotton cloths.

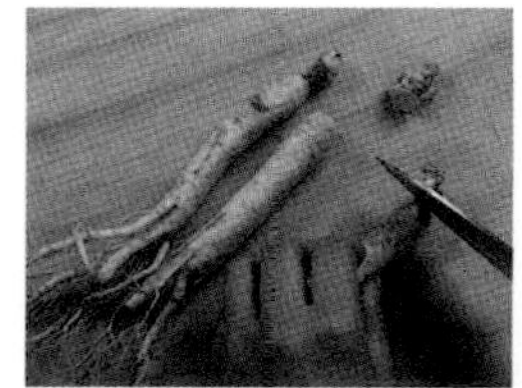

Recipe

1. Put the ginseng, jujube and water into the pot. 【Photo 3】
2. Heat it up for 7 min. on high heat. When it boils, lower the heat to medium, boil it for another 1 hour. 【Photo 4】
3. When the ginseng and jujube soaked fully, sieve, add honey and mix well. 【Photo 5】
4. Put the tea in a teacup, top with pine nuts. 【Photo 6】

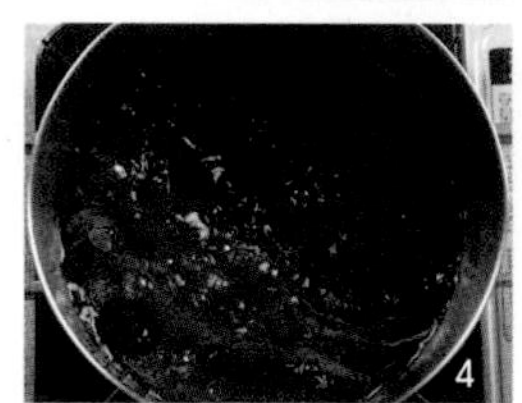

· More sugar and/or ginseng may be added upon taste.

Heating Time	Process	Heat Control
Preparation	Preparing ginseng, jujube, pine nuts	H–heat 7 min. M–heat 60 min.
0 min	Boiling after adding ginseng, jujube and water	
70 min	Sieving through strainer and adding honey. Topping with pine nuts	

Omija-hwachae 오미자화채

Omija Punch

Omija-hwachae is *omija* punch blended with *omija* liquid and honey or sugar, and garnished with carved pear. *Omija-hwachae* is a cold drink that is typically enjoyed in the summer. It has a beautiful color and is high in organic acids which are good for relieving physical fatigue and quenching thirst.

Total weight after cooking	Weight for one serve	Service temperature	Total heating time	Total cooking time	Standard utensil
480 g (4 serves)	120 g	4~10 ℃	0 min	over 5 hours	

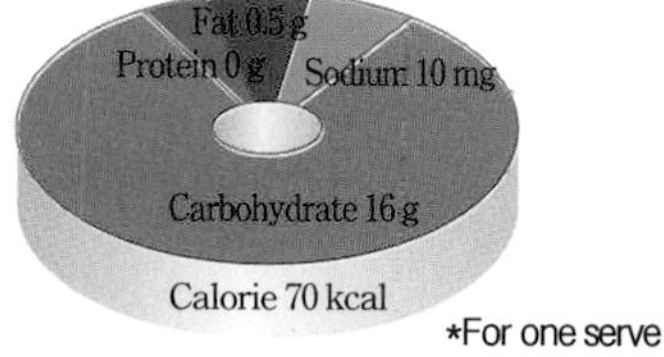

*For one serve

Ingredients & Quantity

20 g ($\frac{1}{5}$ cups) Omija, 400 g (2 cups) water
36 g (3 tbsp) sugar
38 g (2 tbsp) honey
125 g ($\frac{1}{4}$ ea) pear
3.5 g (1 tsp) pine nuts

Preparation

1. Wash the Omija, remove foreign elements, drain water on a strainer.
2. Add water to the Omija and let it sit for 12 hours. 【Photo 2】
3. Remove tops of pine nuts, wipe the nuts with dry cotton cloths.

Recipe

1. When the Omija soaked fully, filter through cotton cloths (352 g). 【Photo 3】
2. Add sugar and honey to the Omija water. 【Photo 4】
3. Peel the pear and slice it into 0.2 cm-thick, carve them into pear flower shape (60 g). 【Photo 5】
4. Put the Omija water into a punch bowl, topping with pear and pine nuts. 【Photo 6】

· Seasonal fruits will be suitable for the season.

Cooking Time	Process	Heat Control
0 min	Preparing Omija	
10 min	Soaking Omija. Preparing pine nuts	
730 min	Filtering Omija water. Adding sugar and honey	
740 min	Carving pear as flower shape. Topping with pear flower and pine nuts	

A Bibliography

[Books]

Inhee Kang, The Korean Taste, Daehan Printing & Publishing Co., Ltd, 1987

Inhee Kang, The History of Korean Dietary Life, Samyeongsa, 1990

Inhee Kang, The Korean Medicinal Food, Daehan Printing & Publishing Co., Ltd, 1992

Inhee Kang, Korean Rice Cake & Gwajeul, Daehan Printing & Publishing Co., Ltd, 1997

Inhee Kang, Table Settings for Korean Food, Hyoil Publishing Co, 1999

Sangbo Kim, The Dietary Culture in Royal Court of Joseon Dynasty, Soohaksa, 1996

The Korean dietetic association, Management Guidebook for Provided Meals, Third Edition, The Korean dietetic association, Third edition. 2000

Ministry of Culture & Tourism, Korean Traditional Food, 2000

Younghee Bae, Dongho Yang, Cooking Training Workbook for Group Meal Management, Kyomunsa, 2005

Chungja Sung and 5 others, Calorie Handbook, Kyomunsa, 2005

Chunja Lee, Gwiyoung Kim, Haewon Park, Byungsuk Bae, Food for the Initiation Ceremonies, Daewonsa Publishing Co, 1998

Sungwoo Lee, The Cultural History of Korean Cuisine, Kyomunsa, 1985

Sungwoo Lee, The Cultural History of Korean Food, Kyomunsa, 1984

Sungwoo Lee, The Social History of Korean Food, Kyomunsa, 1984

Hyogee Lee, The Food Culture in Korea, Shinkwang Publishing Co, 1998

Hyogee Lee, The Taste and Flavor of Korean Food, Shinkwang Publishing, 2005

Choae Yum, Myungsook Jang, Sookja Yoon, Korean Food, Hyoil Publishing Co, 1992

UNESCO-APCEIU, Tasteful Education for International Understandings, Ilchokak Publishing Co., Ltd., 2007

Sookja Yoon, Storable Fermented Korean Food, Shinkwang Publishing, 1997

Sookja Yoon, Korean Traditional Tteok, Cookies and Beverages, Jigu Publishing Co, 1998

Sookja Yoon, Korean Seasonal Food and Festival Food, Jigu Publishing Co, 2000

Seoseok Yoon, The History of Dietary Culture, Shinkwang Publishing Co., 1999

Seoseok Yoon, Korean Food, Soohaksa, 2002

Donghyo Chung and 5 others, The Taste and Science of Food, Shinkwangmunhwa Publishing Co., 2003

Haeok Jung, Understanding of Korean Food, Kyohakyeongusa, 2000

Haeok Jung, Korean Food and Culture, Munjisa, 2002

Jaesun Cho, Seonyun Hwang, Science of Food Ingredients, Munundang Publishing Co., 1984

Hoojong Cho, The Story of Korean Food, Hollym Corp., Publishers, 2001

Kyungryun Cho and 4 others, Experimental Cooking Learning with Flow Charts, Kyomunsa, 2004

Korea Cultural Heritage Foundation, Comprehensive Korean Food 1~6, Hollym Corp., Publishers, 1997

The Korean Nutrition Society, The Criterion of Nutrition Ingestion of Korean 7th Edition, The Korean Nutrition Society, 2005

Bokryo Han, Bap (Cooked Rice), Ppurigipeunnamu, 1991

Bokryo Han, The Royal Court Cuisines in Joseon Dynasty, Institute of Korean royal cuisine, 2003

Youngsil Han, Invitation to Korean Cuisines, Sookmyung women's university press, 2005
Jaehee Hwang, Jungeun Park, Science of Food Ingredients, Hyoil Publishing Co, 2005
Haesung Hwang, Korean Traditional Food, Kyomunsa, 2000
Younghee Hyun and 3 others, Science of Food Ingredients, Hyungseul Publishing Co, 2000

[Thesis]

Soonha Kim, Korean menu preference and buying behaviors on the Japanese residents in Korea, Foodervice Management Society of Korea, vol 7, p129-148. 2004.
Seungjoo Kim, Jinah Cho, Jungsoon Cho, Hoojong Cho, A study on the Standardization and Cooking Properties of Imjasootang, Korean J. SOC. FOOD SCI., vol 15, p197-202, 1999.
Hyeyoung Kim, Yoonseon Jo, A Study on acceptability of food temperature served in Foodervice Operations, The Journal of Living Culture Research, vol 7, p 57-85, 1993.
Hyunkyung Moon, A Study of standardization of menu, food science and industry for the globalization of Korean Food. Korea science and engineering foundation report, vol 27, p38-54,1994.
Kyounghwa Yoon, A study on Korean food tasty expression, MS Thesis, Sejong Univ. 2006
Sunmi Lee, Hyeon-a Jung, Sanghyun Park, Nami Joo, Selection of representative menu and development of standard recipes in middle & high school meals, Journal of the Korean Dietetic Association, vol 11, p 28-43, 2005.
Yaung-iee Lim, Hehyoung Kim, A study on desirable serving temperatures of soups for food service establishment, Korean J. Dietary Culture, vol 9, p303-310, 1994.
Ouk Han, Understanding and acceptance of Korean Food in cultural point of view. Food Technique, vol 8, p 3-34, 1995.

[Report]

National Agricultural Products Quality Management Service of Korea, Standardization of agricultural products, 2006.
Rural Development Administration of Korea, The Science of Rural Life, p289-323, 2000.
Ministry of Culture & Tourism, The Korean Regional Food.
Cultural Heritage Administration of Korea, Korean Traditional Crafts and Food, p135-181, 1999.
Korea Food Industry Association, A Study of facility plan for good menu, 1992.
Korea Science & Engineering Foundation, Development of standard recipe for the mass production of top quality Korean Food and evaluation of operation and control test for industrialization, 2005.
Korea Tourism Organization, Orthography for the travel brochure in foreign languages, 2005.
Korea Health Industry Development Institute, A Study of reference quantity of the food and establishment of the quantity for one serve, 2004.

Index and Glossary of Key Korean Terms

Agujjim	Simmered Angler fish	아구찜
Andong-sikhye	Andong(name of a region) Rice Punch	안동식혜
Baechu-kimchi	Cabbage Kimchi	배추김치
Baechusokdaeguk	Cabbage Core Soup	배추속대국
Baekje	One of the Three Kingdoms in Korea in early age (BC 18~AD 660)	백제
Baekkimchi	White Korean Cabbage Kimchi	백김치
Baesuk	Parboiled Sweet Pear with Ginger	배숙
Banchan	Side Dish	반찬
Ban-sang	Ordinary Dining Table Set with Cooked Rice as Main Dish	반상
Bap	Cooked rice or with other grains	밥
Beoseot-jeongol	Mixed Mushroom Hot Pot	버섯전골
Beoseot-namul	Assorted Mushrooms	버섯나물
Bibimbap	Rice mixed with Vegetables, Beef and Fried Red Pepper Paste	비빔밥
Bibim-naengmyeon	Mixed Cold Buckwheat Noodles	비빔냉면
Bindaetteok	Mung Bean Pancake	빈대떡
Bossam-kimchi	Wrapped Kimchi	보쌈김치
Bugeo-bopuragi	Seasoned dried Pollack Flakes	북어보푸라기
Bugeo-gui	Grilled dried Pollack	북어구이
Bugeo-jeon	Pan-fried dried Pollack with Wheat Flour & Beaten Egg coating	북어전
Bugeotguk	Dried Pollack Soup	북엇국
Bulgogi	Korean Barbecue	불고기
Byeolmibap	Special taste cooked Rice with Vegetables, Seafoods and Meats	별미밥
Cha	Tea	차
Chaloksusu-sirutteok	Steamed Glutinous Corn Cake	찰옥수수시루떡
Chamnamul	An Eatable Wild Herb (Pimpinella calycina - Scientific name)	참나물
Chamnamul-Saengchae	Chamnamul Fresh Vegetable Salad	참나물생채
Choganjang	Vinegar Soy Sauce	초간장
Chonggak-kimchi	Whole Radish Kimchi	총각김치
Chueotang	Loach Soup	추어탕
Daehajjim	Steamed Prawn	대하찜
Dagwa-sang	Refreshment Table Set	다과상
Dak-bibimbap	Rice mixed with Vegetables and Chicken	닭비빔밥
Dakjjim	Simmered Chicken	닭찜
Dasik	Traditional Pressed Sweet Cookie	다식
Deodeok	Roots of Codonopsis lanceolata (Scientific name)	더덕
Deodeok-Saengchae	Deoduok Salad	더덕생채
Doenjang	Soybean Paste	된장
Doenjangguk	Soybean Paste Soup	된장국
Doenjang-jjigae	Soybean Paste Stew	된장찌개
Domijjim	Steamed Sea-bream	도미찜
Domimyeon	Stuffed Sea-bream Casserole with Vegetables	도미면
Dongchimi	White and chilled Watery Radish Kimchi	동치미
Dotorimuk-muchim	Seasoned Acorn Starch Jelly	도토리묵무침
Dubu-jeongol	Tofu Hot Pot	두부전골
Dwaejijok-jorim	Braised Pig Trotters	돼지족 조림
Eobok-jaengban	Boiled Meat Platter	어복쟁반
Eochae	Parboiled Sliced Fish Fillet and Shell Fish	어채
Eomandu	Fish Fillet Dumpling	어만두
Gaeseongmujjim	Steamed Gaeseong (name of a region) Radish	개성무찜
Gajami-sikhae	Fermented Flatfish	가자미식해
Galbijjim	Braised Beef Ribs	갈비찜
Galbitang	Beef Rib Soup	갈비탕
Gamjabap	Cooked Rice steamed with Rice and Potato together	감자밥
Gamjajeon	Pan-fried grated Potato Pancake	감자전
Gamjatteok	Potato Starch Cake similar to Songpyeon	감자떡
Gangjeong	Traditional Korean Cookie made of Glutinous Rice Powder oil-fried and coated with popped Rice	강정

Ganjang	Soy Sauce	간장
Gegamjeong	Crab Stew	게감정
Geopi	Skin off or Thin skin	거피
Geopi–pat	Dark blue, thin skin sweet bean	거피팥
Gimbap	Rice Rolled in Laver	김밥
Godeulbbaegi–kimchi	Korean Wild Lettuce Kimchi (Bitter Taste Kimchi)	고들빼기김치
Goguryeo	One of the Three Kingdoms of Korea in early age (BC 37~AD 668)	고구려
Gomguk	Beef Soup cooked with Brisket, Shank and Intestines	곰국
Gomtang	Beef Soup cooked with Brisket, Shank and Intestines, served with Rice	곰탕
Gomyeong	Garnishes	고명
Gontteok	Pink Rice Cake, kneeded of Rice Powder and oil–fried in Pink Color Oil	곤떡
Goryeo	The 2nd United Kingdom in Korea (918~1932)	고려
Goryeobyeong	See Yakgwa	고려병
Goryeossam	Foods wrapped with Lattuce	고려쌈
Gosarijeon	Pan–fried Bracken Pancake with Wheat Flour	고사리전
Gujeolpan	Platter of Nine Delicacies	구절판
Gukganjang	Concentrated Soysauce (24% of Salinity)	국간장
Guksu–jangguk	Noodles in Clear Broth	국수장국
Guldubu–jjigae	Oysters and Tofu Stew	굴두부찌개
Gungjung–tteokbokki	Rice Cake Pasta and Vegetables , Royal Style	궁중떡볶이
Gwapyeon	Fruit Jelly Slice made of Sour Fruit Juice with Sugar and Honey	과편
Gyeojachae	Assorted Cold Plate with Mustard Sauce	겨자채
Gyeojajang	Mustard Sauce	겨자장
Gyeongdan	Sweet Rice Balls	경단
Gyoja–sang	Large Dining Table	교자상
Haejangguk	A Broth to relieve Alcohol	해장국
Haemuljeongol	Seafood Hot Pot	해물전골
Haemul–kalguksu	Hand–style Noodle Soup with Seafood	해물칼국수
Haemul–pajeon	Seafood Green Onion Pancake	해물파전
Heangjeok	Pan–fried Pork and White Kimch with Mung Bean and Egg York coating after broiled and skewered	행적
Heugimjajuk	Black Sesame and Rice Porridge	흑임자죽
Hobakbeombeok	Steamed and mashed Sweet Pumpkin with Chestnut and Corn, or Lotus Roots	호박범벅
Hobakgojijeok	Pan–fried skewered Pumpkin Flesh with Glutinous Rice Powder Coating	호박고지적
Hobakjeon	Pan–fried Summer Squash	호박전
Hobakjuk	Pumpkin Porridge	호박죽
Hobakseon	Stuffed and parboiled Young Pumpkin	호박선
Hobaktteok	Pumpkin Rice Cake	호박떡
Hongeo–eosiyuk	Steamed Thornback–fish with Rice Straw after skinned, dried and seasoned	홍어어시육
Honghaesam	Steamed minced Beef and Tofu stuffed with Mussel and Sea slug	홍해삼
Horyeom	Coarse Bay Salt	호렴
Huchu	Black Pepper	후추
Huinbap	Cooked White Rice	흰밥
Hwachae	Punch (Drink)	화채
Hwayangjeok	Beef and Vegetable Brochette	화양적
Imjasutang	Chilled Chicken Soup	임자수탕
Insamcha	Ginseng Tea	인삼차
Jaecheopguk	Marsh Clam (Corbicular fluminea–Scientific name) Soup	재첩국
Jaeyeom	Fine Salt (Seasoning Salt)	재염
Janggukbap	Rice in Beef Soup	장국밥
Janggukjuk	Rice Gruel with Beef Broth	장국죽
Jangkimchi	Soy Sauce Kimchi	장김치
Jangtteok	Wheat Flour Pancake with Soybean Paste	장떡
Japchae	Potato Starch Noodles stir–fried with Vegetables	잡채
Japgokbap	A Dish cooked with Barley, African Millet, Fox tail Millet, Bean and Red Bean together	잡곡밥
Jatbaksan	Pine Nut Cookie	잣박산
Jatjuk	Pine Nut Porridge	잣죽
Jeolsik	Festival Foods	절식
Jeonbokjjim	Simmered Abalone	전복찜
Jeonbokjuk	Rice Porridge with Abalone	전복죽
Jeonbok–kimchi	Kimchi made with abalones together	전복김치
Jeonju–bibimbap	Jeonju(name of a region)–style Bibimbap	전주비빔밥

Jeotguk-jjigae	Salt-fermented seafood stew	젓국찌개
Jeuk-gui	Spicy Broiled Pork	제육구이
Jeungpyeon	Rice Wine Cake	증편
Jinganjang	Less Salty Soysauce (16% of Salinity)	진간장
Jogaetang	Spicy Hot Clam Soup	조개탕
Jogi-yangnyeom-gui	Seasoned and broiled Yellow Corvina	조기양념구이
Joraengi-tteokguk	Small Dumbbell Rice Cake Pasta Soup	조랭이떡국
Joseon	The Latest Dynasty of Korea (1932~1910)	조선
Juan-sang	Liquor Table Set	주안상
Juk-sang	Porridge Dining Table Set with Porridge as Main Dish	죽상
Juksunchae	Bamboo Shoot Salad	죽순채
Junggwa	Korean Cookie marinated or braised Fruits in Honey or Sugar	정과
Kimchibap	Cooked Rice cooked with Rice and Kimchi together	김치밥
Kimchi-jjigae	Kimchi Stew	김치찌개
Kkakdugi	Diced Radish Kimchi	깍두기
Kkomak	Ark Shell (Tegillarca granosa - Scientific name)	꼬막
Kkotsanbyeong	Pressed Round Rice Cake stuffed with Red Bean	꽃산병
Kkotsogeum	Fine Salt (=Jaeyeom)	꽃소금
Kongbap	Cooked Rice with Beans	콩밥
Kong-guksu	Noodles in Chilled White Bean Soup	콩국수
Kongjuk	Bean and Rice Porridge	콩죽
Kongnamulbap	Cooked Rice cooked with Rice and Bean Sprouts together	콩나물밥
Kongnamul-kimchi	Kimchi made with Bean Sprouts together	콩나물김치
Kongtteok	Rice Cake stuffed with Bean	콩떡
Maejakgwa	Fried Ribbon Cookies	매작과
Maesilcha	Plum Tea	매실차
Malgeun-jangguk	Clear Beef Soup	맑은장국
Mandu	Dumpling	만두
Mandutguk	Dumpling Soup	만둣국
Maneul-jangajji	Pickled Garlic	마늘장아찌
Mideodeok	Warty Sea Squirt (Styela clava)	미더덕
Minari	Watercress	미나리
Minari-ganghoe	Minari Bundles with Meat	미나리강회
Miyeokguk	Brown Seaweed Soup	미역국
Mosijogaeguk	Short Necked Clam Soup	모시조개국
Muchae	Shredded Radish	무채
Mul-naengmyeon	Buckwheat Noodles in Chilled Broth	물냉면
Mu-malgeunjangguk	Clear White Radish Soup	무맑은장국
Musangchae	Seasoned Radish Salad	무생채
Myeon-sang	Noodle Dining Table Set with Noodles as Main Dish	면상
Nabak-kimchi	Radish Water Kimchi	나박김치
Naengchae	Cold Salad	냉채
Naengguk	Cold Soup	냉국
Naengiguk	Pickpurse Soup	냉이국
Nakji-bokkeum	Stir-fried Baby Octopus	낙지볶음
Nakji-horong	Grilled seasoned Octopus bound over Rice Straw	낙지호롱
Namul	Eatable Wild Herb or Vegetables	나물
Neobiani	Gilled Slice Beef	너비아니
Nokdu-jijim	Mung Bean Pancake	녹두지짐
Nokdujuk	Mung Bean Porridge	녹두죽
Noti	Rice Cake made of Chinese Millet or Glutinous Rice Fermented with Malt	노티
Ogokbap	Cooked Five Grain Rice	오곡밥
Oigapjanggwa	Stir-fried Cucumber stuffed with Beef and Brown Oak Mushrooms	오이갑장과
Oisangchae	Seasoned Cucumber Salad	오이생채
Oiseon	Stuffed Cucumber	오이선
Oi-sobagi	Stuffed Cucumber Kimchi	오이소박이
Ojaengitteok	Rice Cake made of Glutinous Rice sutffed with Red Been into Big Square	오쟁이떡
Ojingeojeot	Salt-fermented Squid	오징어젓
Ojingeojeotkkal	Salt-fermented Squid (=Ojingeojeot)	오징어젓갈
Ojingeo-sundae	Squid Sausage	오징어순대
Omegi-tteok	Millet Cake made of Glutinous Fox tail Millet stuffed with fried Bean or Red Bean Powder	오메기떡

Omija	A Fruit that has Five Taste (Fruit of Chinese Magnolia Vine)	오미자
Omija-hwachae	Omija Punch	오미자화채
Omijapyeon	Omija-flavored Jelly	오미자편
Pa	Green Onion	파
Patjuk	Rice and Red Bean Porridge	팥죽
Pohangcho	Spinach produced in Pohang (name of a region)	포항초
Putgochujeon	Pan-fried unripe Green Pepper	풋고추전
Pyeonsu	Square Dumpling	편수
Pyogojeon	Pan-fried Brown Oak Mushrooms	표고전
Saengseon-gui	Grilled Fish	생선구이
Saengseonjeon	Pan-fried Fish Fillet	생선전
Saengsilgwa	Fresh fruits	생실과
Saeujeon	Pan-fried Shrimp	새우전
Samgyetang	Ginseng Chicken Soup	삼계탕
Samhap-janggwa	Three braised Delicacies	삼합장과
Sangchu	Lettuce	상추
Sanja	Oil-fried Rice Cake made of Glutinous Rice Powder, coated with Honey	산자
Seokryu-kimchi	Pomegranate Kimchi	석류김치
Seolleongtang	Ox Bone Soup	설렁탕
Seomibap	Cooked White Rice with dried Sweet Potato	서미밥
Seon	Steamed or Parboiled Stuffed vegetables	선
Sigeumchi-namul	Blanched and seasoned Spinach	시금치나물
Sikhye	Rice Punch	식혜
Silla	One of the Three Kingdoms in Korea in early age (BC 57~AD 935)	신라
Sinseollo	Royal Casserole	신선로
Sisik	Seasonal on time Food	시식
Soe-galbigui	Marinated and grilled Beef Ribs	쇠갈비구이
Soe-galbijjim	Braised Beef Ribs	쇠갈비찜
Soegogi-jangjorim	Beef Chunks braised in Soy Sauce	쇠고기장조림
Sogeum	Salt	소금
Songi-sanjeok	Pan-fried skewered Jew's Ear Mushrooms	송이산적
Songpyeon	Half-moon shape rice cake	송편
Ssam	Foods wrapped with ~ (ie, Lattuce-ssam)	쌈 (상추쌈)
Ssamjang	Soybean Paste for wrapped Food	쌈장
Sujebi	Soup with Wheat Flour Flakes	수제비
Sujeonggwa	Cinnamon Punch with dried Persimmons	수정과
Sukjanggwa	Pickled Radish, Cucumber, or Garlic in Vinegar	숙장과
Suksilgwa	Marinated Fruits in Honey after boiling or braising	숙실과
Sundubu-jjigae	Spicy Soft Tofu Stew	순두부찌개
Tangpyeong chae	Mung Bean Jelly mixed with Vegetables and Beef	탕평채
Tofu	Bean Curd	두부
Tojangguk	Soybean Paste Soup	토장국
Tteokgalbi	Braised Beef Ribs with Rice Cake	떡갈비
Tteokguk	Sliced Rice Cake Pasta Soup	떡국
Tteokjjim	Braised Rice Cake Rod Stuffs	떡찜
Wandukongbap	Cooked Rice with Pea	완두콩밥
Wolgwachae	Seasoned and stir-fried Young Pumpkin Salad with shredded Beef, Brown Oak Mushrooms stuffed in Glutinous Rice Pancake	월과채
Yakgochujang	Fried red pepper paste	약고추장
Yakgwa	Deep-fried Honey Cookies	약과
Yaksik	Sweet Rice with Nuts and Jujube	약식
Yangjimeori-pyeonyuk	Pressed and sliced Brisket	양지머리편육
Yangnyeom	Seasonings	양념
Yangpajeon	Pan-fried Onion with Wheat Flour Coating	양파전
Yeolmu-kimchi	Young Summer Radish Kimchi	열무김치
Yeonan-sikhae	Yeonan (name of a region) fermented seafood	연안식해
Yeongyang-dolsotbap	Rice steamed with Nuts, Grains, Roots or Vegetables, served in a Hot Stone Pot (Hot Stone Pot with Norishing Staples)	영양돌솥밥
Yeot	Wheat Gluten	엿
Yeotgangjeong	A Kind of Korean Cookie coated with Wheat Gluten	엿강정
Yukgaejang	Spicy Beef and Leek Soup	육개장
Yukwonjeon	Pan-fried Beef Patties	육원전
Yumilgwa	Deep-fried Honey Cookie made of Wheat Flour and Buckwheat Flour	유밀과

Researchers for the 'Research and Development Project for the Standadization of Korean Cuisine'

Principal Researcher

Sookja Yoon, Director, Institute of Traditional Korean Food.

Management Agency Researcher

- Myungsook Lee, Vice Director, Institute of Traditional Korean Food.
- Mija Lim, Researcher, Institute of Traditional Korean Food.
- Bongsoon Choi, Affiliated Prof. at Dept. of Traditional Korean Cuisine, Baewha Women's College.
- Junhee Kim, Affiliated Prof. at Dept. of Hotel Cooking, Kimpo College.
- Jihyun Lee, Prof. at Dept. Hotel Tourism Foodservice, Daelim College.
- Jinhee Park, Affiliated Prof. at Dept. Hotel Cooking, Kimpo College.
- Jaehee Kang, Affiliated Prof. Division of Foodservice Industry, Baekseok College of Cultural Studies.

Cooperation Agency Researcher

Sejong University

- Jonggoon Kim, Prof. at Dept. Culinary & Foodservice Management.
- Joosook Kim, Researcher. at Dept. Culinary & Foodservice Management.
- Jemhee Lim, Researcher. at Dept. Culinary & Foodservice Management.
- Mikyung Choi, Researcher. at Dept. Culinary & Foodservice Management.

Korean Food Research Institute

- Wooderck Hawer, Principal Researcher.
- Jinbong Hwang, Principal Researcher.
- Bae Namgung, Senior Researcher.
- Dongwon Seo, Researcher.

Exploitation Committee Member

- Hyunghee Park, Presiden & Chairman, Korean Foodservice Information.
- Minsoo Kang, Chairman, Korean Food Tourism Association.
- Kiyoung Kim, Prof. at Dept. Foodservice Management, Kyonggi University.
- Ilsun Yang, Prof. at Dept. Food and Nutrition, Yonsei University.
- Hyekyung Chun, Agricultural Researcher. Rural Resources Development Institute, NIAST, RDA.
- Yangho Jin, Prof. at Dept. Foodservice Management, Kyonggi University.
- Inkyeong Hwang, Prof. at Dept. Food & Nutrition, Seoul National University.
- Chulmin Kim, Director, Tourism Industry Team, Ministry of Culture & Tourism.
- Seungjin Jang, Director, Food Industry Section, Ministry of Agriculture & Forestry.
- Jangkun Yun, Director, Export Stratagem Team, Korea Agro-Fisheries Trade Corporation.

Consultation Committee Member

- Soonok Lee, Chairman-Prof.at Dept. Hotel Cooking, Korea Tourism College.
- Wonchul Ha, ex-Section Chief, Koreahouse.
- Yongdo Jung, Director, President Hotel.(Korean a Master Cooking Hand No.4).
- Jincheol Yeom, Prof. at Dept. Traditional Korean Cusine, Barwha Women's College.
- Jongchul Ahn, Prof. Divition of Foodservice Industry, Baekseok College of Cultural Studies.
- Upsik Kim, Prof. Divition of Hotel Cooking Nutrition, Anyang Technical College.
- Eunhee Choi, Prof. Divition of Food & Culinary Science, Howon University.
- Woonjin Kim, Prof. at Dept. Food & Nutrition, Bucheon College.
- Helen C. Lee, Prof. at Dept. Food Science & Nutrition, California State University.
- Kyungja Park, Researcher, Baijing Central National College-Institute of Korean Culture.
- Cheolho Lee, Prof. at Dept. Life Science. Korea University.
- Yonghwan Lee, Principal Researcher, Korean Food Research Institute.
- Yonghyun Chang, Prof. at Dept. Computer Information, Baewha Womem's College.

We would like to express our heartful gratitude to all researchers who have contributed their expertise to the mission of 'Standardization and Globalization of Korean Food'.

Front row from left : President Hyunghee Park, Prof. Soonok Lee, Prof. Jonggoon Kim, Director Sookja Yoon, Researcher Mija Lim

Back row from left : Affiliated Prof. Junhee Kim, Affiliated Prof. Jinhee Park, Prof. Jihyun Lee, Affiliated Prof. Bongsoon Choi, Affiliated Prof. Jaehee Kang